STAN LEE

STAN LEE

THE MAN BEHIND MARVEL

BOB BATCHELOR

ROWMAN & LITTLEFIELD
Lanham • Boulder • New York • London

Published by Rowman & Littlefield
A wholly owned subsidiary of The Rowman & Littlefield Publishing Group, Inc.
4501 Forbes Boulevard, Suite 200, Lanham, Maryland 20706
www.rowman.com

Unit A, Whitacre Mews, 26-34 Stannary Street, London SE11 4AB

Distributed by NATIONAL BOOK NETWORK

British Library Cataloguing in Publication Information Available

Library of Congress Cataloging-in-Publication Data

Names: Batchelor, Bob, author.
Title: Stan Lee : the man behind Marvel / Bob Batchelor.
Description: Lanham, Maryland : Rowman & Littlefield, 2017. | Includes
   bibliographical references and index.
Identifiers: LCCN 2017006405 (print) | LCCN 2017007019 (ebook) |
   ISBN 9781442277816 (hardback : alk. paper) | ISBN 9781442277823 (electronic)
Subjects: LCSH: Lee, Stan, 1922– | Cartoonists—United States—Biography.
Classification: LCC PN6727.L39 Z54 2017 (print) | LCC PN6727.L39 (ebook) |
   DDC 741.5/092 [B]—dc23
LC record available at https://lccn.loc.gov/2017006405

∞™ The paper used in this publication meets the minimum requirements of American National Standard for Information Sciences—Permanence of Paper for Printed Library Materials, ANSI/NISO Z39.48-1992.

Printed in the United States of America

To my heart and soul,
my daughter (and budding author),
Kassandra Dylan.
All my love and more than I can express to
Suzette and Sophia
for endless joy, love, and laughter.

CONTENTS

ACKNOWLEDGMENTS

Stan Lee: The Man behind Marvel is the product of a lifetime of reading, researching, and studying comic books and contemporary American popular culture. I taught myself to read so that I could unlock the joys of *Spider-Man* and the *Avengers*, then later I grew obsessed with the reality-bending *What If?* series. I do not remember a time without Stan Lee, and the "Stan Lee Presents" banner is ever present in my mind's eye.

I never could have written *Stan Lee: The Man Behind Marvel* without a great deal of help, support, and friendship. First and foremost, my thanks to Stephen Ryan, senior editor at Rowman & Littlefield. We are coconspirators, cocreators, and more or less coauthors of this book. His wisdom and way with words made this a better book (perhaps some of Stan's alliterative flourishes are rubbing off on me). I would also like to thank everyone who had a hand in this book at R&L, including the design team for its work on the book cover, the copyeditors, the marketing team, and the production staff—first-rate one and all.

Thoroughly grounded in multiarchival research, *Stan Lee* would not exist in its present form without the wonderful libraries and archives that bring Lee's career and accomplishments to life. My deepest appreciation goes to the American Heritage Center (AHC) at the University of Wyoming. How Lee's papers got to Laramie, Wyoming, is itself a great story. The AHC staff, led by director Bridget J. Burke, is professional and overwhelmingly helpful and gracious. In particular, I would like to thank Amanda Stow, who welcomed me to the library and provided keen insight, and most notably John Waggener, who provided immense help navigating the papers and photographs, as well as served as a kind guide to all things Laramie.

I would also like to extend my hearty thanks to Jenny Robb and the wonderful team at The Billy Ireland Cartoon Library and Museum at The Ohio State University. Materials at the library were essential in completing the book. And, the museum's exhibits gave the researcher a pleasant respite during long stretches of research. Additional comic book resources, including rare books and Marvel materials, were hunted down at the Public Library of Cincinnati and Hamilton County; the Stow-Munroe Falls Public Library; the Lane Public Library in Oxford, Ohio; and the King Library at Miami University and via its vast interlibrary loan consortium. Finally, I would be utterly remiss if I did not acknowledge Marvel for introducing its digital Marvel Unlimited subscription service. The archive opens up the company's back catalog and enables one to trace Lee's work across the decades.

Stan Lee benefits from the insightful analysis I gained from Joe Darowski, Chris Olson, and Norma Jones, who read early drafts and provided thoughtful feedback. Of course, they only improved the manuscript; any resulting errors are mine alone. Beth Johnson, art director at Matter Creative Group, provided sage advice regarding the book cover and art.

I am fortunate to have a fantastic group of mentors and friends whom I can turn to when research, writing, and editing get tough. My deepest thanks to Phillip Sipiora, Don Greiner, Gary Burns, and Gary Hoppenstand. Thank you for being wonderful role models and guides. Many friends offered cheer along the way: Thomas Heinrich, Chris Burtch, Larry Leslie, Kelli Burns, Gene Sasso, Bill Sledzik, Josef Benson, Jesse Kavadlo, Sarah McFarland Taylor, and Heather and Rich Walter and family. I have been lucky to have many fantastic mentors, whom I would like to acknowledge: Lawrence S. Kaplan, James A. Kehl, Sydney Snyder, Richard Immerman, Peter Magnani, and the late Anne Beirne. I benefit from the friendship of a group of like-minded popular culture aficionados: Brian Cogan, Brendan Riley, Kathleen Turner, Norma and Brent Jones, and Leigh Edwards! Thanks to my friend Jason Pettigrew at *Alternative Press* for his support and a timely press pass. I would also like to thank my Miami University colleagues in the Media, Journalism and Film Department.

My family is incredibly supportive considering what writing books means on one's time and energy. Thanks to my parents, Jon and Linda Bowen, for everything they do to make our lives infinitely better. Thanks also to Josette Percival and Michel Valois for their support and many kindnesses.

I cannot express my love and appreciation deeply enough for Suzette and Sophia ("Roberto"). They have brought endless love and laughter. Without Suzette's tenacity, I might have never fulfilled my lifelong dream of meeting Lee. Finally, my daughter, Kassie, is my inspiration, hope, heart, and joy. I can't wait to watch her writing life unfold. I am blessed to have such a wonderful daughter!

PROLOGUE
DAWN OF THE FANTASTIC

"Stan, we've gotta put out a bunch of heroes. You know, there's a market for it," Timely Comics publisher Martin Goodman barked at his editor Stan Lee.[1]

When he sensed a trend in the making, Goodman wasn't shy. His eyes lit up with the thought of cash registers across the country ringing up children's dimes. Those coins would eventually roll into his pockets. He could practically hear those thin dimes hit the cashbox.

Goodman's feeling didn't come from divine inspiration or a lucky hunch. A much more practical business leader, he didn't work that way. Instead, reportedly after golfing with some fellow executives who happened to run the distribution arm of his main rival National Periodical Publications (later simply known as DC), the home of *Superman*, *Batman*, and *Wonder Woman*, Goodman listened in as they bragged about a new line of comic books that were selling fast. In particular, they couldn't stop when it came to a new superhero team that would be getting its own title later in the year. Never willing to let a little bit of competitive intelligence slide, Goodman jumped at the news. Returning to the office, he squawked in Lee's ear about creating a new superhero team to match DC Comics . . . and on the double.

Little did Goodman know, however, that his longtime editor had been suffering from bouts of frustration and despair. Lee could not stomach working in comics any longer. He warred with the idea of chucking a twenty-year career, regardless of bringing home the steady paycheck that Goodman's mediocrity dispensed.

"We're writing nonsense . . . writing trash," he told his wife Joan. "I want to quit," he confided. "After all these years, I'm not getting anywhere. It's a stupid business for a grownup to be in."[2]

Lee had spent decades of his adult life putting out a variety of books that most adults scorned, from silly animal stories to war and romance tales. He had worked alongside Joe Simon and Jack Kirby on the early superhero titles, but they dropped in popularity. The constant flurry of work against tight deadlines and Goodman's follow-the-leader management philosophy became too much to handle. Lee prepped for the leap into something else—anything else—just not comic books.

Glum and exhausted, Lee arrived at home in Long Island after a tiring day at the Madison Avenue office. Gripped by stress and more than a little anxiety, he contemplated alternative careers but wasn't sure which way to turn. What if he couldn't support his family? What would he do? He told Joan about Goodman's urgent directive and asked her advice.

"If you're going to quit anyway, why don't you do a book the way like you'd like to do it, and get it out of your system," she said. "Worst that will happen is that he'll fire you and you want to quit anyway."[3] Lee's life's work hung in the balance—a career that had already spanned more than two decades. It had provided them with a nice home on Long Island, and money was never scarce, unlike his rough early years when his own father faced chronic unemployment.

Fear and desperation can be great motivators. Lee listened to his wife's thoughtful words. After all, Joanie was his best friend and closest confidante. On the verge of giving up and frustrated, he reached a breaking point. Maybe, just maybe, if he took a chance, the job would get better and he could break the spell of monotony. Lee realized that he had no choice.

Although unsure about what the future held and concerned that leaving the job might spell financial doom, Joanie's support and approval gave Lee the boost of confidence that he needed. He would make a last-ditch effort, a final go at the career he had stumbled into as a young high school graduate just looking for a steady paycheck.

Lee decided then and there to follow Goodman's advice—to a point. He would create an original superhero team, one that he concocted, not based on Goodman's typical retread of whatever DC or one of the other comic book companies put out. Lee's boss had even suggested a ridiculous name for the new team: the "Righteous League." Lee saw that idea as yet another in a long list of uninspiring copies of popular DC titles.

No, Lee thought, these heroes would be more based in reality. "This was the chance to do all the things I would enjoy," he said. "To get characters who acted like real people, to try to be more imaginative, to make some stories have happy endings and some not, to continue the stories and set them in the real world."[4]

Lee decided to risk it all—consequences be damned. Whatever happened, he hoped that creating a comic that he would want to read would bring the joy back into his work life and appeal to fans. He started sketching out the new team right away. "I forgot about the publisher. I was off and running: I was going to have fun," Lee explained. "It was very easy for me to control, since I was writing virtually all of them. . . . I could keep them in the style I wanted. I was creating my own universe."[5]

Giving himself the latitude to take chances and be as creative as possible, Lee took up the challenge to create "a team such as comicdom had never known."[6] He realized that this was a go-for-broke moment in his life. "For just this once," he thought, "I would do the type of story I myself would enjoy reading if I were a comic book reader." Joanie's words still rang in his ear: "You could dream up plots that have more depth and substance to them, and create characters who have interesting personalities, who speak like real people."[7] Her words gave him the impetus to go all-out.

After years of churning out monster comics and suspense-filled science fiction titles, Lee drew on what he knew. The new superhero team would contain elements drawn from across popular culture, not only science fiction stories and popular B movies, but also the real-life Cold War tensions with the Soviet Union over space flight and nuclear weapons.

The first swipe Lee took at the traditional superhero was with Reed Richards, the team's leader. Rather than make him muscle-bound and overtly handsome with astronaut good looks, Richards would be a thin, brilliant scientist who liked to show off his smarts. Next, Lee needed a female lead. She wouldn't be the typical, weak girlfriend merely waiting for her man to finish saving Earth. Sue Storm was a full member of the team, not merely pining away for her masked hero. As a matter of fact, he thought, "I was utterly determined to have a superhero series without any secret identities." Lee figured that if he were a hero, he would want the world to know it. "I'd never keep it secret," he explained. "I'm too much of a show-off."[8]

Once he had the two main characters, Lee decided to turn the genre on its ear again. He needed two more characters to keep the banter even. One would be a hotheaded teenager. Rather than make him a teen sidekick, which had always been the case in comic book history, Lee created Johnny Storm, Sue's little brother, a central member with enough firepower to stand on his own. Having a brother and sister would add additional tension. Finally, the team needed muscle. Lee brought aboard a rough-and-tumble, blue-collar strongman named Ben Grimm. The battle between brains and brawn played out with Grimm juxtaposed to Richards, the brilliant scientist leader. The scenario created tension, enabling readers to compare the two, and possibly even forcing them to take sides.

Doodling on a pad, scratching out thoughts in his lefty scrawl, Lee crossed out plot ideas and potential characters over and over again, realizing that the story would not be driven solely by action, like a typical comic book for children or young readers. Instead, he focused on the interaction between the teammates, similar to how families got along and people worked in real life. "I wanted to think of them as real, living, breathing people whose personal relationships would be of interest to the readers and, equally important, to me."[9] Lee also aimed for an older audience, believing that if readers could relate to the superheroes as people, then they would enjoy the book. Television and films were certainly skewing toward the teen and young adult audience, so Lee would aim there too.

Now all the team needed was a way to gain superpowers. Once again, Lee thought about the Cold War tensions over atomic weapons. The possibility of nuclear annihilation terrified the public, so it grew into a mainstay plot twist for stories and films. Lee's team ventured into space in an experimental rocket. When the craft crashed back to Earth, the crew was exposed to cosmic rays, giving them superpowers, but simultaneously nearly scaring them to death. Almost instantly they realized that they had to combine forces for the good of mankind.

Sticking to the alliteration that he liked so much, Lee named his band of misfits the Fantastic Four. In short order, they would not only save Earth and the universe on countless occasions but save Stan Lee's career and change American culture forever.

CHAPTER 1

STANLEY LIEBER, NEW YORKER

Window shoppers tentatively ventured out onto Times Square a few days after Christmas on Thursday, December 28, 1922. They turned up their collars and instinctively grabbed for their hats as a wintry mix of rain and snow pelted New York City. The dark gray clouds matched the city's mood as pedestrians bundled up against the dismal weather. A sudden gust could almost knock a woman off the sidewalk or send a man scurrying out into the street to retrieve his errant cap. All across the East Coast a broad, punishing storm pummeled the region, dumping rain and snow on people in the midst of the national intermission between the Christmas holiday season and the New Year.

In a tiny Manhattan apartment on Ninety-Eighth Street and West End Avenue, Jack and Celia Lieber barely noticed the dreary weather. On this day they welcomed their first child—a son. They named the little tike Stanley Martin.

The newborn entered the world at a peculiar time in American history. Still recovering from the global upheaval and bedlam of World War I, the nation lumbered ahead. With the war over, leaders from across the globe searched for ways to secure a more peaceful future for Europe. At home, the American economy had slipped and sputtered in the wake of war, falling off as companies recalibrated after the frenzy necessitated with war production. Industry was just starting to chug back to life in 1922. Manufacturing picked up as consumer goods companies produced everything from sleek automobiles to new clothing styles and electric kitchen gadgets.

What neither Celia nor Jack could have known on the day of their son's birth was that the gloomy weather outside would be a kind of foreshadowing. The vestiges of the Great War would spiral into the Great Depression and leave the nation reeling. The resulting economic chaos would sweep the Lieber family into near destitution and virtually suck the life out of the parents.

To their credit, however, Celia and Jack raised the boy to believe that he could expect a bright future despite the hardships he experienced firsthand and the countless harsh arguments his parents had about money. Stanley Lieber emerged an optimist, bedeviling the clouds that filled the sky the day he was born and the dark times brought on by the Depression and its aftermath for his little family.

This is how superheroes are born.

Young Stanley Lieber's parents were among the millions of immigrants to enter America in the early years of the twentieth century. Born in Romania in 1886, Stanley's father docked in the New York City harbor in 1905. Hyman, who later went by Jacob or the Americanized "Jack," was a mere nineteen years old. His relative (possibly brother) Abraham, then just fourteen, accompanied him on the voyage. The teens joined the wave of Jewish immigrants from Eastern European countries flooding into the United States at the beginning of the new century. After decades of pogroms (terror campaigns against Jews) across Europe and Russia that left countless thousands of Jews murdered, immigration to the United States skyrocketed from 5,000 in 1880 to 258,000 in 1907. In total, some 2.7 million from all over Europe migrated to America between 1875 and 1924.

Hyman left behind life in gritty Romania, a country in southeastern Europe, at that time sandwiched between Austria-Hungary to the north, Serbia to the west, Bulgaria to the south, and Russia and the Black Sea to the east. Young Hyman Lieber set off during the reign of monarch Carol I, who took control of the nation in 1881 and ruled until his death in 1914. It would have cost Hyman and Abraham about 179 rubles each—about $90, an enormous sum at the time—to make the trip to the United States. Of that sum, 50 rubles were shown to the Ellis Island immigration staff to demonstrate that they could subsist and make a fresh start in the new country.[1]

Hyman and Abraham were among the first large surge of Romanians to leave for America, a wave of one hundred forty-five thousand that left between the mid-1890s and 1920. For most Romanians considering the move, the United States promised economic stability and religious freedom. Like so many Eastern Europeans, the first groups went to America in search of steady wages and the ability to save money, which would enable them to return to their homelands and buy land. The total number of Romanian immigrants paled in comparison to other nationalities. In contrast, some three million Poles immigrated to America between 1870 and 1920.

For Jewish Romanians, the immigration tale is dramatically different, and more typical of the European Jewish immigration that took place during that era. Widespread discrimination meant that Romanian Jews usually stayed in America. Young Jewish men in Romania had few opportunities for meaningful careers. The monarchy forbade Jews to become lawyers, outlawed rabbinical seminaries, and made entrance into medicine almost impossible. The state considered Romanian Jews "aliens" or "foreigners" regardless of how long one's ancestors had lived in the country. According to others who left Romania at that time for the United States, being a minority meant permanent subservience and subsequent discrimination based on religion and ethnicity.[2]

The abuses of power were frequent and pervasive. According to one writer, "Romanians used veiled anti-Jewish legislation while avoiding outward use of barbarous acts and brutality that would draw the attention and disapproval of the civilized world."[3] Yet the psychological terror had significant consequences. Several laws passed in the 1890s outlawed education for Jews, while anti-Semitism was openly taught in Romanian high schools.

The semi-secret pogroms in Romania led to countless anti-Jewish riots and widespread pillaging, which the police and army either did not stop or actively participated in as the rampaging continued. Violence became a constant way of life for Romanian Jews. As one historian explains, "The economic depression that became dire in Romania towards the close of the nineteenth century was accompanied by an increased level of violence, starting with the anti-Jewish riots from Bârlad (1867), Buzău (1871), Botoşani (1890), Bucharest (1897) and Iaşi (1898)."[4] With so few Romanians in the United States, much of this news never reached the states, and thus did not face media scrutiny.

While the teenaged Hyman stayed in New York City, some sixty thousand of the first groups eventually returned to Romania. Other Eastern Europeans moved somewhat fluidly back and forth between America and their native countries. The hardships they endured in getting to the United States and the potential dangers in the manufacturing economy were deemed worthwhile, since the money they earned had transformative consequences for themselves and their families back home. After the initial burst that ended at the dawn of the Jazz Age, however, few Romanians would immigrate to the United States for the next twenty-five years. The numbers remained small and did not really pick up again until the nation faced the threat of Nazi occupation during World War II.

Once they arrived in the United States, the earliest Romanian immigrants faced hardships that transformed the traditional strong family values that they carried with them from their homeland. Most were unskilled laborers, so life in the mills and factories in American industrial cities proved dangerous and difficult. Workplace injuries and deaths occurred frequently among immigrant workers of all ethnicities. For Jewish immigrants from Romania, however, the hardships of life in New York City paled in comparison with what they potentially faced. The American Dream offered them a chance at a better life, despite the challenges of poverty and finding adequate housing. If nothing else, these new Americans gained religious freedom and safety from the wanton violence that took place against Jews in Romania.

Many single men, like the teenage Hyman, left home and the core of their family nucleus behind to scrape out a meager existence. Frequently, these single laborers grouped together in boarding homes or lived with other Romanian immigrant families. For such young men, cultural life, as it existed at the time, meant a revolving set of meeting places, including local restaurants and saloons and church services.

Jewish immigrants also faced potential anti-Semitism, so grouping together with their countrymen provided some insulation from these prejudices. Relatively few of the new immigrants could speak or read English, adding to the kinship ties among countrymen and solidarity when they faced the English-speaking world. Remembering a Romanian-Jewish restaurant on the Lower East Side, Maurice Samuel recalled that people gathered there "to eat karnatzlech, beigalech, mămăligă, and kashkaval, to drink . . . and to play six-six and tablanette," all while speaking in Romanian Yiddish and telling nostalgic stories about Jewish locales in Bucharest. Yet, the stories were also tinged with regret as the storytellers mentioned the anti-Semitic pogroms designed to drive them from the nation.[5]

Hyman Lieber and Abraham both entered the clothing industry in turn-of-the-century New York at a time when the garment district clamored for workers. Many Jewish immigrants were skilled craftsmen (about 65 percent of the total), but there is no way to determine if Hyman had worked in the industry or received any kind of advanced training in Romania. The anti-Semitic education legislation and unfair business practices make this possibility seem improbable. One historian notes, "Upon arrival in the United States, the immigrants became tailors, even if they had not been tailors before, because this trade was in demand in Manhattan."[6]

Like many first-generation families who lived during that era, the Liebers did not talk much about their own pasts or the paths they took to get to America. Although many immigrants brought aspects of their culture with them and continued to hold to those norms as much as possible, often immigrant families focused on adapting to American culture and creating new lives and opportunities for their families. Discussions centered on what the future might hold, not the years of hardships or struggles that it took to get to the United States.[7]

A clearer picture emerges about Lee's parents and his extended family if they are examined within the broader wave of Jewish and European immigrants who moved to New York City in the early twentieth century. The struggles his immediate family faced and the consequences on the youngster were similar to the countless other Jewish families and individuals attempting to assimilate.[8]

In 1910, both Jacob and Abraham lived with Gershen Moshkowitz, a fifty-two-year-old Russian, and his Romanian wife Meintz, on Avenue A in Manhattan. The family had two children, Rosie and Joseph. Both Joseph and Abraham are listed in the census as operators in pocket books, suggesting that the two teens worked together in the same shop. Jacob had already begun his career as a cutter in a coat shop. Like the Moshkowitz children, the census worker listed that both Liebers attended school and could read and write English, but supplied no further details. They almost certainly spoke Romanian Yiddish at home and in the neighborhood.[9]

Ten years later, in 1920, the thirty-four-year old Jacob was still living as a boarder, at this time with the family of David and Beckie Schwartz and their three young children, in an apartment on 114th Street in Manhattan. The Schwartzes immigrated to America in 1914 from Romania. Unlike Jacob, they could not speak, read, or write in English. The connection for immigrants at this time always seemed to center on work lives intermingling with private lives. Both Jacob and David worked in the dressmaking industry. The 114th Street apartment building and surrounding neighborhood was predominantly Jewish immigrants from Russia and Romania, so Yiddish was much more common than English. Both Schwartzes were also considerably younger than Jacob (David at 26 and Beckie 25).

Events would change quickly for Jacob over the next two years. In 1920, he was living with the Schwartz family, but by the end of 1922 he had married Celia Solomon, and newborn Stanley Martin arrived just before the New Year.[10]

As sparse as the Lieber line seems, the family tree does not really straighten out on the Solomon side either. We do know that the Solomon clan consisted of a large family and that they immigrated to America in 1901. The Solomons represent a more typical Jewish immigrant experience at the turn of the twentieth century: they immigrated as a family, a costly endeavor for Jews struggling to save enough money to escape Romania, but important in keeping the family together.

Nine years later, by 1910, the family occupied an apartment building on Fourth Street along with many other Romanian families. Various documents list Celia's father and mother with different first names, his either "Sanfir" or "Zanfer," while her mother's is the more common "Sophia" or "Sophie." Sanfir, born in 1865, and Sophia, born a year later, had eight children. In 1903, Robbie, their youngest child, was the first born in the United States.

Celia's birth year is alternately listed as either 1892 or 1894. In 1910, she worked as a salesperson in a five and dime store. She and her older brother Louis, employed as a salesman at a trimming store, did not attend school, but her four younger siblings living with the family—Frieda, Isidor, Minnie, and Robbie—all did. With the older children working to help support the family and the young members going to school, the Solomon children embodied the typical path to success for immigrants. Similarly to many of their Romanian kinsmen, the family settled into life in the United States, aspiring for a higher standard of living, taking advantage of educational opportunities, and many more readily embracing American popular culture. While Sanfir and Sophia spoke Yiddish, their children gained fluency in English, a significant step toward adapting to their new home. The Solomon family later moved to West 152nd Street.[11]

Lee remembers that the family moved from the apartment on West Ninety-Eighth and West End Avenue to Washington Heights around this time, when his younger brother Larry was born (October 26, 1931).[12] The move definitely signaled a downsizing in the family's fortunes and neighborhood. Like so many others, the Great Depression cut the heart out of the Lieber family and its progress toward fulfilling the American Dream.

Standing outside an Episcopal church on Twenty-Ninth Street in Manhattan, some two thousand men turned up their collars and burrowed their hands deep in their coat pockets against a bone-chilling wind whipping through the city. In the early days of the Great Depression, such lines were commonplace, snaking and twisting up Fifth Avenue. These men heard that the church dispensed food to the poor and assembled in hopes that they might get enough to feed their families. A quarter of them were turned away when the rations ran out. Desperation mixed with fear and many people would go hungry that night.

The sight of these needy New Yorkers and the countless others just like them unnerved the city's residents. Many of those waiting for food were clearly in anguish over accepting charity to survive. Those filling bread lines and taking handouts carried a deep psychological burden as unwilling participants in the country's economic ruin. They did not want to take aid. Americans prided themselves on a strong work ethic and believed that they would be rewarded for this attitude. Most who received welfare, from clothing and rent money to food and medical supplies, did so reluctantly.

The collapse of the national economy at the hands of Wall Street corruption left the country angry and despondent. Money resided at the heart of American culture in the 1920s. The era's brokers and investment bankers rose up and reigned as society's new heroes and celebrities—the kind of men that F. Scott Fitzgerald's Nick Carraway in *The Great Gatsby* might have become if the fictional character were real. Wall Street fluctuations, hot stocks, and trading exploits served as juicy gossip. The overheated economy put the kindling in place; Wall Street greed provided the spark.

The soup line of broken men weaving through Manhattan creates a riveting picture of national despair. Yet, each one of those individuals also represented a defeated family left crippled by the financial collapse. After decades in the United States, falling in love, and starting a family, the Depression devastated the Liebers. Stanley, still too young to comprehend the magnitude of what had happened, did hear the fallout, the anger, and the anguish in his parents' voices. "My earliest recollections were of my parents talking about what they would do if they didn't have the rent money," he said. "Luckily we were never evicted."[13] The struggle for day-to-day essentials forced families into constant alert mode.

When the stock market crashed in late 1929, Jacob had been in the United States for more than two decades. However, nothing could insulate him or his coworkers during such disorder. His work in the garment district simply dried up and went away. According to Lee, his father also attempted to run a diner, but the operation failed, which cost the older Lieber his life's savings.[14]

The chronic unemployment took a toll on Jacob and Celia's marriage. As the daily struggles compounded, the pressure was too much to stand. Stanley, not yet seven, witnessed his parents "arguing, quarreling incessantly." Like a bad record doomed to play over and over again, "it was over money, or the lack of it."[15]

Historically, Romanian families were known for possessing incredibly close ties. Even during the Depression, some patriarchs refused to let their children work, realizing that education still created the path to achievement, regardless of the money woes they faced. For the Liebers, Stanley was too young to contribute. He spent the most difficult years of the Great Depression watching and listening to his parents fight to keep the family afloat.

The constant bickering between Jacob and Celia only halted on Sunday nights, when the boy and his parents gathered around the radio.[16] Young Stanley liked listening to the ventriloquist Edgar Bergen on NBC's *The Chase and Sanborn Hour*, which aired from 8 p.m. to 9 p.m. on Sunday nights for decades. Bergen's wooden sidekick was Charlie McCarthy, a wisecracking, often slyly suggestive mouthpiece for the comedian's humorous skits. Since radio listeners could not actually see that

Charlie was a dummy, the real joy was in Bergen's comedic patter and skill in creating compelling characters.

While Celia cleaned the apartment or cooked in the cramped space, Jacob scoured the want ads, but could not mask his increasing desolation. As a young boy, Stanley watched his father venture out into the city each day to look for work. Exhausted and mentally beaten, the man then returned each evening, more despondent and desperate than before. Jacob, according to his son, just sat at the kitchen table, staring out at nothing, growing ever more depressed as the family balanced on the edge of collapse.[17] Sometimes, Jacob would try to goad his wife into going out to the park for a walk with him and their son. She "hated it," Lee recalled. "They never got along."[18]

Cash-strapped, Celia often had to turn to her sisters for money. In an attempt to save their meager funds, the Liebers moved into a smaller apartment in the Bronx after Stanley's younger brother Larry came into the family. The older boy slept on the couch in the living room, situated—like so many low-rent apartments in the city—in the back of the building. The window looked directly into another building beside it. The cramped confines and additional mouth to feed merely amped up the despair the Liebers faced.[19] Stanley remembered, "All we could see was the brick wall of the building across the alley. I could never look and see if the other kids were out in the street playing stickball or doing anything that I might join in."[20]

Dressed in a dark replica of a sailor outfit, complete with a felt Tam O'Shanter hat perched at an angle atop his head, young Stanley Lieber sits on an antique desk, leaning on his tiny right arm. This is the kind of popular posed photograph that parents forced their kids to endure in the 1920s. Although only a youngster, the boy reveals dark, mesmerizing eyes and a faraway look that seems to hide the key to some distant mystery.

Too young to fully understand his family's plight, Stanley bounced along, relying on his mother's love to overcome his father's anxiety and demanding rules. Celia's sister Jean recalled that Jack was "exacting with his boys." He watched over them and demanded that they do daily routines as he outlined: "brush your teeth a certain way, wash your tongue, and so on."[21] Celia, though, was different. She filled young Stanley with her own hopes and dreams. She bolstered the child at every turn. When he learned to read, his mother realized the importance of education in overcoming their dire straits. "She often asked me to read aloud to her," Stanley remembered. "I enjoyed doing that, imagining I was on some Broadway stage reading for a vast, entranced audience."[22] Celia and Jack might struggle through the harsh realities brought on by the Depression, but Celia attempted to isolate Stanley from its severity.

For a poor kid unable to afford fancy sleep-away summer camps and without many friends, reading helped Stanley cope with his family difficulties, "It was my escape from the dreariness and sadness of my home life."[23] More importantly, reading enabled the boy to hone his sense of adventure and creativity. "Used to scribble my own comics, as far back as I can remember," Lee said. "Used to draw horizon line and add stick-figure people, telling myself little stories all the while."[24]

Celia pushed the boy to excel at school. As a result, "I was always something of an outsider," Stanley said. "My mother wanted me to finish school as soon as possible so I could get a job and help support the family."[25] Hoping to please Celia, Stanley worked hard enough to skip grades and advanced quickly, despite the teasing from older kids and getting picked on. He developed a precocious intellect, but his youth and brightness did not help him socially. He found it difficult to establish friendships with older classmates who had gone to school together for years.

Like many bright students, the boy found a mentor in a young Jewish teacher named Leon B. Ginsberg. Each day, Ginsberg started class by telling the students a baseball story featuring the imaginary slugger Swat Mulligan, always "funny and exciting," according to the boy. Mulligan's heroics created an atmosphere that made learning fun. For a classroom in Lee's elementary school days, this was a rarity. For Stanley Lieber, however, the life lesson drawn from Ginsberg's daily tale was clear: "Whenever I want to communicate to others, I always try to do it in a lighter-hearted way and make it as entertaining as possible."[26]

Telling amusing stories that created a vivid scene and a great deal of excitement also appealed to Stanley's other passion—watching movies. In the late 1920s and early 1930s, when the boy thought about a bigger-than-life future, his idea of heaven was embodied in film icon Errol Flynn. The actor burst onto the scene in 1935's *Captain Blood*, which showcased his good looks, flamboyant charm, and athletic grace. Flynn became the top action film star and drew in young viewers like Lieber with detailed and finely choreographed fight scenes and swordplay, as in *The Adventures of Robin Hood* (1938), Flynn's first color film. For a boy creating his own comic stories and devouring books and magazines, the movies demonstrated how the marriage of visual elements and dialogue drove the action. "There on the screen were worlds that dazzled my mind, worlds of magic and wonder, worlds which I longed to inhabit, if only in imagination," he remembered.[27]

Lee went to the movies at Loew's 175th Street Theatre, one of New York's "Wonder Theatres" built between 1925 and 1930. Originally built for vaudeville, the increasing popularity of motion pictures led to Loew's being transformed for films.

An enormous seven-story-high Robert Morton Wonder organ entertained viewers in the ornate setting. Not just interested in action adventures, Lee also loved the early comedic films of the Marx Brothers and Laurel and Hardy. Within a three-block radius of 181st Street, the youngster could pick from five movie theaters. On Saturdays, they showed serials. Lee eagerly anticipated Tarzan and his other favorite, *The Jungle Mystery*, the adventures of a man-ape. After the films ended, he met up with his cousin Morty Feldman on Seventy-Second Street, where the boys ate pancakes and talked about the movies.[28]

Stanley grew into a self-described "voracious reader." In later years, he often cited Shakespeare as his most important influence, because of the commitment to drama and comedy, which shaped the young Lee's ideas about creativity and storytelling. Lee enjoyed Shakespeare's "rhythm of words," explaining, "I've always been in love with the way words sound."[29] The boy's desire to read had no real boundaries. He took a book or magazine with him everywhere, even the breakfast table, using a little wooden contraption his mother found for him that held the pages open while it propped up the book.

Although he loved reading and film and dabbled with drawing, young Stanley had no illusions about working in comic books. Comic books during Stanley's boyhood years were primarily reprints from newspaper strips and looked more like books or magazines. In the 1920s, black and white strips were popular, particularly the slapstick humor of Bud Fisher's *Mutt and Jeff*, which were reprinted as oversized comic books. He read them, like other children his age, but they did not capture his imagination the way film and novels did. "Creating comic books was never part of my childhood dream," he explained. "I never thought of that at all."[30] He did, however, read *Famous Funnies*, widely considered the first modern American comic book, which Dell published in 1934 and distributed through Woolworth's department stores. He specifically remembered enjoying *Hairbreadth Harry*, a strip created by C. W. Kahles that featured the hero in various melodramatic adventures to keep his rival Rudolph Ruddigore Rassendale from the heroine Belinda Blinks.[31]

As debilitating as the stock market crash was on the nation's economy, the truly crushing blow came from the way it demoralized the American people. The shocking speed of the collapse shook the public's faith in the national economic system. Millions of workers lost their jobs as businesses desperately cut their operations to the bare essentials. Construction in New York City, for example, came to a near halt as 64 percent of workers were laid off soon after the stock market collapsed.

Desperation reigned, and its epicenter was New York City. By October 1933, it counted some 1.25 million people on relief. Even more telling is that another million were eligible for relief, but did not accept it. Some 6,000 New Yorkers attempted to make ends meet by selling apples on the streets. But by the end of 1931, most street vendors were gone. Grocery store sales dropped by 50 percent. Many urban dwellers scoured garbage cans and dumps looking for food. Studies estimated that 65 percent of the African American children in Harlem were plagued by malnutrition during the era.

Tens of thousands of people in New York City were forced to live on the streets or in shantytowns located along the banks of the East River and the Hudson River. These clusters of makeshift abodes were dubbed "Hoovervilles"—a backhanded tribute to President Herbert Hoover. The city's largest camp was in Central Park. Ironically, the Central Park shantytown became a tourist attraction and featured daily performances by an unemployed tightrope walker and other out-of-work artists.

Unemployment in 1929 was about 3 percent, but by 1932 the figure had reached 24 percent. Millions more involuntarily worked in part-time roles. Two years after the crash, some two hundred thousand New Yorkers faced eviction for failure to pay rent. Many who were not evicted sold off their valuables so they could raise the money. Others—like the Liebers—trekked from apartment to apartment. If their furniture had been purchased on credit, many owners left it behind when they could no longer make payments.

For the Lieber family, the crash had lasting and prolonged consequences, yet somehow they managed to keep a roof over their heads and the rocky marriage afloat. On the surface the obvious impact was that Jacob's career virtually disappeared in a complicated game of supply and demand. The number of dress cutters shrank as manufacturing companies struggled to stay solvent. The years after the stock market tanked, Jacob searched for work, but to no avail.

The arguments about money took a toll on the Lieber marriage and created animosity that Stanley could avoid to some degree as he got older. Unfortunately, his little brother, Lawrence (Larry), born nine years after his older brother, suffered more directly and spent his formative years under the stress and strain of a troubled marriage and little hope for better days ahead.

Jacob's unemployment meant that Stanley had to find work as soon as possible; any little bit of extra income might help the family avoid destitution. Consequently, as he reached his mid-teen years, the boy (along with millions of other teenagers) either worked or constantly searched for jobs. Celia's mix of fawning support and pushing him to work through school quickly paid off. The enterprising teen, smart and already a budding storyteller and wordsmith, found a variety of odd jobs, including as an usher at a movie theater, an office boy at a factory that manufactured jeans, and even writing obituaries of living celebrities that would be filed whenever they passed away. Balancing high school and part-time jobs became a constant way of life.

Lieber went to DeWitt Clinton High School, a twenty-one-acre campus at 100 West Mosholu Parkway South and East 205th Street in the Bronx. Described as the "castle on the parkway," the all-boys school stood as one of the largest high schools in the world, enrolling ten to twelve thousand students from across the city and comprising a diverse ethnic population, heavily tilted toward immigrants and the children of immigrants.

In a high school like Clinton, which seemed more like a factory than a school, making a name among the throngs would be difficult, if not impossible. Yet, Lieber's high school years were filled with school clubs and other opportunities that demonstrated his budding showmanship traits. The boy who had whiled away time reading and being alone grew into a handsome, tall young man, though rail thin. He joined the public-speaking club and the law society, where he dreamed of becoming a famous courtroom attorney.

Earning the nickname "Gabby" for his charm and ability to chat up a storm, Lieber predicted big things for himself in the future, a notion echoed by his peers. High school friend Bob Wendlinger remembers thinking that his classmate was headed toward greatness. "You always knew that he was going to be successful," Wendlinger says. "It was a given."[32]

Lieber experimented with a variety of personas as a student, like many good-looking and popular students do while in high school. He gravitated toward publicity and held a position on the business staff of the Clinton literary magazine, the *Magpie*. Despite his own budding writing talents and years of intense reading, he confined himself to "publicity director" for the magazine. Part of the Lieber youthful lore is that before a meeting in the tower, the high-ceilinged part of the school where the *Magpie* staff went to work, he found a ladder left there by a worker on his lunch break. Jumping at the chance to show off and leave his mark, the youngster scurried up the ladder and wrote, "Stan Lee is God" on the ceiling. Perhaps unwilling to risk getting in trouble with the maintenance worker or other high school administrators for defacing the building by using his real name—or just playing around with a stage name—this was his first recorded use of the moniker that would later travel the globe.[33]

The *Magpie* publicity job wasn't a throwaway position in a high school club for the teen. While he dreamed of a variety of careers—including actor—advertising seemed like his true calling. The years of reading magazines created an aura of fascination about advertisements for him. Several of the jobs he held during high school centered on words or selling, including writing publicity materials for a Jewish hospital in Denver, the obituary job, and selling *New York Times* subscriptions to his classmates. Even as a teen, the boy realized that he had a dramatic flair and could be a persuasive public speaker, a skill he had been honing since his mother asked him to read aloud to her as a boy. In high school, he also adopted a magician's persona—calling himself the great "Thimbilini"—and performed sleight-of-hand tricks with small thimbles that drew crowds of curious classmates to his miniroutines. From an early age, Stanley craved attention and a spotlight.

As a fifteen-year-old, Lieber had entered a high school essay competition sponsored by the *New York Herald Tribune*, called "The Biggest News of the Week Contest." The paper, owned by Ogden Reid and his wife Helen, although conservative, pursued local issues in a stylized fashion, emphasizing realism and the city's changing atmosphere. Lieber claims to have won the prize for three straight weeks, goading the newspaper to write the boy and ask him to let someone else win. According to Stanley, the paper suggested he look into writing professionally, which the boy claims, "probably changed my life."[34]

However, the story is apocryphal. The likelier story is that the young Lieber won a seventh-place prize of $2.50 and two honorable mention awards—hardly the rags-to-riches tale that he would identify as the moment he wanted to become a writer. "After all," as one assessment puts it, "Lee is a storyteller, and his account of the *Herald Tribune* essay contest certainly made for a good story, even if it's untrue."[35] While the story veers from the truth, the prize money made an impression on a poor Jewish kid. A year later, in 1939, the teen worked a total of twelve weeks, pulling in $150 via part-time jobs and whatever work he could muster.[36]

Leaving the hallowed halls of the monolithic all-boys DeWitt Clinton High School in early summer 1939, Stanley Lieber entered the job market feeling anxious and under more than a little duress. His high school years coincided with some of the worst years of the Great Depression. Graduating did not mean launching a career but just finding a job. His family needed the money.

President Franklin Delano Roosevelt tried to wrench the United States out of its financial turmoil, only to see gross national product fall 4.5 percent in 1938 and unemployment hit 19 percent. The economic downturn triggered by FDR's misfires did not make the transition easy for Lieber, a young man attempting to make the move from high school student to actually earning a living.

Ironically, Hitler's invasion of Poland several months after Lieber's graduation would spark the nation into war planning and production, thereby reviving the economy. For several years prior to the attacks on Pearl Harbor, the United States shipped products to allies around the globe and simultaneously prepped for its seemingly inevitable entry into the global fight. The economic rebound, however, did not kick in soon enough to aid Lieber.

Duty-bound to help support his family, college would not be an option. As a boy and then teenager, he may have daydreamed about becoming an actor or enjoying a career as a courtroom attorney, but his immediate future meant getting work. He needed a permanent position, not another in a series of humiliating and somewhat menial part-time jobs like the ones he had during high school. The Lieber family suffered during the financial crisis, so Stanley's graduation and subsequent salary might offer his family some financial stability, which it lacked for most of his young life.

For so many families of the 1920s and 1930s, the economic collapse and daily struggle to claw back to normality defined American life. Growing up in New York City during the Great Depression had profound consequences for young Stanley Lieber. He could cling to vague memories of his short life prior to the Wall Street crash, but his worldview would be shaped by his father's inability to find consistent work. The resulting turmoil that unemployment rained down on the Lieber family shook the boy to his core and would remain central to how he approached his own work life.

Lieber's most fundamental thinking was "a feeling that the most important thing for a man is to have work to do, to be busy, to be needed."[37] This notion shaped Lieber as an adult—the desire not only to work, but to feel needed. "Even when I made a good living, my dad didn't think of me as a success," he remembered. "He was pretty wrapped up in himself most of the time. Some of that rubbed off on me. I was always looking at people who were doing better than I was and wishing I could do what they were doing. . . . Part of me always felt I hadn't quite made it yet."[38]

What Lieber would call the "specter of poverty" cast a dark cloud over his parents' marriage, essentially sapping the joy and love they once shared.[39] The fear of unemployment pushed the youngster to value work and earning a living above all else. Lieber had this shared experience with other contemporaries, including fellow comic book veterans, many of whom were first-generation immigrants and Jewish. They knew each other's neighborhoods, and they had similar experiences navigating life in Depression-era America and New York City, including serving as eyewitnesses to the despair of bread lines or watching people around them get booted out of apartments or jobs.

The tumultuous life at near-poverty and his parents' constant battling had lasting effects, despite Celia's frequent doting on him and reiterating how successful he would someday become. One writer describes the consequences these competing factors had on the boy, producing a young man "agonizingly sensitive, desperate for approval and easily influenced by others." Highly intelligent, the youngster yearned for something larger than life that would fulfill his mother's predictions about his future fame and wealth.[40]

CHAPTER 2

TEENAGE EDITOR

Rising up to his feet and towering over a messy desktop with drawings strewn haphazardly about and correspondence littering every square inch, Timely Comics head writer and editorial director Joe Simon reached out his hand to welcome his new young assistant.

Still a little dizzy from how fast he had transformed from applicant to full-time employee, Stanley Lieber vigorously pumped the older man's hand. He beamed with gratitude. Lieber's mind raced as he tried to put it all in perspective.

A steady paycheck . . . $8 a week!

For a kid just out of high school whose family always had money troubles, the meager sum, if nothing else, meant that he might help the family regain its footing. More importantly, however, a full-time job gave the teenager security and a shot at a career in writing and publishing. Words appealed to the boy. Constantly reading as a kid to escape the reality of his father's unemployment and their shabby surroundings in cramped, cheap apartments, he dreamed of one day writing the Great American Novel.

Long before he would get to write anything, though, Lieber would work away the days as an office boy for Simon and the other full-time Timely Comics employee, artist and writer Jack Kirby. Some days the gofer job included refilling the artist's inkwells. Other days he would run out for sandwiches while the famous duo concocted new superhero stories.

The teenager didn't mind the mindless tasks, even if he spent hours sweeping the floors or erasing stray pencil marks on finished pages to prep them for publication. He watched and learned from two of the industry's greats.

More importantly, he had achieved his primary goal at the time, simply finding a permanent position. He had a job! His father's fate would not befall him. Instead, the boy set off on a career.

Many episodes in Lieber's early life are shrouded in ambiguity: some of his ancestors virtually disappear in the early part of the twentieth century, or official records shine down a road to nowhere. Similarly, how the young man bounded from Clinton high school graduate to Simon and Kirby's assistant at Timely involves both a bit of mystery and a touch of mythmaking.

There are several versions of the teenager's Timely Comics origin story. One account begins with his mother Celia, who had urged him to hustle through high school and then helped him search for a job after he graduated early. Clearly Celia put her hopes into her oldest son, particularly since her faith in her husband nearly led the family to ruin.

Celia relayed information to her son about a possible job at a publishing company where her brother Robbie worked. In this version, the young high school grad shows up at McGraw-Hill on West Forty-Second Street with almost no understanding of comic books or even what the company really does. Despite this shortcoming, Simon quickly explains what comic books are and how they come about, and then offers the youngster the position. Basically, he and Kirby are so frantic and overworked from the relentless pace, particularly with their new hit *Captain America*, that they just need someone (anyone, really) to provide an extra set of hands so that they can focus on creating.

Robbie Solomon is at the center of a different story, but here he is the main figure, essentially a conduit between Simon and publishing house owner Martin Goodman. In addition to being Celia Lieber's brother, Robbie married the publisher's sister Sylvia. Goodman liked to surround himself with family members, despite the imperious tone he took with everyone who worked for him. The formal link is never explicitly made, but it seems that having Robbie's stamp of approval and the familial tie to Goodman made Lieber's hire a fait accompli. Simon, then, despite what he may or may not have thought of the boy, basically had to take Lieber in. "His entire publishing empire was a family business," recall two comic book historians.[1] Solomon himself played a suspicious role at the publishing house, a kind of spy for Goodman who ratted out employees that were not working hard enough or were playing fast and loose with company rules.

While the family connection tale is credible and plays into the general narrative of Martin Goodman's extensive nepotism, Lee also offered a different avenue that makes his job at Timely much more coincidental. "I was fresh out of high school," he said, "I wanted to get into the publishing business, if I could." Rather than being led to the publishing firm by his uncle Robbie, Lee explained: "There was an ad in the paper that said, 'Assistant Wanted in a Publishing House.'"[2] This alternative version calls into question Lee's early career move into publishing—and throws up for grabs the date as either 1940, which is usually listed as the year of his hiring, or 1939, as he implies.[3]

As a young man searching for a career, Lieber may have not known much about comic books, but he did recognize publishing as a viable option for someone with his skills. He knew that he could write, but had no way of really gauging his creative talents, and he had little understanding of what took place at a publishing company. Although Goodman was a cousin by marriage, he did not have much interaction with his younger relative, so it wasn't as if Goodman purposely brought Lieber into the firm and groomed him for a leadership role. No one will ever really know how much of a wink and nod Solomon gave Simon or if Goodman knew about the hiring, though the kid remembers the publisher being surprised the first time he saw him in the comics division.

The teen, though bright, talented, and hardworking, needed a break. The youngster could not afford to go to college during the doldrums of the Great Depression. His family's financial instability forced them to rely on handouts from more affluent relatives to make ends meet. His early tenure at Timely Comics served as a kind of extended apprenticeship, as if his work accumulated into an on-the-job type of training at comic book university.

Lieber, for his part, played dutifully with Simon and Kirby, learning the business on the go as the two men scrambled to create content. Since both were known for working fast, the teen witnessed firsthand two of the industry's greatest talents. The lessons he learned on the job would set the foundation for his own career as a writer and editor, as well as a manager of talented individuals as they plied their trade.

Whether young Lieber's job at Timely Publishing came about based on his family connections, the pure luck of being in the right place at the proper time, or some combination of the two, the long-term relationship he developed with publisher Martin Goodman would essentially define his career.

Goodman formed Timely in 1933 to sell cheap, tawdry men's magazines. He had no aspirations to bring great art to the world or innovate in any other way. Goodman was driven by dollar signs. He wanted to make a pile of money in the least taxing manner possible.

The publisher focused on the men's magazine side of the business. An astute businessman, however, Goodman kept a close eye on broad publishing trends and personally demanded that cover art be sensational, revealing, and provocative, particularly when it came to the semi-nude women who graced the covers of the men's pulp magazines he favored, with interesting titles like *Marvel Science Stories* and *Mystery Tales*. Some of the magazines Goodman and his competitors sold were so salacious that they were basically pornographic and had to be sold behind closed doors. The backdoor mentality brought in various underworld elements, including the mafia and mobsters, who saw pulps as a way to make a quick buck and semi-legitimize themselves or their business interests.

From his expansive office perch in the McGraw-Hill building, Goodman excelled at scrutinizing what other publishers produced, figuring out which magazines sold well, and then throwing the full weight of his company into the new craze. Innovation was not his concern. Instead, he wanted to keep the company in business and afford himself a comfortable living. Like all the men who ran pulp publishing houses in that era, Goodman came of age in the rough-and-tumble industry, filled with stories of horrific bankruptcies and corruption, as well as many get-rich-quick schemes that had paid off.

Many publishers had grown wealthy off the tawdry men's pulp content in the 1920s when the demand for magazines skyrocketed. They fed an eager public (with more leisure time to devote to things like reading and the excess money to buy magazines) via advanced print technology that enabled higher-quality photos and better distribution systems. Despite the successes Goodman and others in the magazine business enjoyed, they started to face criticism across multiple fronts due to the raunchy story content and lurid cover images.

In response, many publishers set up dummy companies to play fast and loose with the firm's books. One big company might set up dozens of smaller ones, so that if any single entity went south, it would not topple the whole empire. In this scenario, debts might be loaded onto one operation, which would then go bankrupt and have its assets bought by a secret sister firm at pennies (or less) on the dollar. With little oversight or regulation, the publishers jumped from one fad to the next—from highly sexual adventure stories to true crime dramas with scantily clad damsels in distress to science fiction. Sexual content and pinup covers defined many of these magazines. Titles like *Real Confessions* and *Mystery Tales* played to men's most base desires.

Across the board, the pulps catered to male fantasies, until New York City officials stepped in to clean up the business. They threatened the newsstands first, then the distributors, until they got close enough to the publishing executives with obscenity charges that could land them in jail. In the mid-1930s, while the Depression tore through the national economy, the pulp publishers attempted to skirt the regulations handed down by aggressive district attorneys such as Thomas Dewey, New York City's crusading public advocate and future Republican presidential candidate. Summing up the environment, one writer explains that publishers "managed to follow the letter of public decency laws while selling the most obscenely racist and sadistic sexual fantasies."[4] The publishers kept finding ways to circumvent the regulations and stay just inches ahead of fire-breathing consumer advocacy groups and the politicians they attracted to uphold the popular public decency laws.

What Goodman didn't realize right away was that various forces were aligning against the pulps, ultimately causing another format to grasp the spotlight—comic books. Growing out of the cartoon strips in newspapers, comic books had originally just been reprints bound together and then sold at newsstands. Most of these were aimed at children, like Richard F. Outcault's *Yellow Kid* or Bud Fisher's *Mutt and Jeff*. Later, pulp magazines featured more heroic characters in stories designed to titillate and entertain the magazine-hungry masses. *Tarzan*, *Doc Savage*, and *The Shadow* had superhero powers, secret origins, and extraordinary abilities. Millions of readers gobbled these characters up, thereby creating a kind of intermediary publication that stood between the lurid side of the pulp industry and the kid-friendly comic books.

In 1929, Dell published *The Funnies*, the first comic book comprised of original work, not reprints from the newspapers. The publication only lasted a year, but it gave rise to others willing to try out stand-alone comic books. M. C. Gaines, a salesman at Eastern Color, the company that printed the Sunday comics in color for many large northeastern newspapers, experimented with smaller-sized comic books in the early to mid-1930s and gave them a ten-cent cover price. *Famous Funnies* #1 sold out and other comics were a hit as giveaway promotions for major corporations like Procter & Gamble and retailers like Kinney Shoes. Soon, comic book sales eclipsed the monthly sales mark of one hundred thousand, while the promotional ones reached into the millions. A craze took shape.

The comic book industry in the mid-1930s grew out of the strange convergence of two wild, nearly mythical characters: Major Malcolm Wheeler-Nicholson and Harry Donenfeld. Wheeler-Nicholson had a murky past that he filled with swashbuckling tales of serving in World War I and fighting the Bolsheviks in Russia. Venturing to New York City, his fame grew as a magazine writer who could give readers a realistic portrayal of the hardships and adventures of warfare. Donenfeld, a Romanian Jewish immigrant who grew up on the Lower East Side, learned to hustle there and persuade others to share in his entrepreneurial visions. As he rose through the publishing ranks, Donenfeld formed ties with mobsters. (Rumors circulated that he used his publishing network to help the mafia run liquor during Prohibition.) Donenfeld published smutty pulp magazines that bordered on pornography, most frequently called "girlie magazines," long before Hugh Hefner would create *Playboy*.

The two men's paths intersected when Wheeler-Nicholson agreed to a distribution deal for his new *Detective Comics* line with Donenfeld's Independent News Company. In 1937 and 1938, Wheeler-Nicholson barely remained solvent. Always strapped for cash and facing a large debt to his distributor, he agreed to form Detective Comics, Inc. with Donenfeld to publish the first issue of the new comic book (soon the company would be known simply as DC). Later, Independent News bought Wheeler-Nicholson's National Allied Publications at auction and forced him out of the company. According to comic book historian Gerard Jones, the "Tennessee-born major of the cavalry didn't like Jews," so getting into business with Donenfeld revolted him, but "he made the only choice he could." Donenfeld and his cronies "were obviously interested in calling the shots" and as soon as they gobbled up the major's companies, the move into comic books was nearly complete.[5]

The comic book revolution required one more spark to set off a storm across America. That catalyst ignited in Cleveland, Ohio, at the hands of two earnest, amateur comic book creators: struggling writer Jerry Siegel and artist Joe Shuster, who struck gold with their first creation, Superman. After a long march toward publication, the superhero appeared on the cover of the first issue of *Action Comics* hoisting a car over his head and smashing the front end, pieces flying off the vehicle as onlookers fled in terror. Initially, no one realized what a blockbuster Superman would become, but within several months, Donenfeld saw the sales figures, which backed up what newsstand owners told him: he had a big hit right under his nose. Eventually, *Action Comics* sold more than a million copies a month for Donenfeld's DC Comics line. The independent Superman comic book launched in early 1939 sold 900,000. Sadly, Siegel and Shuster, like nearly all comic book writers and artists, sold away their rights to the character, working initially for $10 a page, thus earning a combined $130 for the first Superman story.

The Superman craze led to marketing the hero across other media, including a newspaper strip, radio show, and a series of animated cartoons. The radio show propelled further expansion, and according to one writer, "the comic strip sold to nearly three hundred newspapers by 1941." The publicist hired to promote Superman for Donenfeld claimed "35 million people were following Superman in at least one medium."[6] Beyond the media avenues, there were countless merchandising pieces for sale, including trading cards, buttons, and metal action figures, which ultimately made the publisher rich beyond his dreams.

Donenfeld even got into the act, wearing a Superman T-shirt under his tuxedo. Out carousing with friends and his mistress at tony bars and restaurants around New York City, people would point at him in awe as the man who published Superman. Never one for indiscretion, Donenfeld would wait for some minor accident to happen, leap up, and rip open his white tux shirt to reveal the hero's logo underneath.[7]

Not willing to sit idly and watch his competitors make money off a popular genre, Goodman jumped on the comic book bandwagon. Frank Torpey, a Funnies, Inc. sales manager who had worked with the publisher at Eastern Distributing, urged Goodman to launch a comic book division. The two shook hands on a deal for Timely to publish the work of Bill Everett and Carl Burgos, two virtually unknown writers who also did the artwork for their creations. Their superheroes, a term used loosely to describe the angst-ridden Namor the Sub-Mariner and troubled android The Human Torch, served as the centerpieces of *Marvel Comics* #1, an anthology published by Goodman at the end of August 1939. Always cautious, he took a wait-and-see attitude toward comic books and outsourced the production of the line wholly to the Funnies, Incorporated team.[8]

The first issue sold 80,000 copies in September alone and ultimately ten times that, actually more than most comics done by Donenfeld's publishing house, even rivaling the sales of *Superman*. *Marvel Comics* soon became *Marvel Mystery Comics*, focusing on its two successful superheroes.[9] Namor and Human Torch became more powerful as the issues piled up, in other words, more Superman-like. They were not the only copycats running rampant across the burgeoning industry. Several dozen publishers rushed into the market. The familiar call rang out across New York City artist and writing communities: "Find me the next Superman!"

Goodman decided to hire his own artists and writers, rather than pay the Funnies, Inc. team. He did not want to become dependent solely on the packager, which would have situated his growing comics business at the whim of outsiders. He offered veteran freelancer Joe Simon a job for $12 a page, much more than the writer/artist had made with Funnies. The editor brought along a young artist named Jacob Kurtzberg, a tough kid from the Lower East Side who had been a gang member but had become obsessed with writing and drawing comic book heroes. His early experience included working in the famous Fleischer Brothers animation house, helping out with *Popeye* and *Betty Boop* cartoons. The young artist could produce pages at an unprecedented rate, which impressed everyone he worked with.

Simon and the artist—using his new pseudonym Jack Kirby—agreed to a partnership. Initially, they worked together on a character Simon created called Blue Bolt for Novelty Press. Many creative teams work well on paper, but Simon and Kirby figured out how to really make it work, particularly since each could do every aspect of the job, from writing and penciling to drawing covers. When people asked about who did what task on a certain project, Simon shrugged and said, "We both did everything."[10] The partnership they forged lasted the next sixteen years until World War II split them apart.

Sensing that Simon and Kirby were supremely talented and that the comic book market was skyrocketing, Goodman bet on their future and offered them a royalty schedule in addition to page rates. In late 1939, he gave Simon a full-time position as Timely's first editor, though the writer had basically been working in that role already.[11] Simon then convinced Goodman to hire on his partner Kirby at a higher page rate than other artists earned, explaining that the artist worked so fast that the steady weekly paycheck would more than pay for itself. Simon and Kirby set up a two-man operation and began developing new concepts for Timely. Goodman purposely kept the comic book division small, not really willing to put funds into the effort until he had a sense it would pay off in a much bigger way.

Content to not micromanage (though he always obsessed over the cover art and whether to add new titles), Goodman basically turned the division over to Simon and Kirby. After a couple of low-selling backfires, including the Red Raven and The Vision, the two hit their stride. Together they came up with Captain America—though both men disputed their roles in the creation to some extent, each giving themselves more of the credit. Steve Rogers got his superpowers from an Army experimental super-serum that made him nearly invincible. Realizing that they had the perfect villain for their patriotic superhero, Simon and Kirby featured Hitler on the cover of the first issue: As evil Nazi soldiers shoot at Cap in vain, he knocks the German leader off balance with a strong right.

With Simon and Kirby in charge of his comics division, Goodman continued his focus on the pulp side of the operation, which consisted of more than two-dozen titles, such as *Gayety*, *Amazing Detective Cases*, and *Uncanny Stories*. Yet, at the same time, his intrusion into comics immediately struck gold with the Human Torch and Sub-Mariner. Then, Simon and Kirby's *Captain America* #1 appeared on newsstands on December 20, 1940 (the cover date for comic books always ran three months ahead, so the official date is March 1941). The comic book, according to one writer, "sold a near-Superman number of one million copies."[12] Suddenly, Timely transformed into a hot comic book publisher. Together, Simon and Kirby shot to fame after creating Captain America, one of the first really successful superheroes not being published by DC Comics, which put out the industry's two hottest commodities, Superman and Batman.

Simon hired Lieber and found a place for him. A little older and more experienced, the twenty-three-year-old Kirby and twenty-seven-year-old Simon were on hand when the modern comic book industry began. Simon had worked in newspapers in Syracuse and knew the rough-and-tumble publishing industry inside and out. Though he did not consider himself a great businessman, Simon saw the power content creators possessed and negotiated deals for Kirby and himself that no one else received at the time—even the *Superman* wonder team of Siegel and Shuster.

The two men grew accustomed to keeping the Timely operation afloat, despite being understaffed and somewhat underappreciated by Goodman and his executive team. A frenetic energy built, though, as Human Torch, Sub-Mariner, and Captain America grew into major superheroes and wild popularity among readers.

Lieber, the young, handsome teenager, with a shock of dark hair and constant smile, joined his new bosses in the cramped offices. In contrast, they were gruff men, almost constantly puffing away on cigars and filling the space with smoke.

At first, Simon kept the new employee busy with menial tasks. "I'd fill the ink wells. I'd run down and get them sandwiches at the drug store, and I'd proofread the pages," Lee recalled. "Sometimes in proofreading I'd say, 'You know, this sentence doesn't sound right. It ought to be written like this.' 'Well, go ahead and change it!' They didn't care!"[13]

Lieber also agitated Kirby by playing a small flute in the office, always yearning for ways to make himself the center of attention. Kirby would throw things at his young protégé and Simon would laugh as his partner's agitation grew. Kirby, the quintessential artist, had a manic—almost obsessive—need to draw, and draw fast.

Simon and Goodman rode the wave of Captain America's popularity, devising more titles that were related to expand the superhero lineup. They created teenage sidekicks for the main stars, Bucky for Captain America, who got to kick Hitler in the stomach in the second issue, and Toro for the Human Torch, a fire-eating circus performer who could also burst into flames and fight bad guys. DC's Batman had Robin, a young sidekick that comic book creators believed would help the superhero appeal to younger readers. Batman's success launched a wave of teen partners. But new titles generated additional work. Kirby and Simon had to bring in some freelancers to keep up, then they threw some odd copy-filler stories to Lieber as a kind of test run to see if the kid had any talent.

The throwaway story that Simon and Kirby had the teenager write for *Captain America Comics* #3 (May 1941), was titled "Captain America Foils the Traitor's Revenge." The story also launched Lieber's new identity as "Stan Lee," the pseudonym he adopted in hopes of saving his real name for the future novel he might write. Given the publication schedule, the latest the teen could have written the story is February 1941, but he probably wrote it earlier. The date is important, because it speaks to Lieber's career development. If he joined the company in late 1939, just after Kirby and Simon and when they were hard at work in developing Captain America, then there probably wasn't much writing for him to do. However, if the more likely time frame of late 1940 is accepted, then Lieber was put to work as a writer fairly quickly, probably because of the chaos Simon and Kirby faced in prepping issues of *Captain America* and their other early creations, as well as editing and overseeing the Human Torch and Sub-Mariner efforts.

Lee later acknowledged that the two-page story was just a fill-in so that the comic book could "qualify for the post office's cheap magazine rate." He also admitted, "Nobody ever took the time to read them, but I didn't care. I had become a published author. I was a pro!"[14] Simon appreciated the teen's enthusiasm and his diligence in attacking the assignment.

An action shot of Captain America knocking a man silly accompanied Lieber's first publication for Simon and Kirby. The story—essentially two pages of solid text—arrived sandwiched between a Captain America tale about a demonic killer on the loose in Hollywood and another featuring a giant Nazi strongman and another murderer who kills people when dressed up in a butterfly costume. "It gave me a feeling of grandeur," Lee recalled.[15] While many readers may have overlooked the text at the time, its cadence and style is a rough version of the mix of bravado, high-spirited language, and witty wordplay that marked the young man's writing later in his career.

Lou Haines, the villain, is sufficiently evil, although we never do find out what he did to earn the "traitor" moniker. In typical Lee fashion, the villain snarls at Colonel Stevens, the base commander: "But let me warn you now, you ain't seen the last of me! I'll get even somehow. Mark my words, you'll pay for this!" In hand-to-hand combat with the evildoer, Captain America lands a crippling blow, just as the reader thinks the hero may be doomed. "No human being could have stood that blow," the teen wrote. "Haines instantly relaxed his grip and sank to the floor—unconscious!"[16] The next day when the colonel asks Steve Rogers if he heard anything the night before, Rogers claims that he slept through the hullabaloo. Stevens, Rogers, and sidekick Bucky shared in a hearty laugh. The "Traitor" story certainly doesn't exude Lee's later confidence and knowing wink at the reader, but it demonstrates his blossoming understanding of audience, style, and pace.

By *Captain America* #5 (August 1941), Lee scored his first "true" comics story, the five-page filler in traditional comic book form, not simply a text piece, titled "Headline Hunter, Foreign Correspondent." Jerry Hunter is a newspaper reporter searching for a scoop in war-torn London. The journalist isn't really a superhero, but displays super strength and cunning, all in a snazzy blue suit and red tie, looking a little like Captain America.

In the end, Hunter foils the Nazi plan to steal Navy cargo route maps between the United States and Great Britain and even blows up a German munitions plant in the effort. "Oh, gosh, it wasn't anything! And besides, boy! Look at the swell scoop I got," Hunter tells the American ambassador at the end of the story. The teen language and golly-gee tone reveal Lee's budding comic book voice. Hunter could be an early incarnation of Peter Parker in the way he carries himself and speaks. The story is decent, given that it is just a filler within the wildly popular *Captain America* comic, but it is leagues better than "Tuk: Cave Boy," an odd rip-off of Tarzan with an exaggerated caveman, that appears in the same issue. At the time, the comics consisted of sixty-plus pages, so the Captain America pieces would take up two-thirds of the space, while filler stories increased the page count, which enabled the reduced postal rate.

Lee could not rest on the laurels of his first superhero publication. His move from office boy to burgeoning writer and editor occurred quickly, basically due to the tremendous growth in popularity of comic books and Timely's need to keep up with demand on limited resources. Timely had a small crew, which essentially necessitated that Lee, even though still a teenager, start producing content *and* new characters.

The combination of Lee's momentum as a writer, the demand for content, and the frantic pace of the publication schedule led the young man to create his first hero. The same month that his first superhero story appeared in *Captain America Comics* #5, he also introduced the character of Jack Frost in *U.S.A. Comics* #1 (August 1941).

Although one of Lee's first solo efforts, the Jack Frost story brims with Lee's dialogue and verve. When "the king of the cold" finds a dying man in his "eternal deathly quiet" kingdom, he vows to bring the murderer to justice, exclaiming: "Dead! I have heard that crime flourishes throughout the world, but it has now reached my land. . . . I will avenge this deed and prevent more like it!" Jack Frost is even a kind of antihero, misunderstood by the New York City police chief he offers to help and made fun of by the chief of detectives. Eventually, Jack Frost rescues the damsel in distress and wipes out a gang of "puny evil-doers." When the police try to arrest him, the story ends with Frost turning against the police, saying, "After this sort of reception I've changed my mind—if I can't work with you, I'll work against you—the next time we meet beware!" The idea that a superhero could be both good and bad, or at least conflicted, had already occurred to Lee.

Given his experience writing for the Captain America line, it is no surprise that Lee used a similar origin point for a highly successful character he also cocreated (with artist Jack Binder) called Destroyer. Appearing on the cover of *Mystic Comics* #6 (October 1941), the superhero is reporter Kevin Marlow, accused of being a spy in Hitler's Nazi Germany and thrown into a concentration camp (before that term was associated with the Holocaust). The tie to Captain America occurs when Marlow is given a super serum that gives him otherworldly strength, turning him into Destroyer, complete with a skull for an emblem. Like Cap, the superhero battles the Nazis, wreaking havoc on Hitler's inhuman forces.

The Destroyer never became a household name, like Captain America, but sales increased as the character fought in war-torn Europe against Nazi forces that were diabolical, gruesome, and drawn as inhuman and animalistic. To mask his identity, Destroyer donned a costume that featured blood-red striped pants and long crimson gloves. The costume made Destroyer appear just as inhuman as the villains he battled.

In some respects, the early comic book era could be defined by the battle for talent. When Simon and Kirby emerged as the hottest creative duo in comics, they found themselves courted by other publishers. The offers were too tempting, particularly for the perpetually money-nervous Kirby. The two had rented a hotel room near the Timely headquarters to use as a studio and spent lunch hours and time after work on freelance projects. At the time the whole comic book business seemed reliant on these kinds of backdoor deals and content creators playing one publisher (or many) off another to get the best rates. Most simply worked for page rates, but Simon negotiated much better deals for himself and Kirby.

According to Simon, Lee often followed the two older men around when they ventured out of the office. One time, he chased after them as the artist and editor snuck off to their hotel studio. Not able to shake their young protégé, they allowed him in. At that point, Lee finally realized that they were working on comic book characters for DC. Simon says he then "swore him to secrecy," despite "my theory that in comics, everybody knew everything. . . . There were no secrets there."[17]

Given Simon's ominous thought and the jealousy in the comic book industry based on who made what amount per page and for which publisher, it could not have been a surprise when they were inevitably found out and fired. In his memoir, Simon remembers working on *Captain America* #10 when several of the Goodman clan who worked for Martin—Abe, Dave, and Robbie—crammed into the Timely office to confront Simon and Kirby.

"You guys are working for DC," Abe accused the duo. "You haven't been true to us. You haven't been loyal to us. You should be ashamed of yourselves," Simon recalled.[18]

Then, Abe delivered the final blow: Once they finished that issue of *Captain America*, they were fired. One quasi-member of the Goodman clan was not there, Simon explained. "Stan was nowhere to be seen."[19]

Although Simon thought the firing was "very humiliating," it enraged Kirby. The artist pinned the firing on Lee, since the timing just seemed too coincidental and the Goodman clan's ties too strong. "Jack always thought Stan had told his uncle that we were working for DC," Simon remembers. "He never gave up on that idea, and hated him for the rest of his life—to the day he died." Simon was not willing to go that far and later, in his memoir, questioned Kirby's implication.[20]

The suggestion that Kirby never got over the firing and hated his counterpart for the rest of his life, however, adds a new twist to the relationship between the creative duo that would later revolutionize comic books. First, they had to get past (or bury) this episode to work together. Then, they needed to find a way to work side-by-side during Marvel's heyday, relentlessly churning out issue after issue, month after month. The animosity that later spilled out as they tangled over who deserved credit for creating the famous Marvel superheroes must have brought Kirby's "hatred" back to the surface with newfound ferocity.

Lee's recollection of the incident is strikingly different. He recalled Goodman personally showing Simon and Kirby the door after discovering that they were moonlighting for the enemy. Lee said, "Unexpectedly, Joe and Jack left Timely Comics! Supposedly it was because they were working on the side for National Periodicals." He then added, "Truth is, I never knew exactly *why* they left. I only knew this: it was suddenly *my* job to be in charge of the comics."[21] Earlier, Lee called their ouster "a surprisingly unexpected development" when "Joe and Jack left Timely in 1941." He also chalked it up to the "luck" that "seems to deal most of the cards in the game of life."[22]

Simon and Kirby's abrupt dismissal is yet another enigmatic episode in Lee's career. Although it would have been completely underhanded for the young assistant to rat out his mentors to his uncle or any of the Goodman crew, the memories of financial struggle just a few years earlier may have fueled a possible betrayal. Or it could be, as Simon suggests, an open secret that Martin Goodman had to challenge. The publishing executive did not abide disloyalty, but the Kirby/Simon team was making him money with the high-flying and bestselling *Captain America* series. Perhaps Goodman determined that Lee or some other creative team could take over the franchise, thus minimizing the loss.

Speculation enables any number of views to emerge, but the evidence demonstrates the high level of duplicity on all sides. First, Goodman and his accountants were ripping the artistic team off, reporting lower sales figures to reduce the share of profits they were supposed to receive. On the other hand, Simon and Kirby secretly did work for DC and other publishers on Timely's dime. They secretly negotiated a $500-a-week combined salary with DC to join the industry's leading firm, but still drew Timely paychecks as they attempted to figure out the transition and continue to make money from both entities.

Even a teenager with Lee's advanced imagination could have never dreamed that he would take over the comic book division at such a young age. Beyond being a teen, what hindered him most was his utter lack of experience managing anything at all. Luckily, the comic division, with Lee as a virtual one-man show, was small, and Goodman did not seem to worry or attempt to micromanage his young relative. Artists Al Avison and Syd Shores continued to draw the red, white, and blue hero, and Lee took over the writing duties.[23]

The success of Captain America, though, did exert some extra pressure on Lee to continue producing. But, he had no time to contemplate what it all meant—the publication calendar slowed for no one. The Captain America duo were working on #10, dated January 1942, when they were forced out, so they left Timely sometime in the late fall.

Thrust into a leadership role that he hadn't planned, Lee did the smart thing—he mimicked Kirby and Simon—working himself to the bone on a variety of projects, a nearly relentless pace. He recalled, "I was responsible for all the stories, either writing them myself or buying them from other people." The range of work expanded too. "Always when I was there—being the editor meant being the art director too, because you can't just edit the stories without making sure the artwork is done the right way so it enhances the stories . . . and the stories have to enhance the artwork. They have to go hand in hand."[24] Suddenly, when his older, more experienced mentors left for DC, the teen became head writer, editor-in-chief, and art director. All the pieces had to come together and his job focused on managing the overall process.

The teen editor had to produce. Rather than give off the vibe that he served as an exaggerated one-man show, he created thinly veiled pseudonyms, thus authoring comic book pieces as "Stan Martin," "Neel Nats," or other plays on his real name. According to Stan Goldberg, who managed Timely's coloring department, Lee served as "the only editor." He had an assistant named Al Sulman, whom Goldberg remembers not doing much work, and two female administrative aides.[25] On the art side, Lee worked with freelancers to pick up the slack from Kirby's departure. Luckily, he had talented artists and writers around, including Alex Schomburg and Burgos and Everett, each a constant presence on their popular comics.

Under intense pressure to write, the teen produced more than anyone else—and faster—perhaps the writing version of Kirby. The quality of the work is debatable.

"Lee's early comic book work was hardly groundbreaking," explains comic book writer and historian Arie Kaplan. "His 1940s-era superhero comics were written just as well as anyone else's, but there was little room for innovation or complex characterization under the watchful eye of Martin Goodman."[26] However, artist Dave Gantz exclaimed: "I thought he was the Orson Welles of the comic book business."[27]

Goodman may have wanted the kid to just keep the seat warm until he could find someone else to run the comic book division, but Lee caught steam and demonstrated that he could handle the task. Plus, as luck would have it, Lee was really the only one left capable of running the division. "I assume he wanted to find someone who wasn't just out of his teens," Lee recalled. "But apparently he had a short interest span and eventually stopped looking." The teen editor thought up a new moniker for himself: "Mr. Timely Comics."[28] Lee began honing his craft as primary writer, editing the work of freelancers, and overseeing the art. He grew up, and into the job.

CHAPTER 3

ARMY PLAYWRIGHT

In 1942, the United States lurched toward full mobilization in fits and starts. The attack on Pearl Harbor may have sent the nation scrambling, but to transform an economy just beginning to emerge from the Great Depression into a global war machine took time and immense coordination.

War is never just about battlefields and strategy. Both the American war effort and the entire conflict itself hinged on the near-total mobilization of the nation's industrial base. Corporations and businesses of all sizes had to create an intricate infrastructure to support the struggle. Although mobilization took a toll on people on the home front, they rallied to do whatever was necessary to aid the troops on the battlefields overseas.

Stan Lee, just nineteen years old, realized that he could not stay home and helm Marvel while countless young men were fighting and dying in the all-out effort against the Nazi war machine. For a young man who earned his first publication credit writing about Captain America—the superhero who had punched out Hitler on the cover of his debut issue—staying out of the war would have been unthinkable. Lee enlisted on November 9, 1942. He would still be a teenager for another seven weeks.

The army needed smart troops, so it evaluated inductees on the basis of intelligence and aptitude using the Army General Classification Test. Recruits fell into one of five rankings, but based on the highly technical and scientific nature of the work in the Signal Corps, the division received a higher number of people in the upper category. Just before Lee enlisted, some 39 percent of its recruits had tested into Classes I and II, but that figure jumped to 58 percent by 1943. Lee's intelligence enabled him to score high enough to get into the Signal Corps.[1]

Goodman felt apprehensive about his editor-in-chief going off to war. No one had any idea how long the conflict would last. Some other artists and writers scrambled to fill pages and waited it out to the last minute until they were drafted. The publisher really could not put up much of a fight—anything else would have been viewed as unpatriotic.

While many comic book creators and artists found themselves overseas—and most, like Jack Kirby, in the thick of enemy fire—luckily for Lee, he remained stateside. The youngster jumped from the Signal Corps to a special division within that unit that produced instructional films and other wartime information materials. Lee's work for Goodman served as useful training. He wrote fast and in a breezy style that recruits and other trainees could comprehend. The army liked these traits as well, because the war effort hinged on strong communications tactics across countless specialty areas.

The proximity to Timely had another benefit for the young military man: He continued writing for the comic book division and Goodman's magazine side of the house, thus keeping his finger on the pulse of his civilian job. So, while many comic book figures virtually disappeared during the war, Lee honed his skills. He worked hard at his army duties—writing and even drawing some cartoon figures—but his workaholic tendencies took over. Lee spent countless off-duty hours writing for Goodman.

During the war, *Captain America* remained Timely's most popular comic book at a time when the industry boomed. By 1943 there were more than one hundred forty comic books on the newsstands, according to one source, "read by over fifty million people each month," though only about a hundred would survive until the end of the year because of paper rationing for the war mobilization effort.[2] Paper challenges limited the growth of the burgeoning industry to some degree, but the demand for comic books by servicemen kept demand skyrocketing. In 1944, for example, Fawcett's *Captain Marvel Adventures* sold fourteen million copies, up about 21 percent over the previous year. Superhero titles drove sales, but publishers also hedged their bets by expanding into other areas like humor, funny animals, and teen romance.[3]

As the sales figures increased, comic book publishers grew rich. Suddenly, it seemed as if Goodman had a golden touch. The steady income from all those captive readers did wonders for Lee, too. He drew his army salary and the extra money that came in from freelancing for Timely. Lee had never been flush, but the war gave him some extra coins to jingle in his pocket.

When he decided to volunteer for the army, Lee had been the editor-in-chief at Timely Comics for about a year. He spent much of that time inventing new characters and keeping the popular comic books going, particularly *Captain America.*

But Lee and Goodman needed to find an editor to replace him for the duration of the war. They turned to Lee's friend, artist Vince Fago, one of the early cartoon animators who had worked on *Superman, Popeye,* and *Gulliver's Travels* for Fleischer Studios, run by the famous Max Fleischer. The animation studio was also one of the places Kirby had worked early in his career. The Fleischer firm competed with Walt Disney, a fierce rivalry for America's animation dollars. Fleischer differed from Disney by focusing on human characters, such as Betty Boop and Koko the Clown, rather than talking mice, ducks, dogs, and other anthropomorphic figures. Later, the Fleischer brothers sold the animation company to Paramount.

"How would you like my job?" Lee asked Fago.[4]

Fago knew that Lee and Goodman hired him to keep the comic book division on track, but it wasn't the same company during the war. Interests shifted and many readers wanted lighter comedic fare. The popularity of Disney's characters and Fleischer's cartoons blew open the children's market. A serial imitator like Goodman didn't need anyone to twist his arm to jump on the cartoon bandwagon. Fago specialized in the kind of funny animals that children craved, so it was a natural progression for him to step into Lee's role. Plus, he could use the steady $250 a week he would earn as Goodman's editorial chief.

Goodman used Disney as a guide, which licensed its characters in comic book form to Dell. Timely transformed into a kind of Disney-lite, putting out a flurry of funny animal comics, in publications like *Comedy Comics* and *Joker Comics.* Some of these characters Lee had devised, like Ziggy Pig and Silly Seal, which he created with future *Mad* magazine illustrator Al Jaffee. The comedy duo—Ziggy was the straight man, and Silly was the less intelligent one—battled with Toughy Cat, who wore bright red pants that were frayed at the bottom and mismatched suspenders. Their antics and the ensuing popularity helped carry Timely during the war years and after. The pair headlined their own book until September 1949.[5]

Timely's titles grew so popular that Fago could barely keep up with demand, a perpetual challenge in the early years. He estimated that each comic had a print run of about five hundred thousand. "Sometimes we'd put out five books a week or more," Fago remembers. "You'd see the numbers come back and could tell that Goodman was a millionaire."[6] The publisher kept his fingers on the pulse of comic book readers and what his competitors put out, so his real acumen centered on taking calculated risks with new genres and seeing what popped based on what his fellow publishers were selling.

Following shortly on the heels of the children's market success, Goodman pushed Timely to go after female readers. Miss America, a teenage heiress who gained superhuman strength and the ability to fly after being struck by lightning, first appeared in *Marvel Mystery Comics* #49 (November 1943), with Human Torch and Toro on the cover thwarting an attacking Japanese battleship. In January 1944, Miss America became the title character of her own comic book. However, when sales were not as strong as Goodman had anticipated, they delayed the next issue until November, renaming it *Miss America Magazine* #2, with a real-life model portraying the character in her superhero outfit. Along with the new look came new content—Fago and his team gradually eliminated the superhero material in favor of teen girl topics.

Lee's basic training took place at Fort Monmouth, a large base in New Jersey that housed the Signal Corps. Research played a prominent role in the division and on the base. Several years earlier, researchers had developed radar there and the all-important handheld walkie-talkie. In the ensuing years, they would learn to bounce radio waves off the moon.[7]

At Fort Monmouth, Lee learned how to string communications lines and also repair them, which he thought would lead to active combat duty overseas. Army strategists realized that wars were often determined by infrastructure, so the Signal Corps played an important role in modern warfare keeping communications flowing. Even drawing in numerous talented, intelligent candidates, the Signal Corps could barely keep up with war demands, which led to additional training centers opening at Camp Crowder, Missouri, and on the West Coast at Camp Kohler, near Sacramento, California. On base, Lee also performed the everyday tasks that all soldiers carried out, like patrolling the perimeter and watching for enemy ships or planes mounting a surprise attack during the cold New Jersey winter. Lee said that the frigid wind whipping off the Atlantic nearly froze him to the core.

The oceanfront duty ended, however, when Lee's superior officers realized that he worked as a writer and comic book editor. They assigned him to the Training Film Division, coincidentally based in Astoria, Queens. He joined eight other artists, filmmakers, and writers to create a range of public relations pieces, propaganda tools, and information-sharing documents. His ability to write scripts earned him the transfer. Like countless other military men, Lee played a supporting role. By mid-1943, the Corps consisted of twenty-seven thousand officers and two hundred eighty-seven thousand enlisted men, backed by another fifty thousand civilians who worked alongside them.

The converted space that the army purchased at Thirty-Fifth Avenue and Thirty-Fifth Street in Astoria housed the Signal Corps Photographic Center, the home of the official photographers and filmmakers to support the war effort. Colonel Melvin E. Gillette commanded the unit, which was also his role at Fort Monmouth Film Production Laboratory before the army bought the Queens facility in February 1942, some nine months before Lee enlisted. Under Gillette's watchful eye, the old movie studio, originally built in 1919, underwent extensive renovation and updating, essentially having equipment that was the equivalent of any major film production company in Hollywood.

Gillette and army officials realized that the military needed unprecedented numbers of training films and aids to prepare recruits from all over the country who had varying education levels. There would also be highly sensitive and classified material that required full army control over the film process, from scripting through filming and then later in storage. The facility opened in May 1942 and quickly became an operational headquarters for the entire film and photography effort supporting the war.

The Photographic Center at Astoria was a large, imposing building from the outside. A line of grand columns protected its front entrance, flanked by rows of tall, narrow windows. Inside, the army built the largest soundstage on the East Coast, enabling the filmmakers to recreate or model just about any type of military setting.

Lee found an avenue into the small group of scribes. "I wrote training films, I wrote film scripts, I did posters, I wrote instructional manuals," Lee recalled. "I was one of the great teachers of our time!"[8] The illustrious division included many famous or soon-to-be-famous individuals, from three-time Academy Award–winning director Frank Capra and *New Yorker* cartoonist Charles Addams to a children's book writer and illustrator named Theodor Geisel. The world already knew Geisel by his famous pen name "Dr. Seuss." The stories that must have floated around that room during downtime or breaks!

Lee took up a desk in the scriptwriter bullpen, to the right of eminent author William Saroyan—at least when the pacifist author came into the office. Saroyan, who had won a Pulitzer Prize for his play *The Time of Your Life* in 1939, spent much of his time working from a hotel in Manhattan. Saroyan had rejected the Pulitzer when he won it, which just made him more popular with readers and other artists. Later, the army sent Saroyan to work on films in London. Lee, along with the others, including screenwriter Ivan Goff and producer Hunt Stromberg Jr., earned the official army military occupation specialty designation "playwright."[9]

Even with a full production company in New York City, some army divisions would need Lee and his colleagues on location. He journeyed to a number of camps on temporary duty (TDY in military vernacular), essentially crisscrossing the Southeast and Midwest, making stops in North Carolina, Indiana, and other locations. Each base had a critical need for easy-to-understand instruction manuals, films, or other public relations materials.

With the influx of men surging into the armed forces via draft or enlistment, thorough training didn't always happen. Whenever he had to write a script, film, or military gadget (or some other subject he knew little or nothing about) that would be used during combat, Lee attempted to simplify the information. "I often wrote entire training manuals in the form of comic books. It was an excellent way of educating and communicating," he said.[10]

One of Lee's temporary posts took him deeper into the nation's heartland—Fort Benjamin Harrison in Indiana, just northeast of Indianapolis—which must have been jarring for a New York City boy who had never really been out into the country. He worked with the Army Finance Department, which seemed perpetually struggling to keep up with payrolls and in need of training manuals and films, since the army couldn't find enough recruits with finance backgrounds.[11]

Looking out at the wannabee-accountants and payroll servicemen marching in various drills, Lee noticed their lack of vigor. So, he penned a song for them to sing while they marched, basically inserting new lyrics over the well-known "Air Force Song." The peppy scriptwriter included memorable lines, like "We write, compute, sit tight, don't shoot," but the song energized the men and livened up the drills.

Another project also demonstrated the kind of army work the young serviceman did during the war years. When the higher-ups in Finance realized that it took too long to train payroll officers, they asked Lee to rewrite the instructional manuals to get the program running more efficiently. Part of Lee's response included creating a cartoon character who added a bit of levity to the training manuals, but also helped the officers learn the proper methods in a lighthearted manner. "I rewrote dull army payroll manuals to make them simpler," Lee remembered. "I established a character called Fiscal Freddy who was trying to get paid. I made a game out of it. I had a few little gags. We were able to shorten the training period of payroll officers by more than 50 percent. I think I won the war single-handedly."[12] Clearly Lee realized that using humor would help the men learn the intricate processes.

Next, Lee moved on to his "all-time strangest assignment."[13] The work centered on creating anti–venereal disease posters aimed at the troops in Europe. Sexually transmitted diseases had plagued armies throughout history, so American leaders took the effort seriously. Even utilizing extensive education programs and making condoms readily available, however, they were still losing men to syphilis and gonorrhea. Prevention required every effort and was a critical concern. For example, the British—culturally less willing to face the STD situation—had forty thousand men a month being treated for VD during the Italian campaign.

Servicemen overseas were lectured extensively, sometimes up to half a dozen times a month and every man was given prophylactic kits when on an overnight pass or furlough. The kits included an ointment, cleaning cloth, and cleansing tissue. Often they were given condoms in packs of three. Another line of attack included education campaigns. Military leaders went to extreme measures to thwart STDs, including the creation of propaganda posters that showed Hitler, Mussolini, and Tojo deliberately plotting to disable Allied troops by the spread of VD. Many of these images, such as the ones famously created by artist Arthur Szyk, depicted the Axis leaders as subhuman animals with rat-like features. The link between them and the disease deliberately created an adversarial image and played on the xenophobic attitudes of the typical Allied soldier.

Lee sat at his desk confounded about what to do for the poster. He had to promote the prophylactic stations the army had set up, in Lee's words, "all over Europe." Soldiers visited the huts afterward and got a series of rough and painful treatments to prevent contracting VD. "Those little pro stations dotted the landscape," Lee said, "with small green lights above the entrance to make them easily recognizable." He wrestled with many different examples and then realized that the simplest message would work best: "VD? Not me!"[14] Lee illustrated the poster with a cartoon image of a happy serviceman walking into the station with the green light clearly visible. Lee's superiors bought it, and countless posters flooded overseas posts. The poster may be one of the most-seen works Lee ever created, but it was also the most roundly ignored.

While it is difficult to quantify the importance of the films, posters, photos, and other materials the Signal Corps produced, the armed forces realized that using films to educate soldiers cut training time by 30 percent. On the home front, Signal Corps troops provided 30–50 percent of the footage for newsreels that played at movie theaters and kept the public informed about the global conflict. Photographers were even able to use new telephoto technology to snap pictures at the front and send them back to the United States almost immediately. Lee, Capra, Geisel, and the other Army "playwrights" did important work for the war effort.

Lee worked on film scripts, posters, and brochures for the Army just as he had back in Goodman's Manhattan headquarters: quickly and efficiently. It got to the point where the other "playwrights" couldn't keep up. The commanding officer ordered Lee to slow down.

A workaholic like Lee used the extra time to keep his fingers dipped in Timely ink and his pockets filled with Goodman's money. The extra income enabled him to purchase his first automobile while stationed at Duke University—a 1936 Plymouth, a beat-up wreck he paid $20 for, but it ran, and even had a fold-up windshield that allowed the warm North Carolina wind to blow in his face.

Lee filled in where he could. Wherever the Army sent him, he received letters from Goodman's editors on Fridays, which would outline the stories they needed. In his spare time, he would type them up and send them back on Monday so that he hit the deadlines the editors established.

In addition to working for Fago in the comic book division, Lee also helped out with the pulp side of the firm. This effort included writing cartoon captions for *Read!* magazine, one of Goodman's publications aimed at adult audiences. An example of Lee's short ditties from January 1943: "A buzz-saw can cut you in two / A machine-gun can drill you right thru / But these things are tame, compared— / To what a woman can do!" The accompanying drawing shows a plump woman feeding her bald husband, who is chained to a doghouse.[15] The ribald humor fit in during that era and certainly within the men's magazines that Goodman put out, which were filled with sexist overtones, racy photographs, and plenty of violence.

Lee also continued to write the kind of mystery-with-a-twist-ending short stories that he had earlier written for Joe Simon in the *Captain America* comics. In "Only the Blind Can See," which appeared in Goodman's *Joker* magazine (1943–1944), the joke is on the reader. What he eventually finds out is that a supposedly blind panhandler, whom people assumed was a phony, actually was blind. Written in the second person so Lee can speak directly to the reader, whom he addresses as "Buddy," one learns that the down-on-his-luck beggar had too much pride to confront those who thought he faked it. He had to get run over in the street by a speeding car before people would realize the truth.[16] These kinds of short stories were the training ground for the science fiction and monster comic books that Lee would later write in the postwar period.

While Lee's after-hours work for Timely went largely unnoticed by his superiors and fellow soldiers, the freelance effort once got him arrested in typical Lee madcap fashion. He routinely picked up his assignments in Friday's mail, which gave him time to write over the weekend when he had more free time. One Friday a bored mail clerk overlooked his letter, explaining that nothing arrived in Lee's mailbox. The next day, however, Lee swung by the now-closed mailroom and spied a letter in his cubby with the Timely return address on display.

Not willing to miss a deadline, Lee asked the officer in charge to open the mailroom. The officer turned him down, telling Lee to drop it and worry about the mail on Monday. Angry, Lee got a screwdriver and gently unscrewed the mailbox hinges, enabling him to get at the assignment. The mailroom officer saw what he did and turned him in to a base captain who did not like Lee. The young man faced mail tampering charges and a potential trip to Leavenworth prison if convicted. Luckily, the colonel in charge of the Finance Department intervened before the dispute went too far and saved Lee's bacon. In this instance, Fiscal Freddy really did save the day![17]

This single run-in with the authorities stood as the one blip on Lee's otherwise spotless military record. He served out the rest of his wartime tenure strapped to a desk, churning out training materials and posters.

Sergeant Lee signed his name and rolled his ink-stained thumb across the single-page army discharge paper. Practically before the ink dried, the young civilian, then just twenty-three years old, jumped into his new car, a large black Buick convertible with hot red leather seats and flashy whitewall tires with shiny hubcaps. The Buick was a noticeable upgrade from the battered Plymouth he had bought in North Carolina.

Lee received a $200 bonus (called "muster-out pay"), which the army gave out so that soldiers could jump-start their return to civilian life, but he skipped the mandatory class that went along with the funds. He deposited half in a savings account prior to leaving. It was late September 1945 and the army had allotted him $42.12 to get back to New York City from the discharge center at Camp Atterbury in central Indiana, about fifty miles south of where he had been stationed at Fort Harrison.

A car junkie, especially admiring long, sleek convertibles, Lee hit the open road. So excited was he to go back to his native city, Lee joked that he "burned my uniform, hopped into my car, and made it non-stop back to New York in possibly the same speed as the Concorde!"[18] He wanted to get back to his helm at Timely, which Goodman had consolidated with his magazine operations in a new headquarters on the fourteenth floor of the Empire State Building. Lee zoomed off on the more than seven-hundred-mile trip back east to the Big Apple.

CHAPTER 4

RETURN TO MARVEL

A ll arms and legs, almost like an animated character careening across the screen, Stan Lee proved a frenetic blur weaving in, out, around, and by agitated pedestrians window-shopping along Broadway. He dashed the two-and-a-half-mile route south from his new two-room abode at the Alamac Hotel to the Timely Comics office in the majestic Empire State Building. Passing the riding stables in Central Park, he sometimes jumped on a horse and spent some time galloping around the hardbeaten paths before getting on with his daily grind at the office. His feet scratching across the sidewalk created a wild beat matched only by the thoughts bursting in his head and the scripts these ideas represented.

The postwar years brimmed with opportunity for go-getters like Lee. Comic book sales had soared during World War II. People wanted a diversion, especially the men on the front or those working on various bases at home and abroad to support the effort. Comic books filled a need for easy, quick reading that was fun filled, exciting, and a diversion from the brutality of the constant media attention regarding death tolls, fierce battles, and innumerable injuries. After the war, industry insiders estimated that 90 percent of children and teens from ages eight to fifteen read comic books on a regular basis.

Because Lee had stayed active in the comic book game during his army stint, he knew that although genres might change periodically, comic book readers were hooked. The nation seemed electric after the war ended. Popular culture in all its variations burst forth in vivid new colors, sounds, and images after the war years defined by rationing and sacrifice. It was a good time to be in publishing.

Lee returned to New York City and Goodman's Timely Comics headquarters after his army hijinks in the great American Midwest. The Alamac Hotel on Broadway and Seventy-First Street was a stately nineteen-story, dark brown brick edifice that had been completed in 1925. The hotel became a home for many jazz groups in the mid- to late 1920s, as well as an away trip locale for major league baseball teams. The Alamac had some six hundred guestrooms, as well as a handful of shops and a restaurant on the ground level. Later, in the early 1950s, the CIA would use the Alamac as a safe house for German scientists and technicians working for American national defense operations during the Cold War.

After being shuttled around to different army bases and training facilities in the middle of nowhere during the war, Lee thrilled at returning to his home city. The Alamac provided a steady flow of new friends and acquaintances. More importantly, it gave him a forty-block walk to the Timely office. Although more than an hour by foot, Lee walked back and forth, his frantic energy keeping his loopy legs loose. He walked almost everywhere in the city, regardless of the distance, because he wanted to stay in shape and work off his excess energy. Lee fully embraced the sights and sounds of the city on his daily commute, from the thrills of Times Square to the towering skyscrapers and mass of humanity coursing through the streets. Sometimes he would rent a boat and row out on the lake in Central Park.

Lee thoroughly enjoyed his job. He felt like he had a new lease on life with a nice place to live, a steady (and growing) income, and plenty of young women to date. Yet there were aggravations, too. "One thing that both irritated and frustrated me," he explained, "was the fact that nobody, outside of our own little circle, had a good word to say about comic books."[1] With most people finding them nothing more than a waste of time, Lee felt as if he were spinning his wheels.

All the outside negativity led to bouts of self-consciousness about working in comics, despite his general happiness in the business. For someone so intent on success and with feelings running through his head almost from birth that he would achieve greatness, exasperation set in. During the war, he had served with some of the great creative minds in the nation; now he was back to being just a comic book writer. Only in his mid-twenties, Lee felt that he still had his whole life in front of him, but what kind of life would it be in an industry that most people thought simply catered to young children, simple teens, and underachieving young adults?

Although Lee bristled at the reaction he received from people who asked him what he did for a living, he really loved the focus on writing and creating at Timely.

Working among his colleagues in the Signal Corps Training Film Division, the young man witnessed firsthand the true value of animation, films, and entertainment as a means to educate and enlighten audiences. If anything, the war demonstrated just how widespread the entertainment and creative industries would become.

Consumers turned to these cultural forms at exactly the moment when they had more money to spend on them and additional free time because of the technological advances made during the war and the booming postwar economy. The United States reached true superpower status and the benefits propelled the creation of thriving middle- and upper-middle classes. Yet, Lee also had to reconcile his daily joy with the sideways glances he got when people found out what he did for a living.

Naysayers didn't know Lee's past and the emphasis that it drove deep into his thinking about having a steady job and paycheck. Like so many of the Eastern European and Jewish artists and writers who populated the comic book industry, Lee's experience with poverty and his father's chronic unemployment weighed on him. Timely provided a job and the editor's position paid well, plus he liked the work. Finding a way to wipe the smirk off people's faces when they found out he wrote and edited funny animal and teen romance comics would have to wait.

In his absence, Goodman had created a small staff to run Timely—most notably turning over the editorial reins to his friend Vince Fago—but that crew had turned out millions upon millions of comic books during the war. Goodman's wallet got fatter and fatter, which made Lee's return to civilian life and the top of the masthead at the comic book company painless. Fago wanted to get back to full-time drawing, so Lee's homecoming went smoothly as the comic book division reverted to the young editor's control.

Timely's focus had changed while Lee served in the military. Fago's expertise in non-superhero comics pushed the emphasis in that direction, while readers grew interested in other topics outside superheroes. Goodman's publishing house was serving an almost entirely different audience when Lee returned. The whole industry had reacted to the growing popularity of Archie and his teenage gang of friends in *Archie Comics*, which had first published in late 1942. Like a good company man, Lee quickly turned his efforts to comics featuring young female heroines and teen humor, which the public craved.

Ruth Atkinson, a renowned artist and writer, created the smash hit *Millie the Model*, which began its long run in late 1945, just as Lee was settling back into the editor's chair. As one of the first females in comic books, Atkinson paved the way for other women to join the industry. She also came up with *Patsy Walker*, a spin-off from the old *Miss America Magazine* series. In typical Timely manner, Lee jumped on any and all bandwagons, creating *Nellie the Nurse*, another nod to the new teen humor/romance category.

As 1945 came to an end, paper restrictions set in place during the war were lifted and the comic book industry took flight. Across 1946, some forty million copies sold monthly at newsstands. While the stalwarts continued to sell pretty well, including Fawcett's *Captain Marvel* and DC's *Superman* and *Batman*, readers moved away from superhero titles and on to crime stories, teen romps, and science fiction.

Late in 1946, Lee tried to mix the popularity of the female heroine stories with the superhero genre by cocreating Blonde Phantom.[2] As secretary to private eye Mark Mason, Louise Grant kept her Blonde Phantom identity a secret. But at night she wore a bright red evening gown and mask, fighting criminals with a mix of martial arts skills and a trusty .45-caliber pistol. Blonde Phantom was in the vein of DC's Wonder Woman and the Timely's own Miss America. Her character was launched as a solo comic, beginning with *Blonde Phantom Comics* #12, which lasted about two years. During that time, she appeared in anthologies in several other Timely collections.

In a kind of last-ditch effort to revive the superhero stories, Lee combined a number of Timely's heroes into a super team, much like DC's Justice Society of America, which had debuted in *All Star Comics* #3 (Winter 1940–1941). *All Winners Comics* #19 (Fall 1946) featured Captain America, Human Torch, Sub-Mariner, Whizzer, Miss America, and their various teen sidekicks. Lee's typical cover blurb jumped out at the reader, promising: "a complete SIZZLING, ACTION THRILLER!" The editor hired famed *Batman* cocreator Bill Finger to script the new superhero team. Finger centered the initial story on a villain's attempt to steal a nuclear weapon. In a sweeping indictment of the decline of superheroes among comic book readers, the *All Winners* team proved a shipwreck of All Losers. The title appeared once more before Goodman canceled it. This decision came on the heels of another team ending, *Young Allies Comics* #20, which had been going strong since its launch in Summer 1941 by Joe Simon and Jack Kirby. For Lee, the evolving marketplace meant throwing every possible genre at the wall to see what would stick.

The comic book industry grew overall, despite the dark clouds over the superhero set. Lee received a major dose of positive publicity in November 1947 when *Writer's Digest* magazine asked him to pen its cover story. Still not yet twenty-five years old when the magazine appeared on newsstands, the boyish Lee chomped on a pipe in the cover image, struggling to look older and wiser than his actual years. Although he still doubted that his long-term future resided in the comic book business, he took on the persona of a seasoned pro in discussing the industry. The field's growing popularity made it a good feature for *Writer's Digest* and gave Lee his first national exposure.

The story: "There's Money in Comics!" offered would-be writers advice for breaking into comic books, including the emphasis on realistic dialogue and its relation to character development. The article is an early and significant indication of Lee's thinking about writing. He would use these same foundational ideas when he later created the tenets of the Marvel style during the company's 1960s heyday. Like many young writers who are working their way through a unique voice, Lee demonstrated that he had a mature vision of what it took to be successful in the field.

While Lee's personal brand started generating interest, Goodman dropped the "Timely" name, fiddling with variations on "Marvel," but ultimately axing those, too. Sales continued to grow across the comic book industry, but publishers scrambled to find the magic elixir that the reading public desired. They jumped from topic to topic, ultimately dipping into different ideas, including the new teen romance field, which Simon and Kirby launched with *Young Romance* (September 1947) for Crestwood/Prize. The longtime creative duo struck gold. As a first-person narrative of "true" stories, *Young Romance* sold in the millions. The success enabled Simon and Kirby to launch and then oversee a mini-empire built on the comic book's tremendous sales. Always on the lookout for talented freelancers, the industry veterans hired a handful of the best to produce the comic book under their attentive, scrutinizing eyes. Some estimates assert that the *Young Romance* books and the various offshoots derived from the title sold about five million copies a month for the rest of the 1940s.[3] The series ran through June 1963, when Crestwood sold the series to DC, which then published it until 1975.

In the postwar era and as the Cold War gripped the nation, the comic book industry endured successive waves of genres that seemed to change annually. Readers bounced from one to the other. Superheroes gave way to teen comedy, which then morphed into romance titles, and next mutated into cowboy comics and true crime books. Of course, Goodman's now anonymous comic book line continued to appear on the newsstands and stay in the upper echelon of publishers, but never with the creative spark that enabled it to gain much ground on the larger firms. As always, he ordered Lee to follow the lead set by competitors. As a result, in late 1947, *Sub-Mariner Comics* suddenly became *Official True Crime Cases Comics* #24, with the latter taking over the sequential order of the superhero title.[4]

As people's entertainment preferences settled on film and television, each medium exerted influence on comics. The popularity of cowboy movie stars—first Gene Autry, then Roy Rogers—sparked interest in western comics. Rogers, along with his trusty horse Trigger and wife Dale Evans, appeared in popular films like *King of the Cowboys* (1943) and *Home in Oklahoma* (1947). From the early 1940s through the late 1950s, Rogers stood as the nation's most popular and successful cowboy actor. His groundbreaking licensing agreement put his image and likeness on countless products, second only to those of Walt Disney. Rogers had released hit records and starred in a long-running radio show that he later moved to television after it became a staple in American homes.

Western-crazed readers turned to Fawcett's *Hopalong Cassidy*, which sold four million copies in 1947 and eight million the following year. DC brought out *Dale Evans Comics* in late 1948 to capitalize on the actress's popularity and connection to Rogers. Goodman published series like *Wild Western* (1948–1957) under the Western Fiction Publishing Company imprint, one of the publisher's ploys for keeping costs spread across the organization. *Wild Western* was a vehicle for the character Kid Colt, but also introduced a rotating group of other heroes, ranging from Apache Kid to Arizona Annie. Lee served as general editor of *Wild Western* and wrote some of the stories himself. A rotating cast of freelancers and staff artists drew the issues.

By March 1948, Lee was fully aboard the cowboy wave, launching *Two-Gun Kid* #1, a singing hero, just like Rogers and Autry. Five months later, *Kid Colt, Hero of The West* #1 hit newsstands, giving the popular character its stand-alone book. The comic featured a fast-draw sharpshooter who kills the bad guy who murdered his father and then hunts for redemption by becoming Kid Colt, despite his fugitive status. The hero that is neither fully good nor fully bad was an early precursor to the superheroes Lee and his team would create a little more than a decade later.

Lee's favorite cowboy character was Black Rider, a doctor by day who donned a secret identity to battle criminals. The comic allowed Lee a rare opportunity apart from his writing and editing duties. Goodman did not get involved with the day-to-day intricacies of running his magazines and comics, especially when titles made money, but he did have a lifelong fascination with covers. He preferred featuring photographs on the covers of his comic books, as he did with early *Miss America* comics and many of his pulp slicks. For one of the *Black Rider* issues, Lee donned the black outfit and mask, appearing on the cover holding two six-shooters and looking ominous.

The shifting interests of comic book readers made publishers nervous. In the frenzy to keep sales figures soaring, it seemed as if the publishers started pushing too hard and began toying with standards of decency, similar to the wave of semi-pornographic slick mags many publishers produced in the 1920s and 1930s. One of the most influential categories that took flight at the end of the decade also brought with it a bout of negativity that would later nearly topple the entire comic book industry—true crime and crime-based books.

In 1948, the crime comics market took off and every publisher launched new titles, some relatively tame, others filled with lurid tales and overt violence. For example, the cover of *Murder Incorporated* (January 1948) from Fox showed a buxom, angry female firing a bullet into a man who had cheated at cards and his reaction as if the bullet had just entered his chest. Although the cover blurb announced "For Adults Only," certainly the creators aimed the stories at a younger audience.

Overall, the popularity of crime comics raised the number of titles published that year by 20 percent over the previous year and up 50 percent over two years. The downside of the crime book mania was that adults saw the violence and lurid images as threats to the morals of younger readers. In 1948, *Time* published an article that implied some juveniles committed copycat crimes after being influenced by reading comic books. The panic grew into a nationwide crisis. Stories about delinquency and crime sold newspapers and magazines, so the media picked up on the story and created further controversy. Frederic Wertham, an influential author and psychiatrist, also fueled the anti-comics propaganda. He organized a symposium that concluded comic books glorified crime, violence, and sexuality. Suddenly, the comic book industry had a real crisis on its hands.

Throughout the postwar years, Lee managed the comic book division, always staying extremely busy. He had boundless energy and an engaging imagination, but did not seem to possess the entrepreneurial spirit to launch his own gig, the savvy that pushed other artists and writers like Joe Simon and William Gaines to resist the indentured servitude attitude held by the publishers. For Lee, the steady paycheck meant something, and he genuinely enjoyed working with the other writers, editors, and artists that teamed to bring out comics, even if he found much of their work derivative. He summed up a typical interaction with Goodman, explaining, "Every few months a new trend and we'd be right there, faithfully following each one. . . . I felt that we were a company of copycats."[5]

Although his career prior to World War II revolved around comic books, Lee grew restless after his return from military service. Perhaps he realized that his words had meaning and power outside of zany animal stories or monster books directed primarily at children.

When Lee did venture away from Goodman's clutches, he focused on safe projects that played to his strengths. The success of the *Writer's Digest* cover story led him to think about the budding industry and how writers and artists might get a foot in the door. In 1947, he self-published the magazine *Secrets Behind the Comics*, which he priced for one dollar, a high price for readers at a time when comic books sold for ten cents. Using comic book–like fonts and illustrations of the writing and drawing process, the book featured "by Stan Lee" in prominent script on the cover and contained his typical zest and enthusiasm. The book's dedication is to Lee's little brother, Larry, and Goodman's children, Iden and Chip.

Ironically, Lee is "Secret No. 1," which answers the reader's questions about who Lee is and why he wrote the book. Accompanied by an illustrated headshot of Lee looking studious, with a pencil behind his ear and a dotted bow tie, the introduction lists the many publications Lee worked on as "Managing Editor and Art Director" at Timely.[6] The Lee trademark writing style jumps out on nearly every page: "NOW, for the first time ever in the world, Stan Lee will show you exactly how comic strips are WRITTEN!!!"[7] In addition to Lee's "secrets," the book had blank illustration areas where readers could attempt to draw the Blonde Phantom based on Lee's script.

Every so often, Lee edited or managed a magazine for adults (or maybe better put, Goodman dangled the chance in front of his young protégé). Although comics sold enormous numbers of copies during World War II, the medium barely registered as a "real" career for adults. The pulps, however, had a bit more respectability, even the schlock that Goodman put out. When he needed extra hands, Goodman would get Lee to work on a magazine, such as the celebrity pinup *Focus* in 1950. Dubbed a "photo bedsheet" magazine because it measured ten inches wide and fourteen inches tall, *Focus* aimed squarely at American male readers (or at least those men interested in looking at pictures) with bikini-clad cover models (including future screen star Marilyn Monroe) and lurid cover headlines. The next year, though, the publisher changed the format to a small pocket-sized magazine, only four by six inches.[8] Goodman notoriously fiddled with magazine cover images, titles, and the physical size of the publication, always hoping that some minor change in a magazine idea he got from one of his competitors would lead to huge sales.

Lee's dissatisfaction continued, but he did not want to rock the boat too much or risk losing his job. Like so many people who remembered the ravages of the Great Depression, Lee carried an inborn fear of joblessness and lack of security. He did not have to go back very deep in his memory to remember his parents arguing about scrounging up the next month's rent and what would happen if the family were evicted.

Lee's boundless energy led to numerous additional freelance opportunities. Many of these went unsigned or were done under someone else's name, since the writer did not want to risk getting fired by Goodman. "I ghosted them under other people's names," Lee explained. The work ran the gamut from television shows and radio programs to writing advertising copy. One of the few he did sign his name to was the Sunday *Howdy Doody* newspaper strip, which ran during the puppet's height of popularity from 1950 to 1953.[9]

The busy editor spent long hours running Goodman's comic book division. However, he also enjoyed the energy and revitalized spirit of postwar New York City nightlife. The city seemed like the best place in the world to Lee, plenty of attractive women to date, many things to do, and a vibrancy that is uniquely New York. In 1947 his life changed dramatically when he met English model and actress Joan Clayton Boocock. Lee's cousin had planned to set him up on a blind date with a model he knew and told Lee to meet her at the modeling agency. However, when he knocked on the door, Joan answered. Lee blurted out that he loved her and had been drawing her face since he was a little boy. Rather than run in horror, she laughed at the offhanded exultation and went out with him. Soon they were an item.

Joan had a successful career as a hat model, but had come to the United States as a war bride after marrying an American officer in Great Britain. Realizing the marriage had been a mistake, she planned to go to Reno, Nevada, for a divorce, since New York state laws made divorce nearly impossible. In the Wild West of Nevada, a woman only had to be in residence for six weeks.

Lee waited nervously while Joan served her time in Reno, but the young model drew many suitors. After Lee received a letter from her addressed, "Dear Jack," he knew he had to take quick action. Throwing caution to the wind, he took a circuitous, twenty-eight-hour plane trip west. When he finally arrived, Lee convinced Joan of his love and they pulled a Reno special: meeting with the judge to nullify the marriage in one room, then walking into the next room over, where the same judge then married them. In a matter of minutes, Joan Boocock became Mrs. Stan Lee.[10]

The young couple took the train back across the nation as the Christmas holiday shopping season descended on the Big Apple. They moved into a tiny apartment in Manhattan on Ninety-Sixth Street, between Lexington Avenue and Fifth Avenue, not far from the Central Park Reservoir, and on the other side of the park from his former digs at the Alamac Hotel. For the city boy who lived almost his entire life in tiny apartments, the place seemed palatial. He and Joanie settled in and got two dogs, cocker spaniels named Hamlet and Hecuba.

Two years later, Lee's mother passed away. Larry, his fifteen-year-old brother, needed a place to stay, so he joined the young married couple. Sensing that they needed a more suburban setting, the little family moved to a small town on Long Island, purchasing an eight-room house on West Broadway in Hewlett Harbor. They bought a green Buick convertible that had been owned by a Blue Angel pilot, and had the novelty of "a huge flying female as a radiator ornament."[11]

Lee and Joan enjoyed the fruits of his successful career (like many men in the late 1940s and early 1950s, he did not want Joan pursuing a career). In 1951, the couple and their young daughter, Joan Celia (born a year earlier in 1950, then called "Little Joan," but later known as "J.C." as an adult), moved into a house not far away at 226 Richards Lane in Hewlett Harbor. Stan and Joan liked the charm of the slightly aged house, built about a quarter of a century before the Lees moved in. The street name in their new home most certainly influenced Lee's decision years later to name the head of the Fantastic Four Reed Richards.[12]

Only a couple miles away lived Martin Goodman and his family. The Goodman children spent a lot of time at the Lee home. Goodman's son Iden even learned to drive in the Lee's driveway.[13] Although Lee distanced himself from his boss/relative and made their relationship seem detached, there is quite a bit of evidence that shows how intertwined they actually were. The Lees needed support of family and friends when their second child, a daughter named Jan, died just three days after her birth in 1953. Unlike many couples that lose a child, Stan and Joan managed to overcome their grief and build a stable, happy family for themselves and J.C.

The Hewlett Harbor carriage house sat on a two-acre property and had a separate room for Lee to work. After moving to Long Island, Lee took the one-hour commute back into Manhattan to meet with artists and get their completed pages but gradually started working from home one or two days per week. Staying on Long Island gave Lee a method for meeting the frantic pace necessary for delivering numerous comic books on a tight schedule. Since his job included managing the staff and freelancers, as well as approving art and editorial, the handful of hours he saved each week made a difference. Goodman's strategy centered on flooding the marketplace with comics. Lee had to create that deluge.

Lee also benefited from being at home with his family. On warm days, he would take his typewriter out to the patio and place it on a bridge table, creating a makeshift standing desk, so he could act out the stories and type while standing up. Joan bought the family a little twelve-foot, round plastic pool to use when the summer sun really heated up. Lee joked that he could "swim" the length of the pool in a stroke and a half. Later, in the Timely office, he would joke with coworkers, "Well, I did 100 laps today."[14]

Committed to making money to keep the upper-middle-class dream alive, Lee hunkered down, pouring his energy into writing, editing, and art direction for Goodman's comic book division. Although prone to visions of grandeur and some wild behavior, like jumping up on desks to act out scenes as his freelancers watched in awe, Lee developed into an energetic, encouraging, and savvy editorial director.

The more scripts he wrote, the more important he became to Goodman's bottom line, and the more page-rate bonuses he earned, which kept the Lee family afloat. Talented and with an inhuman amount of creativity and speed, Lee wrote fast and enjoyed the benefits of being the boss, but he still couldn't shake bouts of depression and worry about his future. Lee called this era his "limbo years." It seemed as if he had slipped into a rut: "Go to the office—come home and write—weekends and evenings. Between stories, go out to dinner with Joanie, play with little Joanie, look at cars."[15] The money afforded the Lees a great lifestyle, but he had to work nonstop to keep it moving.

As the nation slipped from postwar euphoria to Cold War fear and the Truman years transformed into the Ike age, Lee had achieved what most Americans aspired to: gain meaningful employment, start a family, and own a home. But, just like so many others in his shoes, he felt unfulfilled professionally. While he enjoyed the one-on-one relationships with his staff and freelance team, the relentless production cycle created a pressure-filled workplace.

More importantly, he bristled at the perception that writing for comic books wasn't *real* writing. As a result, Lee questioned his future in comic books. When he had the time, he dabbled in outside writing—much of it anonymously—and took on additional opportunities that might enable him to leap out of the business.

Lee wasn't quite sure what he should do next.

CHAPTER 5

PUBLIC ENEMY NUMBER ONE

Comic books burned!

All across America makeshift bonfires blazed in town squares, church parking lots, and on school ball fields meant for athletic events. Adults turned against comic books and whipped children and young people into a frenzy, demanding that they reject the comic books that they loved and had gladly plopped down their nickels, dimes, and pennies to buy. Setting the comics aflame and seeing the smoke lift skyward, both parents and youngsters sent a message to publishers far away in New York City, their local political leaders, and other stakeholders: we will no longer stand for this!

"Criminal or sexually abnormal ideas . . . an atmosphere of deceit, trickery and cruelty"—these are the thoughts that comic books ensconced in young readers' minds, according to the anti–comic book crusader Frederic Wertham, a grandstanding psychiatrist and author of the polemical 1954 book *Seduction of the Innocent.*[1] Since the late 1940s, Wertham had been stirring his troops, constantly railing against comic books and their creators in any newspaper, radio program, or forum that would listen. A national scourge, he argued, a menace that needed to be erased from American culture. In his mind, comic books were a form of evil that surpassed even the wanton cruelty, murder, and destruction propagated by Adolf Hitler.

Wertham saw a direct correlation between juvenile delinquency and the violence, gore, and lurid sexuality comic book publishers proffered. The future of America's children, in Wertham's mind, hinged on the rejection of comics and the inherent immorality the books embodied.

For Wertham, the nation's moral compass stood in the balance!

As far back as 1938, religious organizations such as a Catholic group called the National Organization for Decent Literature (NODL) rallied against "indecent literature." A group of Catholic bishops declared that comics and lewd magazines were "printed obscenity" and "an evil of such magnitude as seriously to threaten the moral, social and national life of our country." Ultimately, the bishops claimed that such publications would "weaken morality and thereby destroy religion and subvert the social order."[2] In 1939, the group calculated that some fifteen million copies of immoral publications were being published and reaching about sixty million readers per month. Bishop John F. Noll, NODL chairman from Fort Wayne, Indiana, took the lead in calling out New York City publishers who preyed on poor children and equated these efforts with Communist infiltration of American society.

The backlash against magazines and comic books abated somewhat during the war years, but in the postwar era, the pendulum eventually swung back to comics. When the media picked up on the rage, the resulting firestorm resulted in local governments trying to prevent comics from being sold and more intense public protest. The criticism of comic books was similar to that of the recent past when film, music, and the literary world all fell under scrutiny. Whether it had been reactions to James Joyce's *Ulysses* or the Hays Code that forced filmmakers to adhere to strict morality standards, mass culture came under criticism. The NODL listed anywhere from forty to one hundred forty comics it found offensive each month in its *Priest* newsletter between 1950 and 1954. Titles on the list included some obviously lurid comics, such as *Crime Detective* and *Love Scandals*, as well as the popular satire magazine *Mad*.[3]

After World War II, economic prosperity and military power combined to propel the nation. Simultaneously, however, more free time gave people the impetus to worry about issues and ideas that might be perceived as outside the norm. In an age of conformity, anything labeled atypical actually stood way beyond what mainstream tastemakers found appropriate. In the late 1940s, numerous national news outfits ran anti–comic book pieces, including ABC radio, the *New Republic*, and *Collier's*.

The comic book industry played into the hands of reformers by publishing an avalanche of crime books and horror comics that featured extensive explicit, violent, and sexual content. Some of the publishers realized that the gathering storm could really imperil their industry. In late 1948, several leaders banded together, hiring

Henry Schultz as "comic book czar" to lead the new Association of Comics Magazine Publishers (ACMP). Schultz had served as an attorney and member of New York's Board of Higher Education. Over time, the ACMP made inroads, but never gained full membership, so publishing houses outside its purview simply ignored the group's work. By 1950, the organization had withered away.[4]

Goodman's little knockoff shop, no matter how well it did in sales, was not considered an industry thought leader, so the self-appointed culture police like Wertham or the members of the NODL did not target him or Lee specifically. While Lee claims to have participated in a series of debates directly with Wertham or one of his minions in the early 1950s, there is no evidence to support the claim.[5]

Whatever his actual interaction with the comic book-burners and rabble-rousers, Lee did take a shot at Wertham in *Suspense* #29 (April 1953), a story illustrated by one of Lee's closest friends and freelancers, Joe Maneely, who would later die in a tragic train accident. Demonstrating his typical bombastic style and lack of subtlety, Lee titled the story "The Raving Maniac" and featured himself in an invented argument with a Wertham-like figure. After listening to the intruder rail against comics, the editor forcefully pushes him into a chair and delivers a blistering freedom of speech soliloquy, explaining, "In a dictatorship, people try to change your mind by force! You should be grateful you're in a land where only words are used!!" The story's twist ending—one of Lee's specialties—is that the intruder is an insane asylum escapee.

At the end, returning home, Joan and J.C. greet Lee. Then he rocks his daughter to sleep and begins the bedtime story about the "excited little man." It is impossible to know if this fictional account ever reached Wertham's desk or an associate's, but Lee took a huge gamble in publishing the story and placing himself front and center.[6] "To me, Wertham was a fanatic, pure and simple," Lee explained. "I never cease to be amazed at the gullibility of human beings."[7]

As a result of the publicity and the mania that attacks on comics roused, the United States Senate launched an investigation, forming the Subcommittee on Juvenile Delinquency in 1953. Senators realized the power in televised hearings after a similar subcommittee on organized crime led by Estes Kefauver generated extraordinary television ratings, which nearly propelled the Tennessee Democrat to the presidency. Robert Hendrickson (R-NJ) led the investigation, joined by Kefauver and four other senators. Like its predecessor, the board televised its proceedings, which took place in several locations, including Denver, Boston, and Philadelphia. The senators looked at different causes of juvenile delinquency based on the hearing location, then Hendrickson announced that the focus for the New York proceedings would be comic books. The star witness would be Wertham himself, who was happy to be in the national spotlight, as it sold more copies of his book, published earlier in the year. The testimony served as the culmination of the psychiatrist's efforts for many years to draw attention to the negative influence of comic books on young readers.

The hearings opened in late April and early June 1954 in room 110 of the federal courthouse in New York City. A parade of experts from education, sociology, and child services pinned a great deal of negativity on the publishers and creators, but surprisingly the evidence against comic books to most observers wasn't overwhelming. Of course, Wertham made the most damning points. At one point, he explained, "I think Hitler was a beginner compared to the comic book industry. They get the children much younger. They teach them race hatred at the age of four, before they can read."[8] The senators seemed to take their cues from his *Seduction* book, using it as a kind of playbook. Kefauver and his colleagues did not question Wertham's findings or the book's legitimacy.

The tide turned for good on April 21, 1954, when Kefauver, always on the lookout for publicity, enticed EC publisher William Gaines to answer a series of questions about decency. In preparation for his testimony, Gaines had stayed up all night working on his remarks by popping Dexedrine diet pills (a kind of middle-class wonder drug at the time, prescribed to men to overcome fatigue). The publisher believed that once people heard the issues from his perspective that they would come to their senses. Kefauver had different ideas, which he would debut as the television cameras rolled.

Herbert Beaser, one of the committee's counsel, baited Gaines into generalizations, ranging from how comics were captioned to what might be considered good taste. Kefauver patiently laid in wait for his moment to strike. Gaines, who later admitted that the Dexedrine wore off and left him feeling deflated, had difficulty keeping up the pace.[9] As if on cue, Kefauver pulled out his key piece of evidence: EC's *Crime SuspenStories* #22. The issue's cover displayed a gruesome close-up of a man holding a bloody ax in his right hand and a blond woman's severed head in the left. The woman's mouth dripped blood, as did the axe, and her bare legs were splayed on the floor below. Gaines did not budge, insisting the cover was okay for a horror comic book. That exchange became the defining moment for those watching the spectacle on television, as well as the front-page story in the next day's *New York Times*. Later, Gaines would be chastised by newspapers and magazines across the nation, including *Time* and *Newsweek*, which had far-reaching influence.[10]

The resulting furor led to Gaines jettisoning his crime and horror comics. He claimed it was in response to what parents demanded, but no distributor would work with him after such a fiasco. Gaines stood as the figurehead for everything wrong with comic books. All across the industry, other publishers folded. The firms that stayed in business had to make do with steep sales declines. Goodman's comics division dropped from 15 million a month in 1953 to 4.6 million in 1955.[11] "Parents everywhere were forbidding their children to read anything that even hinted at action or adventure or any sort of gripping conflict," Lee said.[12] The only genres that sold were the female leads, like Patsy Walker, some science fiction titles, teen humor, funny animals, and westerns—as long as they weren't deemed too violent. Goodman and Lee had enough of these titles to continue in business, but no longer needed additional staff or as many freelancers.

Public disapproval of comic books—spurred on by the Senate investigations and Wertham's incredible influence—overwhelmed the industry. The demand for change grew louder until it could be no longer ignored. The psychiatrist used his bully pulpit to call for reforms, which ultimately led to the 1954 editorial code adopted by the Comics Magazine Association of America (CMAA), the organization the publishers formed to regulate the industry.

The Comics Code forced publishers to submit their comic books to a review board, which then determined if anything might be found offensive, including such seemingly innocuous things as vampires and using words like "horror" on the cover. If the book passed through the review board, it could print the Comics Code Authority "Approved By" stamp on the cover. In effect, the consent became mandatory, because distributors were not willing to risk trafficking in comics that were not sanctioned.

The idea behind the Comics Code was similar to the stringent Hays Code that governed film for many years with tight restrictions on how movies could depict certain topics. Like the Hollywood studios, comic book publishers took action to self-police rather than face potential sanctions, which were mainly meant to scare distributors and newsstands from carrying titles that repeatedly violated the Comics Code. Whether or not they regarded the regulations as infringements on freedom of speech, many accepted the oversight as a safeguard.

Goodman felt the dip in sales and once again forced Lee to cut staff members and freelance contracts. The publisher again hightailed it out of town and left the dirty, face-to-face firings to Lee. "The market for comic books disintegrated," Lee said, "with artists and writers being fired by the barrelful. I was amazed that Martin kept me on, but then, he had to have somebody to fire all those other people for him."[13] After a dreadful situation of canning his friends and coworkers, Lee struggled to remain positive, wracking his brain in an attempt to devise a genre that Wertham and his cronies wouldn't attack.

While the comic industry caved in to the external pressure brought by Wertham and the Senate hearings, Goodman's company kept churning out titles across numerous genres. Goodman pushed Lee toward whatever he saw his competitors selling. For Lee and his small team of freelance artists, colorists, and inkers, that meant tackling romance, animals, war stories, crime tales, and westerns, churning out issues to meet the print deadlines. At Goodman's firm, quantity categorically trumped quality.[14] "I was the hackiest hack who ever lived," the young editor lamented. "Goodman," remembered colorist Stan Goldberg, "left it all up to Stan. . . . I don't think Martin ever came into Stan's office, and I never saw him in the bullpen."[15]

As the comic book industry turned even more conservative, Lee wrote innocuous comic book titles that no one could find offensive. Many of these books were mostly silly to the point of absurdity, featuring stereotypical characters that engaged in harmless adventure experiences, such as the long-running and benign *Nellie the Nurse* and *Millie the Model*. Lee considered the material beneath him. "I felt I was a better writer. . . . I shouldn't be wasting my life on this," he remembered. The only positive was that he enjoyed the process of working alongside other creative talents. "I'll stay just a little bit longer," he told himself, "because this is fun."[16]

In the wake of the downturn due to Wertham and the anti-comics fanatics, Goodman decided to vacate the Empire State Building for smaller offices at 655 Madison Avenue, the heart of the American advertising industry. Most of the operations were dedicated to his magazine business—Magazine Management, Inc.—a variety of genres and themes, perhaps only a half step removed from the bawdy slicks he had published during the era of the pulps. Lee settled into a small office and attempted to resurrect the comic book division, while all the other editors and writers basically ignored him, finding his work appalling at best and at worst depraved.

On the heels of the disastrous Senate hearings and the implementation of the Comics Code, Goodman made several business decisions, some of which nearly destroyed the comic book department Lee created and managed. Regardless of the cyclical nature of the comic book industry, Goodman could always get his products on newsstand racks because he owned his own distribution firm. The battle for prime placement went on and on, but the comics and magazines would be on the shelves.

In 1956, Goodman searched for ways to squeeze more money out of production costs. He decided to close his own distribution operations and go with the industry's largest player—American News Company (ANC). The company stood as the largest book wholesaler in the world and the primary distributor for an overwhelming majority of magazines and comic books. On the surface, the move made sense. Behind the scenes, though, ANC had been waging a battle to the death with antitrust regulators for four years. There were also rumors that ANC had mob connections. These ties gave the government added incentive to pursue the giant. Goodman gambled, but the move quickly turned sour.

The publisher had changed Timely's name to Atlas Comics in the early 1950s, but did not want to tie the entire corporation's future to the comic book division, which seemed like a sinking ship. Just as Goodman put the company's future in ANC's hands, the shaky situation worsened for the distributor. In January 1957, two of ANC's most successful magazines, *Collier's* and *Woman's Home Companion*, folded. Then, in a catastrophic setback, ANC's largest client, Dell Publishing, decided in April to find a new distributor for its comics and paperback books. In a last ditch effort to stay alive, ANC shuttered its comic book arm. That year the national behemoth lost $8 million and fired eight thousand employees. Two months after the comic book division closed, ANC went completely out of business.

The ANC debacle looked like the end for Goodman and Lee. The editor declared, "It was like we had been the last ones to book passage on the *Titanic!*"[17] ANC's failure had lasting consequences. Many magazine and comic book publishers were forced out of business as well. The remaining independent distributors leaped into the power vacuum and took control, often forcing publishers to bend to their will or close down. Nearly everything changed about American magazines as a result, from publication frequency to the actual physical size. The entire industry would become more uniform, while marginal titles and topics would nearly cease altogether. For Goodman, the ANC collapse threatened not only Lee's comic book division, but also placed Goodman's entire life's work in jeopardy. He now had no way to get his magazines onto shelves or into the hands of consumers.

In a last ditch effort to save his publishing empire, Goodman begged his main rival, Independent News (owned by National Periodical/DC Comics), to distribute Atlas's entire catalog, both his popular magazines and comic books. After watching ANC fight antitrust charges, Independent News executives feared the repercussions or sanctions they might face if they turned Goodman away. Although desperate, Goodman also had something to offer. Independent knew that they could make money on the deal, particularly by distributing the magazines. Realizing their strong negotiating position, they signed an agreement with Goodman, but with harsh stipulations: Atlas could only publish eight comic books per month. Goodman also had to agree to a ten-year deal, which would ensure that Independent News controlled his company's future.

Overnight, the comic book division plummeted. Despite the downturn after the comic book scare and the number of freelancers who left the industry as a result, Lee had still been publishing sixty to seventy titles per month. He wrote or scripted most of them, while also overseeing all editorial work and art. In one fell swoop, though, Independent News neutered its competitor and thwarted Goodman's main strategy, which had been to flood the market with knockoff titles when a new genre caught on. Goodman and Lee decided to publish sixteen bimonthly comic books, culling the bestselling ones across genres, including stalwarts *Millie the Model*, *Patsy Walker*, *Strange Tales*, *Wyatt Earp*, and *Two-Gun Kid*. The backlog of artwork and scripts from all the canceled titles were later used in the remaining sixteen, which meant that freelancers who had stayed with Lee after the fallout wouldn't find much work from him for the foreseeable future.

Despite his reputation for toughness and the ability to melt employees to the core with an icy stare, once again Goodman left for a Florida vacation, leaving Lee the onerous task of firing staff members who were no longer needed. Lee also had to trim the freelance roster. Venerable artists like John Romita and Joe Sinnott turned in their remaining work with no new jobs on the horizon. Firing his friends and teammates, Lee recalled, "was the toughest thing I ever did in my life."[18] Some of the freelancers weren't even paid for the work they were doing at the time. As a result, many artists left the business for more stable positions in advertising or the corporate world.

Lee hunkered down in a cubicle and got back to producing, ever fearful that Goodman would axe him next. The editor had several things on his side: he worked fast, was an extended family member, and Goodman did not want to miss out on the next comic book wave, even if the profits were scaled back dramatically. He knew that he needed Lee to capitalize on the next big trend that readers would embrace when they started buying comic books again.

Both a people-pleaser and dedicated company employee, Lee reacted badly to having to fire his friends and coworkers, alternatively transitioning between fears of his own unemployment and the escalating unhappiness with his career path. "I couldn't shake that gnawing feeling of depression," Lee explained. "It was like I was chasing my tail all the time. I could never shake that feeling of vague dissatisfaction."[19] He didn't think that his skills could translate into a job in magazines or screenwriting for film or television, though, so he continued to abide Goodman's rule and wait until another opportunity surfaced, even though he wasn't sure what that might be.

While the comic book industry suffered in the years following the Senate investigations, Goodman's publishing machine grew. The magazine business produced a mix of conventional titles about Hollywood, the burgeoning television industry and its stars (like Jackie Gleason), and romance magazines, along with more racy titles aimed at titillating young men. These efforts included an *Esquire* copycat titled *Stag* and others, including *For Men Only, Man's World,* and *Male. Stag* and the others emphasized explicit and sensational photographs and content (nearly bordering on pornographic), but many first-rate writers published with Goodman, including Ogden Nash, Graham Greene, and William Saroyan (Lee's old Army officemate).

Lee bounced back and forth between the two parts of Goodman's business, chiefly searching for security, but also on the lookout for respectability. Ironically, at the time, it seemed to him (and other adults outside publishing) that a brassy Hollywood pinup magazine like *Focus* was more prestigious than writing and editing comic books, even though the former featured risqué photographs, provocative drawings of women, and stories heavy on sexuality and intrigue, such as "I Kidnapped the King's Harem Girl" and "Divorcees are Dynamite." These lurid tales trafficked in sexuality, innuendo, and either complete nudity or semi-nudity.

In 1956, Goodman tried to copy the success of *Mad* magazine with *Snafu* and even had Lee assemble an all-star cast of artists, including Bill Everett and Joe Maneely. Despite Lee's best efforts, *Snafu* did not catch on and lasted a meager three issues.[20] The quick cancellation was a Goodman trait. He rarely allowed magazines to build momentum. If he sensed that the audience moved on or wasn't interested, he dumped the product and searched for the potential next big thing. If that didn't appear right away, Goodman might attempt to repurpose content elsewhere, like slapping new titles on old articles and running them as original essays in different magazines. Several times throughout his career, Goodman faced sanctions from the Federal Trade Commission for publishing practices that either skirted the letter of the law or were entirely illegal.

In June 1958, Lee put in calls to two artists that he had worked with in the past: Steve Ditko and his old boss, Jack Kirby. Both men needed work, especially Kirby, who had burned bridges while working for rival DC Comics and saw his partnership with Joe Simon evaporate in the industry downturn as Simon went off into the advertising business. There simply weren't enough assignments to go around and many of the remaining ones were at a reduced page rate. Kirby had few options. Goodman, virtually ignoring Lee's comic book work, barely noticed that his editor had hired back its former star artist, even if there might be some leftover resentment between the two about old *Captain America* profits.

Lee put them to work on science fiction and fantasy titles. Ditko's fluid style and gripping sense of shapes and sizes worked perfectly in these genres. Kirby was less happy, but committed to the paycheck. From a similar background as Lee, yet more hardscrabble and poorer, Kirby had a manic drive to support his family. He drew the monster books that Lee requested, even though it didn't require his best work.

Both Lee and Kirby had reservations about the comic book business, but they also needed the work, sharing a level of determination that few could match. Lee edited and wrote for Goodman's magazines, but thought that the publisher purposely snubbed him because of the weakness of the comic book division. Lee remembered his boss/relative walking straight past him without saying a word. The silence was deafening and sent a clear message. Lee realized, "It's like a ship sinking, and we're the rats. And we've got to get off."[21] For his part, Kirby said that he felt "shipwrecked" at Goodman's company.

Little did Lee, Kirby, and Ditko realize that they would soon revolutionize the comic book industry and popular culture forever.

CHAPTER 6

BIRTH OF THE NEW HERO
THE FANTASTIC FOUR

Barely looking at the road in front of him, Stan Lee barrels toward Long Island in a souped-up Buick convertible. Jack Kirby, chewing on a cigar, sits in the passenger seat to Lee's right. John Romita, another one of Lee's favorite artists, grips the back of Kirby's seat. With one eye on the duo in the front and one on the traffic, Romita is a captive audience, fearing for his life.

Lee can't stop talking. Over the onrush of air and booming sounds of the city, he barks out soliloquies about the intergalactic adventures of a quartet of superheroes. Shot through with gamma rays after crashing a spaceship back to Earth, each member has developed a superpower. With their newfound powers, they vow to battle evil together.

Kirby punctuates his ideas with a jab of his stogy. Even in the swirl of wind, he shifts the cigar from one side of his mouth to the other, waiting for Lee to pause. The arguments over plots and scenarios began as soon as Lee's foot stomped on the gas.

Nonchalant, Lee swerves and jukes between passing vehicles. Kirby focuses on the plot, seemingly unfazed by Lee's daredevil driving. As they bicker over how the stories should play out, each battling for his point of view, Romita realizes that neither is actually listening to the other. "They would both come in with their ideas," he recalled, "they would both ignore each other. . . . I never really knew which way they would go because both of them had a different aspect on the story."[1]

The bickering doesn't end until Lee drops Kirby off at his house in East Williston on Long Island, a bucolic little village of less than three thousand souls. The tiny hamlet is far removed from the great artist's youth growing up on the crime-ridden streets of the Lower East Side.

Such story conferences, whether they took place in a whizzing convertible shooting toward Long Island, over the phone, or in Lee's cramped office, came to define the way he and Kirby created superhero stories in the 1960s. Neither the writer nor the artist probably realized it at the time, but in these arguments and countless others they had actually reinvented the way comic books were created.

The new writing style mixed storytelling, plot, and visual representation (later dubbed the "Marvel Method"). Both the writer and artist had a say in how the final product unfolded, rather than the artist merely following a script, as had been done in the past. When readers went nuts for the new superhero team, Lee and Kirby realized that they were at the dawn of a new era.

It all began with those gamma rays and the Fantastic Four!

From the planet-smashing opening burst to the pistol shot and train churning headlong around a bend and nearly right at the viewer, *The Adventures of Superman* gave audiences chills up and down their spines. The orchestra blared, while the announcer proclaimed that the hero fought for "truth, justice, and the American way." Tall, with dark slicked-back hair and a broad chest, actor George Reeves brought Jerry Siegel and Joe Shuster's character to life. *The Adventures of Superman* blazed across the 1950s, and television sets across the nation were tuned to the program.

Julius "Julie" Schwartz, the editorial director of DC Comics, Goodman's chief competitor, realized *The Adventures of Superman*'s success gave DC an opportunity to rekindle interest in superhero-driven comic books. He had been editing Wonder Woman, Flash, and Green Lantern since 1944. Despite the ongoing challenges with Wertham's crusades and television's lure, Schwartz figured that if the company focused on superheroes, their fortunes might be reversed.

Beginning in 1956, the editor gingerly pushed the company back into the superhero game, bringing out remodeled, updated versions of the Flash, Green Lantern, Hawkman, and The Atom, among others. One hit led to another. Then, the early success of the Flash led him to introduce a superhero team, modeled after the Justice Society of America, which had run its course in 1951. The new group, with the slightly different name of the Justice League of America, first appeared in *The Brave and the Bold* #28 (March 1960).[2] Although Superman did not appear on the cover with the superhero team, both he and Batman were revealed as members. The combination of the Superman television show and his inclusion in the new super-hero lineup helped National Comics stay at the top of the industry.[3]

Schwartz wasn't the only comic book insider to see the resurgence of Superman and its consequences. As usual, Martin Goodman smelled a trend in the making and wanted to pounce. Innovation did not interest him—he cared about profit. Goodman had a seemingly simple directive: move mountains of paper as fast as possible. Although he had a lifelong affinity for cowboy stories and some interest in science fiction, this was about as complex as he got about magazines and comic books. Both were merely products to be exploited.

Goodman's fundamental business acumen centered on watching to see what worked for his competitors and then brazenly copying them, whether this meant setting up a series of shell corporations to prevent any one piece of his publication empire from toppling the rest or latching onto a hot genre being pushed by a competitor and riding it until the next fad appeared. It seemed as if much of the industry ran on this notion of watching the market leader and then following along. Many of the men who ran comic book houses knew each other well, playing cards and drinking, dining at the same high-end restaurants, golfing, and even vacationing near one another in Miami Beach. Though they attempted to outdo one another on the newsstands, they shared the commonality of comic books and publishing, which made them a kind of odd tribe, since comic books and magazines were hardly seen as reputable concerns.[4]

From the mid-1940s through the early 1960s, Goodman cut every corner possible to make money. Often, he dipped into rather seedy and unscrupulous tactics and content in search of sales. Titles like *For Men Only* and *Stag* appealed to people's most sordid interests, essentially soft-core pornography, horrific crime scene photos, and pirated movie stills of famous Hollywood stars to heighten the sensationalistic content. Goodman even urged employees of his magazine business and freelance staffers to pose as models for the magazines, which saved him hiring real models or actors.[5] The bonus for Goodman was that *Stag* and other lascivious magazines were sold for twenty-five cents versus the comic books at just ten cents.

In the cutthroat publishing business, profitability meant keeping costs down and averting risk at all turns. Goodman believed that the people buying comic books consisted primarily of preteen and teenage boys, simply interested in rock 'em, sock 'em stories with excessive fight scenes and action-filled pictures, and a large base of dimwitted adults. According to Goodman, they did not give a hoot about quality. Instead, he had his editorial staff push conventionality. The publisher famously followed in the wake of competitors who launched new trends and genres, exclaiming, "If you get a title that catches on, then add a few more, you're in for a nice profit."[6]

Stan Lee did not have notions of high artistry. At one time, he dreamed of writing a great novel or getting into movies, but years of work for Goodman knocked those ideas on their ear. He knew the reality—publishing was a moneymaking venture. His number one priority centered on creating products that would sell. Yet Lee also realized that there might be more to it than simply generating profits. He understood that comic books could play a more significant role in young people's lives, such as helping youngsters learn to read, or sparking their imaginations in ways that would help them later in life.

These impulses warred inside Lee. The monotony of writing and editing comic books at the relentless pace essential to make Goodman's strategy work pulled at his conscience. He served as the comic book division's editor, writer, and art director, but felt like he was spinning his wheels. Am I wasting my life on comic books? he wondered. "I felt we were merely doing the same type of thing, over and over again with no hope of either greater financial rewards or creative satisfaction."[7] In 1960, approaching two decades in the business, Lee hung at the end of his rope. Depressed and desperate, he thought he should travel some other career path—anything, really, to get away from the banal topics, plots, and characters that filled comics.

Still a couple years removed from forty years old, Lee considered other options, his usual optimistic outlook curtailed by thoughts of his own family history. After living through his father's fight with internal demons brought on by chronic unemployment during the Depression, the mere thought of leaving his job demonstrated Lee's deep-rooted despair. Jacob Lieber had been just a little older than Stan was now when he lost his job and the resulting fallout left his small family in tatters. Stan never forgot how his father's chronic unemployment sparked tense fights between his parents and left their marriage shattered.

Lee had a decision to make. He balanced two conflicting notions: a regular paycheck that provided a stable, happy life for his family, on one hand, and the relentless despondency he experienced by grinding out uninspiring comics, on the other. As the primary writer and editorial director, Lee spent long days scripting and editing teen romance and humor comics such as *Teen-Age Romance* and *Life with Millie*, and perennial westerns, such as *Rawhide Kid*, *Wyatt Earp*, and *Two-Gun Kid*. Monster stories featuring surprise or twist endings, including *Strange Tales* and *Journey into Mystery*, also took up much of Lee's time.

Lee added up the pieces and realized that the comic book business seemed doomed. Sales figures that had taken off in the 1950s plummeted at the end of the decade. Public outcry had hurt the industry, which added to Lee's unhappiness. "There we were blithely grinding out our merry little monster yarns," Lee said. "We were turning out comics by the carload, but nothing much was happening."[8] No matter which way he turned, Lee felt pressure: Stay in comics and continue his malaise for a regular paycheck, keep churning out derivative characters to satiate Goodman's demands, or leave behind the only career he had ever known.

In the summer of 1961, Lee took action. He decided to create a superhero team that would put the consistently second-rate publishing house on the map. He immediately got to work piecing the team together. Contrary to the Justice Society and the Justice League, which were formed by disparate individuals, Lee determined that his team would be a family, and like a regular family, would confront the challenges people faced in the real world. The only difference, Lee thought, is that these seemingly typical people would have to deal with gaining superpowers that they never asked for. Lee wondered: How would people who lived next door or down the street react to living through a rocket crash to find that they had abilities that could enrich or destroy the world?

I wanted to "make the unreal real," Lee said. "Take extraordinary people, put them in extraordinary circumstances, and then have them behave like ordinary people. No audience of ordinary people could resist." He thought back to what attracted him to books he had read and radio programs he had listened to in his youth and mirrored the kind of storytelling that attracted him. "Plop an earthly superhero into a familiar setting, and you've got some classic pulp fiction."[9]

Like a compelling dramatic film (and just like at the heart of most families), Lee began with the love story between the central characters Reed Richards and Susan Storm. Then, he upped the drama and family dynamic by adding her hot-tempered younger brother Johnny. Lee rounded out the new team with Ben Grimm, the group's everyman. When Grimm became the Thing, the group gained both comedic relief and a sense of humanity. The monster's exterior concealed a sensitive soul. The team's interactions—both as superheroes and individuals coping with a new world and one another—served as the jet fuel to send the comic racing. Lee saw that action as the central facet, explaining, "I like to have characters to work with as though it's a movie or a soap opera, where the characters' own personal lives would help write the dialogue and come up with situations."[10] The quartet would be a loving, but dysfunctional family, held together by affection, but dealing with a myriad of challenges brought on by their newfound might.

Lee pulled from current events to give the origin story context. The team took a risky spaceflight "to the stars" in an attempt to beat the Soviet Union into space, referred to as "commies," in the parlance of the day. The Russians had actually beaten the United States into space, initially with the launch of Sputnik (the first satellite), then in 1960, sending the dogs Belka and Strelka into orbit, so Lee's plot served as a kind of revisionist history.

When the group battled Mole Man, its first super villain, they were on red alert because the evildoer struck an "atomic plant behind the iron curtain" and a French facility in Africa. These references to reality—even keeping the team unmasked in a nod to the burgeoning celebrity culture of the age—made the team more interesting. The familiar territory and use of common lingo helped readers relate to the plight the heroes faced.

Finding an artist to draw the epic was Lee's easiest decision. Jack Kirby had been dutifully crafting covers and stories for Lee for years, essentially creating a house style for the company. Kirby excelled at space epics and illustrating action scenes that made readers feel the force of a roundhouse punch or the ground shake as an enormous intergalactic monster shambled through a cityscape. "I didn't discuss it with Jack first," Lee explained. "I wrote it first, after telling Jack it was for him because I knew he was the best guy to draw it."[11] Kirby, according to his cocreator, "has the uncanny ability to visualize unforgettable scenes so clearly in his mind's eye that all he has to do is put down on paper what already exists in his incredible imagination."[12]

A horrifying green monster pushes up through the city pavement, clutching a half-invisible blond as a human flame circles in flight. A handful of citizens react in horror. The reader sees another character from behind, a kind of monster, while the fourth seems to have limbs that stretch, loosening ropes that entangle him. A call-out box tells us their names and announces that they are "Together for the first time in one mighty magazine!"

The Fantastic Four have arrived!

The scene is dramatic and intense, but what really draws the reader's eye is the bold red, fanciful script used to title the comic book. It leaps from the page, a representation of the atomic age in the early Cold War. Next to the title is a tiny box with a capital "M" atop a smaller "c." Already, Lee and Kirby were thinking "Marvel Comics" as a way to differentiate this book from the company's other titles.

Inside, the *Fantastic Four* comic is a four-part story that Lee decided to tell in a nonlinear narrative. Although we know from the cover that the heroes will battle a monster, the reader doesn't reach this event until the third act. The first two sections introduce the team and tell its origin story.

Initially, when Richards uses a "4" smoke signal to assemble his teammates, citizens and the police react with terror. The Thing is viewed as a monster, and the police wonder if this being portends "an alien invasion." They try to shoot him before he uses the city's sewer system to evade a further confrontation. Later, the government launches jetfighters against the Torch, shooting at him with nuclear missiles. Mister Fantastic saves Johnny—and the city—as he "hurls the mighty missile far from shore where it explodes harmlessly over the sea."

The next section begins with an argument between Reed and Ben over the safety of the experimental rocket and the possible consequences of flying through "cosmic rays." Although he doesn't want to pilot an unsafe ship, Ben is manipulated by Susan, who invokes the dreaded "Commies" as rationale for the danger. Then, she infers that Ben is a "coward." Soon after, decked out in dark plum-colored spacesuits and blue helmets, the team sneaks past a guard and into the rocket. In what might be Kirby's strongest panels in the entire book, the rays pulse through the ship, causing Ben to collapse and Johnny to combust. You can almost smell the teen's flight suit go up in flames.

After the ship crashes back to safety, the team emerges from the wreckage dazed and angry. Susan is the first to be impacted, slowly turning invisible as the others look on in horror. "Wha—What if she never gets visible again?" her brother asks in amazement. Next, as Ben and Reed start to get angry, the former turns into the Thing, an orange-skinned monster, like a giant rock pile gone amuck. He reveals his secret longing for Susan, exclaiming, "I'll prove to you that you love the wrong man, Susan," and swings a tree trunk at Richards. The latter eludes the violent burst by stretching his body and neck. Then, using his newfound ability, he wraps Ben up using his arms as ropes. Finally, Johnny bursts into flames, which starts a brush fire. They collectively think, "We've changed! All of us! We're more than just human." Speaking for the group, Ben declares that they "gotta use that power to help mankind." They band together under the "Fantastic Four" moniker.

The final two sections of *Fantastic Four* #1 find the team—back in their purple jumpsuits—tracking a mysterious threat to "Monster Isle." There, they battle a flying three-headed monster, a giant rock monster, and various other gargoyles, including the green giant from the cover. Using Torch's immense heat, they thwart Mole Man, ultimately entombing him and the monsters underneath Monster Isle. The team flies away in a private jet, grimly facing the future.

The Kirby-Lee partnership brought *The Fantastic Four* to life, but neither had grand expectations for its success. "Okay, that's it," Lee figured, "I'm going to get fired. I got that out of my system."[13]

Lee was proud of the work and willing to go out on a limb, but neither he nor Kirby had the luxury of waiting to hear if *The Fantastic Four* would be successful. Comic books were actually released about three months prior to the month printed on the front of the book and it took another handful of months for the sales figures to trickle in. Plus, the writer and artist couldn't really stop working, given the ten to twelve issues that had to be produced within the stipulations of Goodman's punitive agreement with the DC Comics distribution arm, which included the next issue of *The Fantastic Four*.

As Lee and his team pushed to meet the tight printing and distribution deadlines, they experienced something totally new—fan mail started to arrive at Marvel headquarters, an avalanche of fan mail. Readers were crazy for the new superhero team. According to Lee, getting any mail at all was virtually unprecedented. Previously, fans only wrote in when an issue had some mechanical defect and a reader wanted a refund.

Rather than get the ax, Kirby and Lee had struck gold. "We were swamped with it," Lee recalled, "and it just kept growing with each new issue."[14] The sales figures that came in months later reiterated the comic book's popularity. The success took Lee by surprise: "I never realized it would sell that well."[15]

In response to the mail, Lee started answering fan letters within the pages of the comic and writing up a chatty column that let readers in on insider information about Marvel and its staff. On the surface, the jokey, easygoing interaction with fans seemed frivolous. Over time, however, it became an important link in establishing Lee as the central public persona of not only Marvel, but the comic book industry. Lee seemed like every reader's favorite uncle, always willing to share a wisecrack and some insider gossip going on behind the scenes at the company.

The play between reader and writer/editor turned many young people into lifelong fans. Readers felt as if they were there in New York City with Stan and his "bullpen" collaborators, whom they imagined they knew based on the colorful nicknames the editor gave them and the way he touted both their skills and quirky personalities. A born showman, Lee used the space at the back of the comics to express his newfound happiness. His personal gamble in creating *The Fantastic Four* paid off.

Although *The Fantastic Four* sold extremely well, Marvel did not list the title among its 1961 sales figures, since it had been released so late in the year.[16] If the comic was the company's bestselling issue that year, though, one can infer its sales exceeded *Tales to Astonish*, which ranked fortieth with about one hundred eighty-five thousand issues sold. In comparison, *Uncle Scrooge* (published by Dell) ranked first in 1961 with more than eight hundred fifty thousand in paid circulation, while DC's venerable *Superman* stood at eight hundred twenty thousand. Based on how publishers reported circulation, *The Fantastic Four* would not appear on the official roll until 1966, when it placed nineteenth for the year at three hundred twenty-nine thousand copies.

The combination of fan enthusiasm and the mountain of mail streaming into Marvel's Madison Avenue offices served as an indication of the watershed moment in Lee's career. In 1961, DC's *Justice League of America* won the Academy of Comic Book Arts and Sciences (Alleys) comic book of the year award. The next year, however, *The Fantastic Four* won the award. The Marvel revolution had begun.

Although years later Kirby and Lee would contest who deserved credit for creating *The Fantastic Four*, thereby setting the Marvel Age ablaze, they each brought special talents to the process, like all great creative duos, whether musicians, filmmakers, or athletes. Without Kirby's inimitable artistry, the superhero team would not have burst off the page, generating so much energy and action that a reader could almost feel the void of deep space or what it felt like for a man's arm to stretch hundreds of yards or another to burst into flames. Lee is all words. He delivered a distinct dialogue and narrative patter that left his own unique mark on the team and its thrilling collection of archenemies.

The fact of the matter is that by 1961 both men were seasoned professionals, having spent nearly their entire adult lives in the comic book business. Soon they would become legends. It is easy to forget, too, in the generations of praise they have received since they created *The Fantastic Four*, that Kirby and Lee each felt personally and professionally stuck at that time. Both had been deeply unsatisfied. They felt anxiety and fear regarding the future for themselves and the industry they had dedicated their careers to building. Later—particularly as Lee's career shot skyward and Kirby felt jealous and used—a personal cold war enveloped the duo. But when *The Fantastic Four* hit newsstands for the first time, the two barely looked up . . . the writer from his one-finger, clickety-clacking typewriter and the artist from his worn-down drafting table. They did not realize that they were creating a masterpiece. For them, it was just another product, one among many that kept them chained to the business.

Headstrong and talented, Lee and Kirby were also intense workaholics and deeply driven. They had contrasting personalities, but the combo worked on a mix of fear, concern, pride, and passion It is clear that the Marvel Method perfected by Lee and Kirby worked, because of the talents each willingly put on the table. There are glimpses of how they worked that have had comic book historians arguing over who deserves credit for what for decades.

Years ago, Lee stumbled across his original two-page synopsis of *The Fantastic Four* #1 and shared it with *Alter Ego* magazine editor Roy Thomas, Lee's onetime protégé and later replacement as Marvel editor-in-chief. One of the surprises the manuscript uncovered was that Lee had obviously run some parts of the story and its characters by the Comics Code Authority. Directly in the origin story, for example, Lee informs Kirby about the Human Torch character, passing along that the CCA warned that he "may never burn anyone with flames, he may only burn ropes, doors, etc.—never people." Thomas speculated that Lee cleared the character prior to writing the overview, because he feared potential outcry that might delay the comic.[17]

This episode also reveals two sides of Lee's work as writer/editor. While Lee experienced newfound joy in creating a new kind of superhero team, he had to be businesslike and strategic in getting the Code censors' approval, particularly when time and deadlines played such an important role in his work. Talking to an early interviewer about "King" Kirby, Lee praised his partner for mixing storytelling and visualization like no one else in the business. He explained that Kirby often plotted the comics himself, admitting, "We're practically both the writers on the things."[18] Kirby also took on the role of unofficial art director, training new artists in the company style, which really was just his own style applied to Marvel's superhero lineup.

Lee's budding showmanship grew and his confidence increased as a result of the super team's increasing popularity and sales. By the third issue, when the Fantastic Four took on the seemingly invincible Miracle Man, Lee took the brash step of tattooing the phrase: "The Greatest Comic Magazine in the World!!" just below the series title. From issue four on, a slightly altered slogan appeared above the title: "The World's Greatest Comic Magazine!" No one could miss the blaring letters, essentially daring the reader to disagree. The publicity generated by the tagline increased the notoriety, which Lee anticipated. Always willing to go out on a limb to spark sales, the writer explained, "I figured a line like that would certainly get attention, if only for its flagrant pretentiousness."[19] Lee knew that he took a risk, but no one could really prove or disprove his claim. Like a great fastball pitcher or rock and roll guitarist, the declaration drew a line in the sand and told competitors: "we're the best comic book company in the world."

The success of *The Fantastic Four* served as a hurricane-force wind thrusting Lee and Kirby deeper into the psyches of their hero team. Lee remembered that after ten issues, "we had both gained new insights into the FF and their ever-menacing antagonists." These were more than comic book creations, Lee explained, "Reed, Sue, Ben and Johnny seemed like part of our own families by now." For the longtime writer, "I felt comfortable writing their scenarios. It was increasingly easy to imagine what they would say or do in almost any given circumstance, for they had become as familiar to me as my own friends."[20] The family saga intensified as the Fantastic Four continued saving the world and dealing with the strains this effort caused them as individuals and a team.

For many fans, Ben Grimm/Thing was the group's go-to hero. Kirby modeled the hero after himself and added many of the tough guy characteristics he had acquired himself as a kid on the Lower East Side battling among gang members. According to Lee, Grimm epitomized what he hoped to create: "I realized there was no monster, no funny, ugly guy who's a hero. . . . When this guy becomes very powerful, he also becomes grotesque. It had a touch of pathos."[21]

The creative duo also specialized in inventing super villains evil and nasty enough to cause the reader anxiety. For example, they brought back Bill Everett's Prince Namor, the Sub-Mariner, as a misunderstood, majestic villain who just wanted his underwater kingdom to be left alone—that is, until he determined that Sue should rule the seas by his side, thus giving Reed constant fits as Namor moved in on his fiancée.

Doctor Doom proved even more interesting and despicable, a criminal genius and physically powerful foe who caused global mayhem from his home base in Latveria, an imaginary Eastern European kingdom that Lee concocted. In one of their sometimes dazzling and often argumentative story conferences, Kirby and Lee talked about a villain that would put the FF to the test. Lee latched onto the name "Doom," but Kirby was skeptical. Still, they found a way to work through their differences, despite having strong opinions. Lee recalled, "Whenever something is really right, it never takes long to put it all together. Each little idea led to another, more exciting one."[22]

Making Doom as sinister as possible, Kirby sketched him in a suit of armor, with his face hidden behind a cold gray steel mask. The villain first appeared in *Fantastic Four* #5 with a short origin story that would later be given a fuller treatment. The issue begins with one of Lee's soon-to-be famous in-jokes—Johnny Storm reading the new issue of *The Hulk*, which in reality had just reached the newsstands. Johnny teases Ben, "I'll be doggoned if this monster doesn't remind me of the Thing." In dysfunctional family fashion, Ben sets off after Torch, resulting in a broken table. Reed and Sue have to intervene, dousing her little brother with a fire extinguisher, while Reed ties Ben into knots. Reed laments, "What's the matter with the four of us? Whenever we're not fighting some menace to mankind, we end up fighting among ourselves!" Lee's heavy-handedness may be showing, but fans loved seeing the superheroes fight and bicker just like in their own living rooms.

After Doctor Doom ensnares the team in its skyscraper headquarters, Reed recognizes that their masked foe is actually his college classmate Victor Von Doom, "a brilliant science student . . . only interested in forbidden experiments" in "black magic." Doom takes Sue hostage, and then whisks the whole team to his fortress. Using a time machine of his own devising, Doom sends the three male members back in time to capture "Blackbeard's treasure." The teammates draw on their superpowers to battle the overmatched pirates and seize the treasure. Instead of giving it to Doom, however, Reed realizes, "If Doctor Doom wanted it, there must be some dangerous power which it possesses, and we've got to see that he never gets it!"

Ben, whom the pirates believe is Blackbeard, decides he likes being the outlaw and orders his crew to turn on Reed and Johnny. Moments later, though, a tornado rips apart the ship, nearly causing Johnny to drown. Later, Reed and Johnny discover Ben washed up on shore. He apologizes, "I musta got carried away by being accepted—as a normal man—even if it was only by a band of cutthroat pirates! I—I just lost my dumb head for awhile!" Ben gives Lee a new way to tell stories in comic books. The monster who just wants to be human keeps the tension high because he always yearns to give up his superpowers. Ben's internal struggle and how it plays out publicly when he appears as a monster adds to the pervasive sense of conflict at the heart of *The Fantastic Four*.

When Doom brings the men back to his castle through a time portal, he understands that they tricked him. Locking the team in a vault, the villain starts to cut off the oxygen. Sue, however, is able to turn invisible and stop the attack, thereby saving her teammates. The heroes escape Doom's fortress, but they cannot capture him. He rockets away using a portable jetpack.

By allowing the villain to escape, Lee and Kirby veered from the traditional comic book plot, refusing to neatly wrap up the story by the end of the issue. Essentially, the creative duo invented a comic book that read like a serial or soap opera, revealing more about the protagonists in each episode, while also benefiting from the continuity that episodic entertainment provides. Using these methods, Kirby and Lee infused *The Fantastic Four* with context and a history that fueled future issues. The level of suspense would remain high.

As with the launch of *FF* #1, fan mail about Doctor Doom piled up in Lee's office almost immediately. In short order, Lee and Kirby realized that Doom was "probably Marvel's very top villain, in appearance, in power, personality, and plain sheer reader appeal."[23]

The image of Reed angrily storming away and the seemingly incomprehensible notion of Doctor Doom as part of the team graced the cover of *Fantastic Four* #10. Despite this intriguing setup, what readers could not have overlooked is the appearance of Lee and Kirby in the lower left hand corner with their backs to the reader, actually commenting on the issue.

Inside, three team members have to deal with their growing celebrity, each avoiding fans who either want a piece of them or think they should be reined in somehow when they attempt to answer the Thing's distress signal. When they arrive at the apartment of Ben's blind girlfriend, Alicia, they realize that he is not in trouble. However, the mention of Sub-Mariner causes an argument between Reed and Sue. She blurts, "I'm not even sure of my own feelings." Just then, the story cuts to Kirby and Lee at Marvel's Madison Avenue offices, adorned with images of Hulk, Thor, and other superheroes, as the creative team attempts to create another super villain.

Suddenly, Doom walks into the office. He removes his mask, causing Lee and Kirby to recoil in horror. Doom then threatens their lives, saying, "You are searching for a story—well I shall give you one! Here, phone Mr. Fantastic—say what I tell you if you value your lives!" He shoots a ray out of his index finger, destroying Lee's ashtray as a show of force. Doom waits for Reed to arrive, and then ambushes him with sleeping gas. Next, Doom teleports himself and Richards to his secret lab.

Using knowledge he acquired from an advanced race of space aliens called the Ovoids, Doom transports his brain into Richards's body using telepathy, while Richards is stuck in the Doom armor. Tricking the Fantastic Four into helping him, Doom is able to lock Richards away in an underground chamber that only has an hour's worth of air left. Ultimately, Reed escapes, but he is knocked unconscious by Sue at Alicia's apartment. When the rest of the team (minus Doom in Reed's body) shows up, they realize that he might actually be telling the truth. Johnny and the Thing trick Doom into showing his true colors and in a moment of weakness, the two men are transposed back into their own bodies. Doom is accidently hit with a shrinking ray that makes him so small that he vanishes. Thus, Doom is thwarted again.

Drawing themselves into the comic and actually playing a role in the story may have seemed like a farce, but the issue helped further establish that Marvel books would be categorically different than the competition, especially the staid do-gooder superheroes at DC Comics. Just as important, the issue introduced them to readers as heroic figures, able to engage with their creations at will, even being more than a little scared of Doom, just as one would be in real life. Suddenly, the names adorning the issues—"Stan Lee & J. Kirby"—had meaning. And, as Lee explained, fans called out for the distortion, which he called "perhaps the first super hero take in which our featured players are aware that they are characters in a comic book. It was produced in response to many, many letters requesting such a story, and it was a real hoot for me to script the yarn."[24] Blurring the line between real and imagined showed Marvel readers the playful nature of the company and its primary writer/artist duo.

Just shy of Lee's thirty-ninth birthday, *FF* #1 appeared on newsstands. Created at a watershed moment in his life, as well as Kirby's, *The Fantastic Four* seemed almost a last ditch effort, as if their careers really did hang in the balance. After the tumultuous 1950s and the public backlash against comic books, many people thought the entire industry might collapse, including Lee. The cyclical nature of the business made the possibility that it could fall apart a reality. How many more of these boom-and-bust periods could one take?

Instead of his swan song, however, Lee found himself inundated with fan mail, which had never happened before. Usually, the only gauge for a comic book's success was sales figures, which wouldn't be reported for many months after a comic book launch. As Lee examined the letters, he realized that readers in the twelve-to-fifteen-year-old age group had stumbled on the title and dug the angst they found inside. They begged for more, which bolstered Lee's flagging spirits. After producing titles in bunches without much interaction from fans, the outpouring of support gave Lee what he needed at exactly the right moment.

Ever the curmudgeon and cautious, Kirby reacted with less enthusiasm, not willing to jump on the emotional roller coaster he had been on with so many other "hit" comics in his career. He continued to write and draw; always churning out pages at an astonishing clip. Lee viewed the letters and cards he received as vindication of his idea that if he just created a comic book that he would enjoy as a reader, others would enjoy it too.

The Fantastic Four did more than set the stage for Lee and Kirby to conceive more superheroes—it rejuvenated the entire comic book industry. After a career built on creating knockoff titles as fast as possible, Lee realized that he could assume a different role: trendsetter, rather than follower. He trusted in his instincts, his ability to tell stories that readers enjoyed, and Kirby's phenomenal artistry.

CHAPTER 7

SPIDEY SAVES THE DAY!

Bursting from the page and seemingly swinging right into the reader's lap, a new superhero is all lean muscles and tautness. He is masked, only alien-like curved eyes reveal human features, no mouth or nose is visible. His power is alarming—casually holding a ghoulish-looking criminal in one hand, while simultaneously swinging from a hair-thin cord high above the city streets. In the background, tiny figures stand on rooftops, looking on and pointing in what can only be considered outright astonishment.

The superhero is off-center, frozen in a moment, as if a panicked photographer snapped a series of frames. The image captures the speed, almost like flight, with the wind at his back. The hero's deltoid ripples and leg muscles flex. Some mysterious webbing extends from his elbow to waist. Is this a man or creature from another world?

The answer is actually neither. Looking at the bright yellow dialogue boxes running down the left side of the page, the reader learns the shocking truth. This isn't a grown man, older and hardened, like Batman or Superman, one an existential nightmare and the other a do-gooder alien. No, this hero is just a self-professed "timid teenager" named Peter Parker. The world, he exclaims, mocks the teen under the mask, but will "marvel" at his newfound "awesome might."

Spider-Man is born.

The 1962 debut of Spider-Man in *Amazing Fantasy* #15 happened because Lee took a calculated risk. He trusted his instincts, honed over decades of working in the chaotic comic book industry, which often seemed to run on trial and error more than logic. On the long path from the publisher to the newsstands, sales determined what each publisher offered. Fickle comic book fans frequently switched interests, leaving editors like Lee scratching their heads and trying to predict the next fad.

Rolling the dice on a new character also meant potentially wasting precious hours writing, penciling, and inking a title that might not sell when that same time could be used on more profitable books. In an industry driven by talent and always against the clock, there were never enough good artists and writers to spare time for a series that did not sell. The business side of the industry constantly clashed with the creative aspects, forcing fast scripting and artwork to go hand in hand. The creative teams always raced against stringent monthly deadlines.

In more than two decades toiling away as a comic book writer and editor, Lee watched genres spring to life, and then almost as quickly, readers would turn their attention to something else. War stories might give way to romance titles, which would then ride a wave until monster comics became popular, and then be super-seded by aliens. In an era when a small group of publishers controlled the entire industry, they kept close watch over each other's products in hopes of mimicking sales of hot titles.

Lee calls publisher Martin Goodman, "One of the great imitators of all time." Goodman dictated what Lee wrote after ferreting out tips and leads from golf matches and long lunches with other publishers. If he heard that westerns were selling for a competitor, Goodman would visit Lee, bellowing, "Stan, come up with some Westerns."[1] Every new fad meant immediately switching to those kinds of titles. The versatility necessary in this environment had been Lee's primary strength, based on swift writing and plotting many different titles almost simul-taneously. Lee had been working under these conditions for so long that he had mastered the techniques for easily creating multiple storylines and plots, using gimmicks and wordplay to remember names and titles, like recycling the gun-slinger Rawhide Kid in 1960 and making him into an outlaw or using alliteration, as in *Millie the Model*.

When certain comic genres sold well, publisher Martin Goodman gave Lee breathing room, but when sales dipped, he exerted pressure. A conservative ex-ecutive, Goodman rarely wanted change, which irked Lee. The writer bristled at his boss's belittling beliefs, explaining, "He felt comics were really only read by very, very young children or stupid adults," which meant "he didn't want me to use words of more than two syllables if I could help it. . . . Don't play up characterization, don't have too much dialogue, just have a lot of action." Given the precarious state of individual publishing companies, which frequently went belly-up, and his long history with Goodman, Lee admitted, "It was a job; I had to do what he told me."[2]

Despite being distant relatives and longtime coworkers, the publisher and editor maintained a cool relationship. From Lee's perspective, "Martin was good at what he did and made a lot of money, but he wasn't ambitious. He wanted things to stay the way they were." The publishing industry remained highly competitive, but most American business executives were not cutthroat captains of industry. Goodman pushed Lee, but the writer recalled: "He hired a good friend of his to be his business manager, and they would spend two or three hours a day in Martin's office playing Scrabble."[3]

Riding the wave of critical success and extraordinary sales of *The Fantastic Four*, Goodman gave Lee a simple directive in line with his general management style: "Come up with some other superheroes."[4] For the publisher, the order made sense: superheroes seemed to be the next big genre to catch on, so that would be Timely's new direction. Yet, *The Fantastic Four* subtly shifted the relationship between editor and publisher. With sales doubling because of the new superhero team, Goodman looked away a bit, which enabled Lee to wield greater influence and authority. From the publisher's perspective, the popularity of superhero books meant simply jumping on the bandwagon until it died out. Lee, though, used some of the profit to pay freelance writers and editors more money, which then offloaded some of the pressure he felt in writing, plotting, editing, and approving the company's limited number of monthly titles. In launching *Spider-Man*, however, Lee did more than divert the talents and energy of his staff. He actually defied Goodman.

For months, Lee grappled with the idea of a new kind of superhero in the same vein as the Fantastic Four, with realistic challenges that someone with superpowers would experience living in the modern world. The new character, however, would be "a teenager, with all the problems, hang-ups, and angst of any teenager." Lee came up with the colorful "Spider-Man" name and envisioned a "hard-luck kid" both blessed and cursed by acquiring superhuman strength and the ability to cling to walls, sides of buildings, and even ceilings, just like a real-life spider.[5] He knew Spider-Man would be an important character for the company and its efforts in the superhero genre.

Lee recalled going to see Goodman, "I did what I always did in those days, I took the idea to my boss, my friend, my publisher, my cohort," even embellishing the story of Spider-Man's origin by claiming that he got the idea from "watching a fly on the wall while I had been typing."[6] He laid the character out in full: teen, orphan, angst, poor, intelligent, and other traits the young man would possess. Lee thought Spider-Man was a no-brainer, but to his surprise, Goodman hated it and forbade him from offering it as a stand-alone comic book.[7]

The longtime publisher had three major complaints: "people hate spiders, so you can't call a hero 'Spider-Man'"; no teenager could be a hero "but only be a sidekick"; and a hero had to be heroic, not a pimply kid who isn't popular or strong.[8] To Goodman, a hero who isn't a hero or even particularly likeable sounded like a "comedy character." Irritated, he asked Lee, "Didn't [he] realize that people hate spiders?"[9] Given the litany of criticisms, Lee recalled, "Martin just wouldn't let me do the book."[10]

Goodman thought featuring a teenager would also make his company a laughingstock among comic book publishers, a concern that the executive worried about incessantly. No matter what the company's success, Goodman felt the ups-and-downs of the industry too keenly, so he pushed back on ideas that he thought would fizzle and kept looking to pick up on the successes of other publishers. Goodman hated everything about Spider-Man. He usually took a hands-on approach only during downturns, but when Lee brought him the new character, the writer opened himself up to Goodman's insecurities and fears regarding status in the marketplace and among competitors.

Realizing that he could not completely circumvent his boss, Lee made the executive decision to at least give Spider-Man a try in as low-risk a manner as possible. The best case for the experiment would be to place the character on the cover of a series that had bombed up to that point—*Amazing Fantasy*. The comic-buying public simply had little interest in the *AF* run, which usually featured thriller/fantasy stories by Lee and surreal art by Steve Ditko, Marvel's go-to artist for styling the macabre, surreal, or Dali-esque. At one point, Lee even put the word "Adult" directly into the title, hoping that "Amazing Adult Fantasy" would get readers interested. Facing Goodman's disdain and the woeful *AF* sales figures, it seemed as if there were already two strikes against the teen wonder.

Despite these odds and his boss's directive, Lee remembered that he couldn't let the nerdy superhero go, saying, "I couldn't get Spider-Man out of my mind."[11] He worked up a *Spider-Man* plot and handed it over to Jack Kirby. Lee figured that no one would care (or maybe even notice) a new character in the last issue of a series that would soon be discontinued.

In this fast-paced environment, where Lee served essentially as Marvel's managing editor, writer, copy editor, and overall creative director, he turned to artists that he trusted because they needed little direction and worked quickly. Often, Lee would dictate a storyline and then the artist would take that plot and begin to draw the issue. Later, the writer would add the dialogue and extra information, allowing time to edit or add in what the artist might have overlooked.

With Spider-Man, however, Kirby missed the mark. His early sketches turned the teen bookworm into a mini-Superman with all-American good looks, like a budding astronaut or football star. With little time to pause and think about what was essentially a throwaway character, Kirby turned to other projects and Lee put Ditko on the title. He did the art for *Amazing Fantasy* anyway, and his style was more suited for drawing an offbeat hero.

Ditko nailed Spider-Man, but not the cover art, forcing Lee to commission Kirby for the task, with Ditko inking. Despite Kirby's last-minute effort on the cover, Lee could not have been happier with Ditko's version of the teen. He explained: "Steve did a totally brilliant job of bringing my new little arachnid hero to life."[12] They finished the two-part story and ran it as the lead in *AS* #15. Revealing both the busy, all-hands state of the company and their low expectations, Lee recalled, "Then, we more or less forgot about him."[13] As happy as Lee and Ditko were with the collaboration and outcome, there is no way they could have imagined that they were about to spin the comic book world onto a different axis.

Lee's new writing style established a voice for *Spider-Man* comic books and the company as a whole. Breaking down the invisible barrier between writer and reader (commonly referred to as "the fourth wall") on the first page of the initial Spider-Man *AF* debut reveals how Lee established a friendly, homespun voice that also gently guided the reader on the hero's journey. This second-person method stood in stark contrast to the more formal, distant language of other superheroes, primarily the competitors at DC—Superman, Batman, and Wonder Woman.

From the start, Lee lets us in on a secret, explaining that "confidentially," people in the comic business call superheroes "long underwear characters" and that they are "a dime a dozen." Yet, the reader is also informed that this new character is "just a bit . . . different!" At about a hundred words into the story, then, Lee has already formed a relationship with the reader and created the context for Spider-Man as something new versus other superheroes. The tongue-in-cheek tone emphasizes how "different" this hero will be in a deliberately easygoing style.

On page two, Lee shows how adults generally like Parker, including his surrogate parents Aunt May and Uncle Ben and his teachers, who are "fond" of the "clean-cut, hard-working honor student!" Yet, as quickly as the reader realizes that Parker is a good guy, Lee shows us how his classmates alienate him, particularly in contrast to school stud Flash Thompson. Parker asks a girl out and she refuses, turning instead to "dreamboat" Thompson. As the popular gang speeds off in a red convertible, they laugh at him for suggesting that they go to a science exhibit. "You stick to science, son. We'll take the chicks," one of his classmates sneers. In the next frame, Parker is crying as he enters the science lab, declaring, "Someday they'll be sorry!—Sorry that they laughed at me!"

The elegance in juxtaposing Parker as a regular guy versus the "in crowd" makes the teen sympathetic. Most readers can instantly relate to Parker because every school has a Flash Thompson who basks in the attention and seems especially gleeful in pushing the smaller, frail Parker aside. Again, Lee addresses the reader directly, saying: "Yes, for some, being a teenager has many heart-breaking moments." The writer establishes that Parker has feelings and that being an outcast hurts.

Rather than simply hinging the story on Parker as an outsider, Lee exposes the young man's full range of emotions, while the story grows darker and more foreboding. Once the atomic-powered spider bites the teen, he stumbles into his newfound power blindly, eventually entering into a professional wrestling contest to test his strength and get some quick money. Parker's lack of confidence causes him to put on a mask to avert the possibility of being a "laughingstock," but he challenges the muscled bruiser Crusher Hogan anyway, who calls the boy "a little masked marvel." Lee's wordplay, using "marvel" here and on the cover, subconsciously creates an association between the character and the future company name, which the writer/editor had been contemplating.

In one of several ominous scenes, almost immediately adults search for a way to exploit the teen's powers. A "TV producer" promises the masked Parker a "fortune" and an appearance on the era's immensely popular *Ed Sullivan Show*. Under the tutelage of the TV man/agent, Spider-Man becomes a sensation, inhaling what is described as the "first sweet scent of fame and success." The celebrity goes to the youth's head, though, and when he has the chance to stop a thief that a policeman is chasing, he does nothing, despite his massive powers. Parker, as Lee demonstrates, has strength, but not yet the wisdom to transform into a real hero.

Later, when the now-familiar story of Uncle Ben's death unfolds, Parker loses his cool, becomes Spider-Man and hunts down the fugitive. In the only frame in the entire comic that shows his pupils through the mask, Spider-Man realizes that the thief is the same one he could have stopped earlier. The boy does not kill the criminal, instead dangling him from a web and lowering him to the police below. However, Lee depicts the anguish the teen suffers, accepting the burden of his actions. In the final frame, Lee wrote the famous line that sums up Spider-Man: "Aware at last that in this world, with great power there must also come—great responsibility!"

Finally able to apply his innovative ideas about voice and style directly to the new superheroes, Lee captured the reader's attention by formulating a hero that had genuinely human traits. Peter Parker, a wallflower kid picked on by his peers for being different, actually grew out of Lee's own feelings of being bullied as a kid. "Because I was the youngest and the thinnest, I was never the captain or leader, and

I was always the one getting pushed around." So, when searching for Parker's voice, Lee explained, "I figured, kids would relate to a concept like that. After all, most kids have had similar experiences. Turns out I was right."[14] Lee put the *AF* issue to bed and scurried off onto the next title that demanded his attention.

The hectic pace of the comic book business did not allow anyone to slow down, let alone stop to contemplate how the public might react to a particular title—which may account for why "Spider-Man" is listed in *AF* #15 both correctly and as "Spiderman" and "the Spiderman." Lee and his small crew of artists were already off onto new titles, working against the relentless deadlines.

But, although the sales figures would be unavailable for several months, Lee realized that Spider-Man had found an audience when letters from readers poured into the office by the satchel, just as they had a year earlier when the Fantastic Four debuted. Lee recalls getting about a hundred fan letters a day and sometimes more, which he dutifully read and answered.

The fateful day sales figures finally arrived. Goodman stormed into Lee's office, as always awash in art boards, drawings, mockups, yellow legal pads, and memos littering the desk.

Goodman beamed, "Stan, remember that Spider-Man idea of yours that I liked so much? Why don't we turn it into a series?"[15]

If that wasn't enough to knock Lee off-kilter, then came the real kicker: Spider-Man was not just a hit, the issue was in fact the fastest-selling comic book of the year, and indeed the decade. *Amazing Fantasy*, perpetually at the bottom of the sales charts, skyrocketed to number one with issue #15, due to Lee's efforts to bring the character to life.[16] Although it had been months since Lee and Ditko had created Spider-Man, the overwhelming popularity meant that the creative team would need to begin work immediately to turn the character into a series.

Despite Goodman's initial negativity and the indifference Kirby had about drawing Spider-Man, the success of *Amazing Fantasy* #15 elevated Lee and Ditko, since the new character would be the keystone of Marvel's superhero-based lineup. More importantly, the combination of the Fantastic Four and Spider-Man transformed Marvel from a company run by imitating trends of other publishers to a hip and relevant hot commodity.

Because of the long lag in obtaining sales figures and the length of the printing and distribution system, it wasn't until six months later that the new Spidey comic book debuted. To make way for the new title, Lee had to drop one, since the distribution agreement with Independent News only allowed Marvel to carry eight titles, regardless of the number of pages. Thus, a little less than a year after its debut, *The Incredible Hulk* ceased publication based on limited sales. In March 1963, *The Amazing Spider-Man* #1 burst onto newsstands.

When *The Amazing Spider-Man* finally arrived, comic book fans could not believe their eyes. The teen superhero seemed suspended in midair and encased in clear tubing, captured by none other than Lee's supergroup, the Fantastic Four. The Human Torch blazes up to eye level as if checking on the captured hero, while on the ground the Thing shakes his powerful fists, eager for a fight.

The appearance of Marvel's other breakout hit—the Fantastic Four—in Spider-Man's debut revealed how Lee hedged his bets and hoped to boost sales by bringing the two hot commodities together in one book. This idea seemed to carry over from the final issue of *Amazing Fantasy*, when Lee told readers to look forward to the next issue, even though the comic book faced cancellation. Lee always left the door open to possibilities, probably because he had experienced so much change in the industry over the preceding two decades of ups and downs. Goodman's sales figures showed just how popular Spider-Man promised to be, but using the Fantastic Four as reinforcement made good business sense and spurred a new creative form along the way.

For the cover image of *The Amazing Spider-Man*, Lee once again turned to veteran Kirby, which worked well, particularly since he was the artist and cocreator of the Fantastic Four. The difference between Kirby's cover and Ditko's work on the rest of the issue is immediately noticeable on the splash page. Here, Spidey seems slightly less muscular and truer to his creature namesake. A crowd led by publisher J. Jonah Jameson calls out: "Freak! Public Menace!" as the hero retreats to a web, gripping a tendril for balance. Lee's call-out to the audience is full of hype and hyperbole, "There's never been a story like this one—because there's never been a hero like—Spider-Man!"

The first *AS* issue carried two separate stories, which was not uncommon in comic books of the era. The two stories were connected, but had different purposes. The first focused on recounting the hero's origin story, a much-needed rehashing for fans that might have missed the *Amazing Fantasy* issue but eagerly looked for the debut. The second half of the book brought Spider-Man face-to-face with the members of the Fantastic Four and introduced the first stand-alone villain that the teen hero would face.

The first Spider-Man story emphasizes the plight Parker and Aunt May face with no money and the lengths the boy goes to to support the family. His efforts are thwarted, however, when his manager writes him a check for his "town hall" show and the bank won't cash it. Then, Jameson publishes a headline labeling the hero a "menace" and lectures around town, declaring, "Spider-Man must be outlawed! There is no place for such a dangerous creature in our fair city." The newspaperman offers his son, test pilot John Jameson, as an example of a real hero, as he is about to orbit Earth in a space capsule.

When the orbit mission goes awry, Spider-Man springs to action, even though the pilot's father is the source of his inability to make money performing. When the older man calls Spidey out for being a "publicity-seeking phony . . . trying to grab a headline!" the hero responds in Lee's smart-alecky style, saying, "Instead of flapping your lips, mister—just watch and see what I can do!" Within minutes, Spider-Man is hanging onto the shooting missile and replaces a control unit that enables Jameson to land safely.

Rather than celebrate the heroics, the newspaper editor resumes the fight, explaining that the difficulties were a "plot by Spider-Man to steal the spotlight . . . sabotaging the capsule." Later, Parker is shown listening to a crowd of workers demanding that the hero be "run out of the country" and reported to the FBI. Even Aunt May turns against Spider-Man and the episode ends with Parker nervously wondering if becoming "a menace" is the "only course left for me."

In the second story, Parker decides that he will show off his powers to the members of the Fantastic Four and that they will invite him to join them. Showing off, he breaks into the Baxter Building. When the super group picks up his arrival by camera, Johnny Storm quips, "Why didn't he phone for an appointment, like anyone else?" Thing answers: "Cause he's a teen-age cornball show-off, just like the Torch."

Later, the group squares off with the teen, trying to contain him. They basically battle to a draw, then Spider-Man announces his plan, exclaiming, "I'm worth your top salary." Sue Storm tells him, "We're a non-profit organization," while Reed Richards explains, "We pay no salaries or bonuses! Any profit we make goes into scientific research!" Johnny, like Parker, a sarcastic teen, says, "You came to the wrong place, pal! This isn't General Motors!" Lee's ear for teen-specific dialogue captures the cadence and sarcasm of the era.

Meanwhile, Spider-Man is about to face his first super villain—the Chameleon—a highly intelligent criminal who can disguise himself as anyone, even the teen hero. Chameleon orchestrates a plan to frame Spider-Man by stealing secret missile defense plans. The real Spidey escapes from the police and slingshots himself across New York to catch the villain's helicopter. He speeds out in a motorboat to a waiting

Soviet submarine, uses his webbing to keep its hatch from opening, and then takes control of the helicopter.

Chameleon then uses a number of tricks to escape momentarily, including impersonating a policeman, forcing the real police to grab Spider-Man. The police realize the ruse, but the hero scampers up a wall, "in a fit of white-hot fury," and vows to let the officers catch the criminal, rather than try to help. As Spider-Man flees the scene, he tears up, thinking, "Nothing turns out right. I wish I had never gotten my super powers!" The Fantastic Four is then shown wondering if Spider-Man will ever turn evil. The ten-page story ends with Lee's narrative: "And the whole world will have to wonder—until our next great issue! Don't miss it!!"

Over the course of the next year, Lee and Ditko introduced almost every one of Spider-Man's most significant super villains, from Vulture and Electro to the Lizard and Doctor Octopus. While battling these criminals provided the comic book with the requisite action of a superhero comic book, it was the large supporting cast around Peter Parker that propelled the stories. Peter's interactions with Aunt May, Jameson, and a series of love interests made the youth seem more convincing as a teen who stumbled into his role as a superhero.

As a comic book author, Lee used Spider-Man to introduce several innovations that separated him from other writers. Besides narratives directed at the audience that transformed the force of the superhero books, Lee also pulled the reader deeper into the story via thought balloons. As Lee explained, they "let our readers know what a character was thinking as often as possible . . . and add a whole additional dimension to the story."[17] These advances in style and voice shouted at readers to pay attention, while simultaneously making them aware that a *person* existed within the pages. Lee's easygoing manner let you know that he was a friend and just as excited about what you were reading.

Another Lee and Ditko novelty centered on using New York City as Spider-Man's stomping grounds, having the youth living in a cramped apartment in Queens with his surrogate parents. Lee and Kirby had done the same with the Fantastic Four, plopping them down in Manhattan, but while they jetted around the globe and universe, Spider-Man stayed central to the city, bringing it alive on the pages. For readers familiar with the city, the stories came to life at the mention of Manhattan or the Brooklyn Bridge, while others could imagine Spidey swinging through the steel and concrete canyons created by the city's massive skyscrapers. "Instead of living in a fictitious Gotham City or Metropolis," Taking a swipe at his DC Comics competitors, Lee explained, "[Spider-Man] has his digs in good ol' New York City and . . . might be found running after a taxi anywhere from Greenwich Village to the Upper East Side."[18]

Placing all his heroes in and around the Big Apple enabled Lee to accurately depict the setting in his native city and gave him another innovation—having superheroes casually (or not so coolly) run into one another. Beginning with *AS* #1, the "guest starring" notion kept comic book audiences thrilled at the idea that Spider-Man could engage with (and potentially battle) the Fantastic Four, the Hulk, or other characters.

The web slinger's growing popularity also enabled Lee to use him as a means of introducing new characters or sprucing up existing ones. Fans could not get enough of the teen hero, so Lee and Marvel pushed the limits. For example, Spider-Man appeared in *Strange Tales Annual* #2 (September 1963), a seventy-two-page crossover between him and the Human Torch. And in *Tales to Astonish*, which had moved from odd, macabre stories to superheroes, Spidey guest-starred in #57 (July 1964), which focused on Giant-Man and Wasp. When *The Amazing Spider-Man Annual* #1 appeared in 1964, with Lee dubbing himself and Ditko "the most talked about team in comics today," it featured appearances by every Marvel hero, including Thor, Dr. Strange, Captain America, and the X-Men.

Spider-Man now stood at the center of a comic book empire. Stan Lee could not have written a better outcome, even if given the chance.

All this from a risky run in a dying comic book!

CHAPTER 8

HORDE OF SUPERHEROES

"**A** monster!" Martin Goodman turned on his heels, shaking his head. Following the success of *The Fantastic Four*, the publisher wanted Stan Lee and Jack Kirby to create another superhero team. When Lee told him that he had a different idea, a solo book centered on what he described as an "offbeat" monster, Goodman audibly sighed and walked away. The notion of not following up on the popularity of the superhero team with another one—derivative or not—seemed ludicrous to Goodman. Lee watched his boss leave the room, dreaming of the powerful behemoth that he and Kirby had been kicking around.

"I had been wracking my brain for days, looking for a different superhero type, something never seen before," Lee said.[1] The new character had to have super strength, but not mirror the Thing or the competitor's venerable Superman.

Mountains of fan mail had poured into Marvel's Madison Avenue office in support of *The Fantastic Four*. But the insatiable fans also pleaded for a new superhero. Although he had created hundreds of comic book characters over the previous two decades, Lee agonized over a follow-up to the hit supergroup. A victim of his own success, Lee felt the pressure to keep up the momentum.

Lee pulled from classic stories and familiar narratives. Like other great artists in that era, whether Bob Dylan reimagining old folk songs into protest anthems or novelist John Updike transforming the Peter Rabbit story into a 1960s existential everyman named Rabbit Angstrom, Lee turned to his deep reading of classics. He would give fans what they wanted: an almost invincible monster as antihero. Lee created the Hulk out of traces of Mary Shelley's *Frankenstein* and Robert Louis Stevenson's

Dr. Jekyll and Mr. Hyde. Then, to add to the dramatic tension, he contextualized the comic with heavy doses of Cold War anxiety. As the world wrung its hands about the potential devastation of atomic technology, Lee made nuclear weapon testing the cataclysmic event that turns a brilliant young scientist into a rampaging behemoth. Introducing the Incredible Hulk, a brooding—somewhat terrifying—monster and convoluted antihero to the Marvel family, Lee and Kirby took another intellectual leap forward, deducing that fans would gravitate to the giant's failures and frailties, just as they had with the Fantastic Four.

The ongoing success of *The Fantastic Four*—measured by mountains of fan mail, critical acclaim, and later, sales data that confirmed the heady circulation numbers—and the quick introduction of Hulk, Thor, and Iron Man, along with other heroes, set off a two-year run that changed the way people looked at comic books and their creators. Lee and Kirby became celebrities. Lee gave them monikers that readers would adopt: Jack "King" Kirby and Stan "the Man" Lee.

As a creative duo, Lee and Kirby caught a star as it shot skyward, able to bring dazzling characters to life and contextualize their stories with content drawn from what was happening in the real world around them. These heroes were different from past ones or those of the competition—they talked differently, inhabited a world that seemed authentic and right outside the window, all the while turning on fantastic plots and strong visuals.

Lee no longer had to simply kowtow to Goodman's request to copy the superhero team concept. But he still had to turn out new concepts to keep Goodman at bay. Under this pressure, but finally being allowed to create the kinds of comic books that he had imagined doing over the years, Lee and his artist cocreators churned out a succession of superheroes that captured the attention of rapt fans and turned others into readers for the first time. Lee now headed the hottest comic book publisher in the business, and he grew into the voice bringing those superheroes to readers around the world.

Lee felt flabbergasted when fans started writing in after *The Fantastic Four* debuted. Subsequently, he read the letters and put admin staff on the task of writing back. Taking the notion of using fans as a kind of focus group, Lee also asked them to write more in the pages of the comics, because he knew that he could use the insight later in developing new characters.

Many of those letters, Lee remembered, screamed "more innovative characters." When he sat down and stared at a blank piece of paper in his typewriter, he considered these missives. He drew on what he considered the craziest idea possible, "Think of the challenge it would be to make a hero out of a monster," he asked himself. "We would have a protagonist with superhuman strength, but he wouldn't

be all-wise, all-noble, all-infallible."[2] That monster would have elements of Frankenstein, but turn the idea on its ear by making the townspeople chasing him the real
monsters, while the monster would turn heroic, though always misunderstood.

Readers picking up *The Incredible Hulk* #1 could get a sense of the character
on the splash page. Kirby drew massive, tree-trunk arms, but also faraway, almost
pleading eyes, capturing the Hulk's pathos and internal strife. A few pages later,
when brilliant but meek scientist Bruce Banner endures gamma bomb rays and
transforms into the Hulk for the first time, the monster bats young Rick Jones
away, demanding, "Get out of my way insect!" Via Kirby's masterful artwork, Hulk
(initially with gray skin) seems to burst from the page, charging at the reader. "Lee
had come up with the perfect vehicle for exploring the notion of what it would be
like to possess super powers in the real world," one comic book historian explained.
"Kirby's chunky, monster style art" gave the hero/monster energy and also added to
the existential angst and inner id that Hulk represented.[3]

This single panel embodies the essence of the character, as well as the achievement of its creators. Readers almost feel like they are inside the art, watching Jones's
feet lift off the ground as the monster shrugs him off. In terms of capturing the
giant's bewilderment, Lee decided to use the word "insect," which provides immediate insight into the Hulk's strength and feelings about "normal" human beings. He
shreds the wall of the military base to escape, then demolishes a jeep that runs into
him in his escape. "Have to go! Have to get away . . . to hide," Hulk murmurs as he
"storms off, into the waiting night."

Just six months after the debut of *The Fantastic Four*, *The Incredible Hulk* shot
out of the gate in May 1962, but struggled in subsequent months. Readers lost interest quickly, perhaps giving credence to Goodman's criticisms. Lee couldn't provide
the comic with room to grow because the egregious distribution contract limited the
number of titles Marvel could ship. When Lee grasped Spider-Man's popularity, he
had to cancel a title to make room. So, the Hulk was cut to make room for the first
issue of *The Amazing Spider-Man* in March 1963, less than a year after the rampaging hero had debuted.

The failure of the Hulk book also highlighted the incredible pressure on Lee.
Goodman reviewed the sales figures and wondered what was going on with the book,
always urging his editor to cancel titles that undersold. In only six issues, Lee had
made wholesale changes to Hulk, so he transforms into the monster at nightfall, then
later when angry; next, he kept modifying the character's intelligence, sometimes
making Hulk imbecilic and other times having him keep Banner's super-genius ca-
pabilities. The strangest Hulk occurred in the final issue when Hulk transformed but
kept Banner's human-sized head. This version had to don a Hulk mask to keep his
identity secret. When he faces off against Metal Master, he exclaims: "Don't look so

surprised, peanut! Everyone on earth isn't a puny weakling!" Clearly, the character had gone off the rails and Lee took the revisions into absurdity.

The distribution restriction forced Lee to come up with creative methods of getting characters space, especially when fans demanded more of them, which was the case with the Hulk. In October 1964, Lee brought the green goliath back in *Tales to Astonish* #60, one book featuring two separate superheroes: a renewed Hulk and Giant-Man. Since early comics were anthologies containing several different stories, like the ones Lee worked on early in his career with Simon and Kirby, he kept that idea going with the team books. From the reader's perspective, it almost seemed as if these comics were delivering more action than a solo title.

Hulk would star in the *Tales to Astonish* series and play a role in other titles, including *Spider-Man* and *The Avengers*. When the draconian distribution deal ended and Marvel's popularity surged to the point that the company could launch books at Lee's whim, he had the new *Incredible Hulk* #102 take over the *Tales* numbering in March 1968. It had taken years, but one of Marvel's premiere superheroes would now carry on the existential mantle and grow more popular as he appeared across varying media, such as animated television, and on lunchboxes, T-shirts, and other licensed materials.

Realistic superheroes were Marvel's strength, but dating back to the late 1930s and Superman's tremendous impact, the industry revolved on near-invincible characters that possessed almost unimaginable powers. Lee understood that he needed a superhero "bigger, better, stronger" than his creations to date. After dozens of failed attempts, from outlandish concepts like "Super-God," to mountains of discarded doodles and sketches in his left-handed scrawl, Lee figured, "since we were the legend makers of today, we'd simply take what had gone before, build on it, embellish it, and come up with our own version." Instead of "God," Lee focused on Norse mythology to create a "god" with a small "g" that would unfold the "continuing saga of good versus evil—god-wise," just the kinds of stories that human beings had been telling for centuries.[4]

The Norse god that Lee and Kirby birthed would be named Thor and powered by the magical Uru hammer. The hero debuted in *Journey into Mystery* #83 (August 1962), which would replace *The Fantastic Four* in its former slot as a bimonthly book when the superhero team moved up to monthly status. The awful distribution deal that Goodman had to sign with his rival years earlier to get books on the newsstands still hampered the company. As a result, Thor and other new creations debuted in existing anthology books, rather than burst onto the scene as solo efforts. The unfavorable distribution system did, however, give Lee the opportunity to bring a new superhero along slowly and gauge fan interest prior to committing full-time resources to it.

Given the publication schedule and somewhat limited title range, Lee had to switch back and forth between the teen and western and superhero titles. In response, he searched for other writers to fill in the gaps. For Thor, he gave the scriptwriting duties to his younger brother Larry Lieber (who kept the family name). "Stan would give me a plot, usually typed," he says. "Then he'd say, 'Now, go home and write me a script.'" Initially, Lieber worried about his ability to write, because he "thought like an artist," yet Stan, he claims, "did teach me" to write, providing him with insight about how to make stories positive and exciting using strong language. "Everything he said was much better than what I wrote," Lieber explains. "I worked and I learned a lot from him."[5]

Teaming his younger brother with Kirby as penciler worked well. Lee created the plots and the artist added and expanded them, because he was particularly proficient in the kind of mythic tales Thor necessitated. Soon, though, Lee took over the writing completely, in part because he liked the character and wanted Lieber to take on more western titles, which remained extremely popular, even in the superhero age.

Writing *Thor* enabled Lee to draw from his study of Shakespeare, which he had read out loud as a kid. Other sources, like Edgar Allan Poe and the swashbuckling works of Alexandre Dumas, allowed him to try different dramatic voices to give the Norse god added depth. From a lifetime of watching and analyzing film, he recognized the significance of rhythm and pacing and applied it to his budding superhero writing style. He also looked to Arthur Conan Doyle's Sherlock Holmes, deciding that he epitomized the ultimate superhero, because "a superhero should be believable. There was never a more believable character than Sherlock."[6] Many of Lee's creations were implausible, but their torment and anxiety appealed to the growing number of high school and college readers.

When Lee told Goodman about his desire to create a superhero who was also a handsome tycoon and weapons manufacturer modeled after Howard Hughes, Goodman said flatly, "You're crazy."[7] Insane or crazy like a fox, Lee figured that Goodman hadn't said "no" and created Tony Stark/Iron Man with artist Don Heck.

With the Cuban Missile Crisis still fresh on people's minds, as well as former president Dwight Eisenhower's harsh words about the growth of the military-industrial complex in his farewell address, Lee thought Stark should be the antithesis of other superheroes: wealthy, suave, and handsome, a weapons dealer seemingly without a care in the world. Lee pulled from real-world topics, which contextualized the stories, especially when creating a new character. As a result, the Hulk embodied the nation's conflicted ideas about science and the potential negative consequences of innovation. For Iron Man, Lee would again draw on technology, but also place the hero's origin story in a little-known nation on the other side of the world called Vietnam, long before anyone really knew anything about the Asian nation. Iron Man, the metallic alter ego of industrial titan Stark, first appeared in *Tales of Suspense* #39 (March 1963).

Iron Man peers out from the cover in gunmetal gray and looks stiff, more robotic than human, with no distinguishable facial features except slits for eyes and a mouth slot. Littered with Lee's typical excitable tone, the reader is asked to speculate about "the newest, most breath-taking, most sensational super hero of all," but also told that the character comes from the same "talented bull-pen" where the other famous Marvel superheroes "were born." In early 1963, trust is already a defining matter for Marvel readers. Lee asks them to have faith in the new hero (and essentially Lee's role as leader of this flock).

Stark, like many Lee characters, is a scientist but also a "glamorous playboy, constantly in the company of beautiful, adoring women." Much of the plot (created by Lee, but written out by Lieber) is told in flashback, tracing Stark's transition from Hughes-like industrial leader to armored superhero. A booby trap in the jungle fells Stark and his military protectors, which allows him to be captured by the enemy. Later, at the "guerrilla chief's headquarters," the reader learns that Stark is alive, but expected to die, because a piece of shrapnel is lodged near his heart. Wong-Chu determines that he will trick the American inventor into creating bombs until the moment he dies from the steel moving closer to his heart.

Realizing that his time is limited, Stark declares: "This I promise you . . . I shall build the most fantastic weapon of all time!" Then he begins crafting a suit designed to keep him alive and defeat Wong-Chu's forces. With the help of Professor Yinsen, a renowned physics professor imprisoned for not helping build weaponry, Stark creates the Iron Man suit using his powerful transistor design. Yinsen fits the suit on the American just in time, and Stark stirs back to life just as the guerrilla's forces kill Yinsen. Iron Man declares that he will avenge the professor and flies into the building's shadows to hide until he can concoct a plan.

Confronting Wong-Chu, the superhero tosses him aside and then uses a transistor to reverse the trajectory of the soldiers' bullets, which causes the soldiers to run. After using his "electrical power" to extricate himself from under a heavy cabinet that Wong Chu has pushed on top of him, Iron Man shoots a stream of oil at an ammo dump that the leader is trying to reach. He then lights the stream with a torch, and Wong Chu is blown up. Iron Man frees the other prisoners and walks away, covering himself in a long brown jacket and fedora. The superhero ponders his new fate as Iron Man, asking, "Who knows what destiny awaits him? Time alone will provide the answer! Time alone . . ."

The partnership between Heck and Lee in bringing *Iron Man* to life centered on Heck learning and adapting to Lee's new storytelling mode, which seemed foreign for many artists who had worked at other publishers. As a matter of fact, when Heck first got a story synopsis from Lee, he balked at the process. Later, though, he grew to enjoy the creative freedom and trust that developed. "Stan would call me up and he'd give me the first couple of pages over the phone, and the last page," Heck remembers. "I'd say, 'What about the stuff in between?' and he'd say, 'Fill it in.'"[8] While some artists found it difficult to adjust, Heck and many others flourished. The Marvel Method is similar to the way many television and Hollywood scriptwriters work: many smart minds tackle a script after the central idea has been established, which adds depth and nuance, even if it is birthed by one person on the team.

When Lee finally had comic books that readers were eager to buy, he created tactics for additional superhero stories to get into their impatient hands. Rather than just load up each issue with filler and old monster tales, he decided to add more superheroes to the mix in the handful of stories necessary to complete the book. For example, the Fantastic Four's Human Torch became the primary star of short pieces that ran in the anthology *Strange Tales*, a leftover title from Marvel's monster era. Lee's intuition paid off and sales shot through the roof.

The character Steve Ditko and Lee created as a companion piece to the Human Torch grew out of Stan's childhood listening to a radio program called *Chandu, the Magician*. Lee's version became *Dr. Strange*, which benefited from Ditko's psychedelic imagery and magical portrayal of the enchanted world. The story centered on Stephen Strange, an arrogant surgeon who suffers a debilitating injury to his hands, rendering him unable to operate. After hitting skid row, he journeys to visit the "Ancient One," a mystical healer and wise man. After studying with the wizard, he becomes a supreme sorcerer and returns to set up shop on Bleecker Street in Greenwich Village. Unknown to the world at large, which sees him as a fraud, Dr. Strange battles the dark arts that people cannot see all around them.

Since Dr. Strange was essentially a magician, Lee had him speak in an elevated tone, rather than in the corny stage magic "hocus pocus" banter of pulling a rabbit from a hat. Lee reveled in the character and the new words Dr. Strange used. "I can lose myself completely while putting them together, trying to string them on a delicate strand of rhythm so they have a melody all their own," he explained. "When it came to Dr. Strange I was in seventh heaven, . . . I had the chance to make up a whole language of incantations."[9] Reading the comic, one could immediately hear Lee's cadence and voice in Strange's interesting speech traits and in catchphrases like his frequent "by the hoary hosts of Hoggoth," always alliterative and beguiling.

It did not take long for older teens and college students to catch on to Lee's words and Ditko's groovy artwork. Many tried to dissect Dr. Strange's odd cadence and assess the literary origins. Lee barely had the heart to tell them that he made most of it up. If it was derived from anything, it was the phrases and symbols that came from Lee's reading science fiction greats when he was growing up. When Ditko abruptly left Marvel, Lee continued writing the series, working with artists Bill Everett and Marie Severin. The mystical sorcerer attained an important place in the Marvel Universe. Dr. Strange took on villains that embodied evil itself, such as the dreaded Dormammu and the Living Tribunal. In occupying this dark realm, a case could be made that Stephen Strange was Marvel's most powerful superhero.

The Fantastic Four surprised everyone when it became a hit, so Goodman never let go of his idea that Lee should come up with another superhero team. If one group of heroes sold well, then the natural inclination would be to add more to the roster. Plus, Goodman had reworked the deal with Marvel's distributor, allowing them to publish more titles per month.

This deal was purely a financial decision on the part of Independent News. Independent wanted to capitalize on Marvel's popularity, even though rival DC owned the distributor. No one thought that Goodman and Lee would actually catch up to the market leader, so the thinking was that merely allowing a few extra titles a month would just make everyone more money. Some of the men who ran Independent probably thought that they were pulling the ultimate irony over on their golf buddy Goodman: the better his comics sold, the more money it made for his bitter rival. DC execs would never have envisioned that they were essentially letting the fox into the henhouse.

Just as the fan letters had given Lee insight into the popularity of the Fantastic Four, he gathered information from mail that poured in asking him to create teams of Marvel's heroes. Again, with DC's *Justice League of America* team in mind, Lee determined that the Marvel group would consist of its most powerful characters. Since Kirby drew so many of the heroes in their other comics, Lee tapped him for *The Avengers*, comprised of Thor, Ant Man, Hulk, Wasp, and Iron Man. Finally, Lee had the roster of superheroes that could form a potent counterpoint to DC's group.

Lee and Kirby combined to give the Avengers an aura of superiority, as if this supergroup were the best-of-the-best in the Marvel Universe, but also added the touches of realism that had pushed sales skyward for the other comics. Similarly to the Fantastic Four, the members of the Avengers wouldn't always get along or agree. They too resided in New York City, in a building donated by Tony Stark. Lee called these points the "fashioning of a world for the characters to live in" and a "mood of realism to be created so that the reader feels he knows the characters, understands their problems, and cares about them."[10]

When *Avengers* #1 (September 1963) appeared on newsstands, the action jumped off the cover—Thor's swinging hammer, Ant-man and Wasp swooping in, and Hulk and Iron Man prepping for a fight. The reader only sees Loki, the "god of evil," in a glimpse from behind, as if a camera has taken a snapshot over his right shoulder. The perspective makes it seem that you are there viewing the confrontation firsthand. Although Kirby's Thor and Hulk, because of the way he drew all faces, look like cousins, the cover's layout provides a brilliant introduction to the new superhero team.

Inside, Loki unleashes a sinister plan to draw out his brother Thor using the Hulk as bait. All the heroes respond to a distress call from Rick Jones's Teen-Brigade after the guest-starring Fantastic Four can't help because they are busy on a different mission. Eventually, the heroes find Hulk, who has disguised himself as Mechano, a super-strong robot performing in a traveling circus (the monster is in an odd brown jumpsuit and orange shoes and has white makeup around his mouth). Thinking that Hulk derailed a passenger train, they try to stop him. Meanwhile, Thor returns to Asgard to confront Loki. After fighting Loki and thwarting a series of traps, Thor returns Loki to Earth, revealing the plot to the other superheroes. When the god of evil turns radioactive, it seems he will fight Thor again, but Ant-Man and Wasp trap him in a lead-lined container designed for trucks to "carry radioactive wastes from atomic tests [and] dump their loads for eventual disposal in the ocean." After stopping Thor's evil brother, the group decides to band together, convincing the Hulk to join. Lee's final panel announces "one of the greatest super-hero teams of all time! Powerful! Unpredictable! . . . a new dimension is added to the Marvel galaxy of stars!"

The second issue of *The Avengers* begins with Thor criticizing the Hulk, who threatens him in return. Here Lee is placing the supergroup directly within the realistic confines of his other characters. Thor and Hulk itch to fight one another, placing Iron Man in the mediator role. Wasp pines for Thor, whom she calls "adorable" and "handsome." Their foe, the Space Phantom, can take the identity of others, so he replaces the Hulk and starts a fight with the others inside Stark's mansion. Hulk gets away and is later confronted by his teen sidekick, Rick Jones, who mistakenly tells him that he can turn back to "Doctor Don Blake when you want to!" (a Lee slip-up that demonstrates the fast pace of comic book production, since Blake is Thor's secret identity). Summoning the Norse god, the Avengers defeat the Space Phantom, but in the melee with Hulk, they reveal their suspicion of the green goliath. As a result, he quits the Avengers and leaps off into the future.

While only the second issue, Lee has already changed the team (also adding Giant-Man) significantly and presented Hulk as a nearly indestructible force. Over the next several issues, the group will battle Hulk when he teams up with Sub-Mariner. Later, the Avengers find Captain America and bring him into the fold. In a call-out box, Lee trumpeted the return of the red, white, and blue super soldier, telling the reader that Kirby had drawn the original and that his first story was a Cap tale: "Thus, the chronicle of comicdom turns full circle, reaching a new pinnacle of greatness!" Lee also urged fans to "save this issue," more or less pushing the notion that comic books could be collector's items, explaining, "We feel you will treasure it in time to come!"

The Lee/Kirby creative team set 1963 ablaze with quirky superheroes who seemed quite a bit like real people who happened to stumble into their tremendous powers and had to deal with the ramifications. Fearing that readers might get tired of these accidental heroes, Lee broke the mold and thought up a team of individuals who were born with "unique abilities." This team, he recalled, would be "mutants . . . an aberration of nature." Together, Lee and Kirby created two groups—one good and one evil—which Lee thought had "an air of freshness and surprise."[11] He stumbled on the word "extra," as in the extra powers the characters possess, after Goodman shot down his original title: "The Mutants" for being above the heads of young readers. The publisher agreed to "X-Men" (as if that made more sense), so Kirby and Lee sat down to brainstorm, plot, and plan.

The world that Lee and Kirby created centered on the idea that human beings continued to evolve and some people were born with special powers that came to light when the person hit puberty. They reasoned that teenagers with amazing powers would delight young fans. Such mutants, like Cyclops, who shot laser beams from his eyes, and Jean Grey, who had telekinetic powers that enabled her to move objects at will, attended Professor Charles Xavier's School for Gifted Youngsters. There they learned to harness their abilities and build on them for the good of humankind.

The *X-Men* series enabled Lee to explore the alienated feelings that many teens experienced, while also providing the group with kinship via their relationship with Professor Xavier, who provided a father figure for them. The school turned into an extended family for the youths, many of whom had faced discrimination for having abilities that "regular" humans did not understand. Their powers were a blessing and a curse. Only the wise counsel of Professor X and their experiences battling evil as a team could provide them with a semblance of normality, which always seemed fleeting.

Running from 1963 to 1970, *X-Men* never really generated strong sales, despite the high hopes Lee had for it. He and Kirby faced tremendous pressure to work on the comics that did sell, so when the artist asked for a replacement, Lee granted his request. Later, the writer moved himself off the book to concentrate on better-selling titles.

Once the superhero business took off, Lee created a system that centralized his control over nearly every aspect of the creative side of the comic books division. Some of these work responsibilities were the continuation of what he had been doing in art, editorial direction, and general management, but other aspects grew out of necessity, since Marvel changed as it became more popular. Lee may not have been trained to be a manager or talent scout, but his years in the business honed these skills.

Lee not only knew when to move an artist onto a different piece of work, like the critical decision to replace Kirby with Ditko on the early *Spider-Man* efforts, but he also respected the freelance artists who served as the backbone of the comic book world. He recognized talent and assembled a crew of artists to infuse Marvel with a new spirit. The superhero comics married the art and writing in a way that the business hadn't seen before. Strong freelance artists served as visual partners for the snappy dialogue and personality traits that he and other writers used to differentiate the company.

Lee's unique ability was to mirror the voice and style of the early 1960s and bring it into comic books. As a result, Marvel readers get the humor and satire that actor Peter Sellers brought to *The Pink Panther* (1963) and *Dr. Strangelove* (1964) while also appreciating the full-throttle heroic characters, like Ian Fleming's James Bond, whose action-packed films like *Goldfinger* (1964) encompassed a mix of sophistication, violence, and superhero-like deeds. Popular culture was changing. Lee found a groove with realistic superheroes who balanced great power with existential angst, an idea surging through mainstream media. He explained:

> We try to write them well, we try to draw them well; we try to make them as sophisticated as a comic book can be. . . . The whole philosophy behind it is to treat them as fairy tales for grown ups and do the kind of stories that we ourselves would want to read.[12]

As editor and art director, Lee guided the voice and style of the company by working with artists and writers he trusted. When he found a person who possessed first-rate abilities, Lee deliberately indoctrinated the artist or writer into the company's distinctive process. For example, Lee quickly realized the beauty in the artwork of George Tuska, a stylist who some insiders felt had the most unique ability in all of comic books. It did not take long for Tuska to become one of Lee's favorites. According to *Daredevil* artist Gene Colan, "Stan always would hold [Tuska's] work up as the criteria of how he wanted the other artists to draw." This kind of management style enabled Marvel to be distinctive, yet also gave his artists a template that emphasized the kind of work he needed done, and completed quickly.[13]

In a business that could often be cold and ruthless, Lee cultivated talent. He had to do so, since Marvel lagged well behind DC Comics, its rival perched at the top. He needed talented freelancers for his vision of producing quality comic books that people would hold to a higher standard to work, so Lee took chances on young artists and writers.

At the start of his career, for example, Colan could not get into DC, which had locked down its talent and locked out others who wanted in. For the venerable industry leader, he simply did not have enough experience. Colan recalls, "Stan could see something in my work that no one else could see. . . . That's what really got me started, Stan's faith in my ability. Although it wasn't completely there at the time, I was too young and had a lot to learn."[14] The other harsh reality staring Lee in the face was the relentless publishing schedule that placed a real premium on not just speed, but efficient speed.

For artists who expected to get committed to a specific script (or were used to that treatment at other comics and magazine firms), Lee's style changed their outlook. Colan remembered Lee giving the artists "such unprecedented freedom," which translated to happier artists. "I'd talk with Stan about a plot over the phone, and I'd tape record his whole idea—it'd just be a few sentences." Lee would tell him: "This is what I want in the beginning, the middle, and what I want in the end . . . the rest is up to you." For Colan and the other trusted freelancers, this set a precedent.

"I had all the characters work for me, what they looked like was up to me—except those that were already established. But whatever I did, I could do."[15]

Despite his growing public persona that turned him into the face of comic books for the general public, the day-to-day Lee understood the volatility of the market and its consequences. As a result, many artists grew into big Lee supporters. The camaraderie that developed had important ramifications: they worked long hours to meet the company's needs, but Lee rewarded them by keeping steady work coming their way. Colan, for example, spoke about the grueling hours necessary to produce two complete pages a day, which then translated to about two full books per month. Maintaining this schedule took much longer than forty hours per week. The artistic freedom represented by the Lee method, then, balanced the physical necessities.

The core group of freelance writers Lee took under his wing received a master class in comic book writing. Dennis O'Neil, a former journalist who started his comic book career as a staff writer at Marvel and later became widely known for his work on *Daredevil*, *Batman*, and *Green Lantern*, explains, "That first year working for Marvel, my job was to, in effect, imitate Stan." For the young writer and his colleagues, the message was clear and direct: "Stan's style really was Marvel."[16]

For O'Neil, Roy Thomas, and the other writers, Lee served as a commanding general, but with a level of benevolence that most driven leaders do not possess. He didn't spend a lot of free time mingling with his staff—primarily based on age difference—but their admiration ran deep because they really were the first of Lee's "true believers." O'Neil says, "I learned the basics. I learned the basics by imitating Stan, and he was, by a huge margin, the best guy to imitate back then." For O'Neil, they did revolutionary work and under the guidance and training of the industry's pioneer: "The best comic book writer in the world."[17]

Lee's eye for talent, though, is clear, seeing what the writers and artists he commissioned would later go on to do in the business. In the years that Marvel began its ascent on the backs of the characters Lee, Kirby, Ditko and others created, the company served as a kind of comic book university, teaching the next generation how to build and expand what would become famous as the "Marvel Method." The new style of creating a comic book actually grew out of Lee's determination to keep freelance artists working. If they had to wait around while he finished writing a script, they were essentially losing money.

Marvel's success with superheroes upped the pressure on everyone in the creative process to perform at a faster rate, even Lee, who neared the limits of how quickly a person could write. He famously hired three secretaries and would dictate stories to them in order, running through one as the other two typed out the notes.

"In the beginning, I was writing almost all of the stories for Marvel. I couldn't keep up," Lee said. Comic book production demanded that all the various creators be kept busy at all times. For the freelance artists the need was much more basic: if you aren't drawing pages, you aren't getting paid. Lee developed a way to keep them active. He remembers that they would pace around after they dropped off their work, always wanting more. Too often Lee simply had no way to keep up with the demand, so he changed the system: "I couldn't stop what I was doing . . . [instead] I would tell him generally what I wanted. He would go home and draw it any way he wanted, bring the illustrations back to me, and then I would put in the dialogue and the captions."[18]

Without really planning a new system for creating comic books, Lee came up with the Marvel Method or, as he explained, it "happened purely through need." The process played on the strengths of Lee's freelance artists. He recalled: "These guys thought like movie directors. They were really visual storytellers." As a result, Lee could give them lots of latitude to interpret what he wanted from a quick story conference or brief phone discussion. "When I would give them a plot, they knew how to break it down—how to begin it, how to end it, where to put the interesting parts." When the artists missed the mark, Lee discovered that he could amplify the artwork with sound effects or extra dialogue. "It started as an emergency measure—it's the only way to keep these guys busy—but I realized that you get better stories that way."[19]

The unimaginable successes Marvel experienced in the early 1960s took place as Lee and Kirby cemented their creative bond. It put Marvel's future directly on their shoulders. The most logical and straightforward aspect of their relationship centered on mutual respect. Later, it grew convoluted. There were inherent difficulties, certainly, even as they worked on the characters that would serve as the foundation of the Marvel cosmos. In the 1960s, Kirby worked for and reported to Lee, even though he had been Lee's boss when the writer/editor started as a teenage office boy. Though their roles were reversed, the truth was they were dependent on one another.

Perhaps even more pointedly, neither realized the immense frustration each secretly held. They both detested many facets of the comic book industry and its seemingly continuous boom-and-bust financial cycles. Lee and Kirby were friends and had a long professional history, but their friendship did not carry over to the point where they would share intimate details about their hopes and dreams. If either had actually opened up to the other in this fashion, it might not have changed the way their relationship unfolded, but it might have enabled them to see that they had more in common than they ever believed.

Clearly they needed each other as professionals. After decades of keeping the comic book division of Goodman's empire alive, Lee recognized talent and knew Kirby was one of the best pencilers in comics. As editorial and art director, he decided that Kirby's style would serve as the company's signature style, just as his own writing became the de facto voice. Artist Gil Kane, who worked for Marvel on and off for decades, most memorably drawing many of their covers in the 1970s, recalled:

> Jack's point of view and philosophy of drawing became the governing philosophy of the entire publishing company and, beyond the publishing company, of the entire field. . . . They would get artists, regardless of whether they had done romance or anything else and they taught them the ABCs, which amounted to learning Jack Kirby. . . . Jack was like Holy Scripture and they simply had to follow him without deviation. That's what was told to me, that's what I had to do. It was how they taught everyone to reconcile all those opposing attitudes to one single master point of view.[20]

The entire Marvel line revolved around the Kirby style. For example, Jim Steranko passed the Marvel employment test by inking two of Kirby's penciled pages for S.H.I.E.L.D. He then worked with Kirby on three Nick Fury issues as a kind of apprenticeship. According to writer Chris Gavaler, "Becoming the Marvel house style seems to have required Kirby to regularize his layouts, presumably so they could be more easily imitated. Variation and innovation are not qualities easily taught, and they do not produce a unified style across titles."[21] Yet, Steranko built his later reputation on irregular page layouts, which introduced art deco, postmodernism, and new-wave impulses into Marvel's pages.

All DC could do, despite its own iconic superheroes, was try to keep pace with Marvel. By the time DC recovered—sort of—by producing its own colorful, exciting covers, the leap Marvel had taken created the foundation for Goodman's firm to eventually take over the top spot in the comic book business. In the battle between Marvel and DC, fans were voting with their nickels, dimes, and quarters.

As a result, an innovative, colorful, and exciting character like Metamorpho, created by DC mainstays George Kashdan and Bob Haney in late 1964, seemed like a Marvel clone rather than a new superhero. But there was reason to think that DC simply attempted to mimic Marvel. The Metamorpho cover (*The Brave and the Bold* #57) mirrored the kind of language that Lee popularized, exclaiming: "See the amazing powers of the world's most fantastic new hero." The book also used dynamic imagery and colors, yet Marvel had already created a beachhead in the war over the comics fans would determine to be "hot." It took some time for the upstart to displace the market leader, but few doubted the excitement that Lee and Kirby created down on Madison Avenue. Once Marvel had a couple hit titles on the books, Lee wanted to add to its roster to keep the forward progress. "I was like a crapshooter rolling one great pass after another," Lee said. "You just don't stop when you're on a winning streak."[22]

In the back of his mind, Lee believed that the superhero boom would eventually crash, just like all the other cycles he had experienced. As a result, he moved fast to generate new titles and new characters to capitalize on the trend. He kept his freelancers hopping, driven by his own seemingly endless supply of optimism and energy. Under relentless publishing deadlines, Lee had to live and breathe the constant balance of creativity and commerce, artwork versus commodity. Under his leadership, Marvel would spend the rest of the decade solidifying its universe.

Marvel Comics publisher Martin Goodman (1941) holding *Captain America Comics* #11, the first Lee wrote as editor after Goodman fired Joe Simon and Jack Kirby. *Photofest*

Lee during World War II, a copy of *Terry-Toons Comics* #25 (Oct. 1944) is on his desk; a sketch of his famous "VD? Not me!" poster is over his left shoulder at the top of the photo. *Stan Lee Papers, Box 138, American Heritage Center, University of Wyoming*

Lee's Army portrait, a "playwright" in the Signal Corps' Training Film Division, 1943. *Stan Lee Papers, American Heritage Center, University of Wyoming*

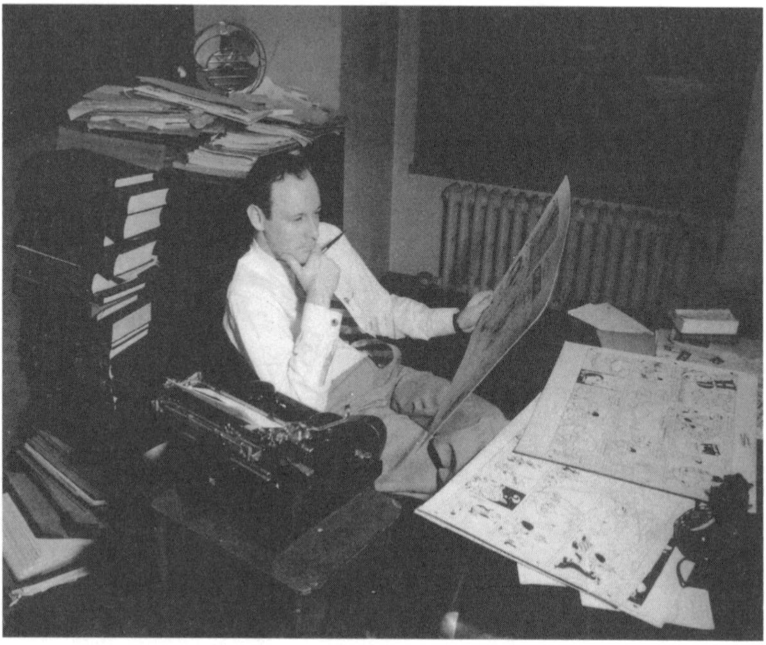

Lee at his editor desk, reviewing comic book copy. *Stan Lee Papers, American Heritage Center, University of Wyoming*

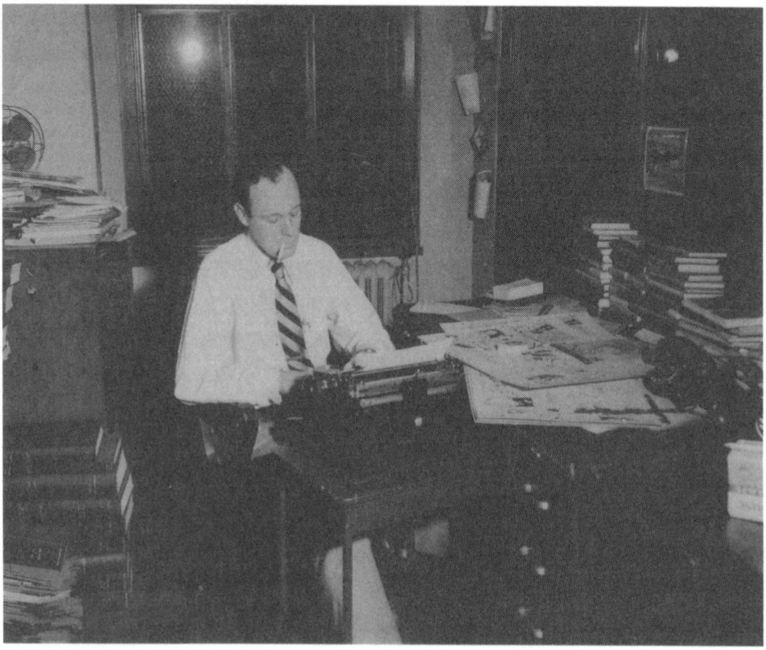

Lee at his desk typing, circa 1950. *Stan Lee Papers, Box 145, American Heritage Center, University of Wyoming*

Lee with wife Joan Boocock Lee, circa late 1940s. *Stan Lee Papers, American Heritage Center, University of Wyoming*

Lee posing with his book *The Origins of Marvel Comics*, 1974. *Stan Lee Papers, Box 133, American Heritage Center, University of Wyoming*

PERSONNA DOUBLE II

30 Second TV Commercial

"Stan Lee"

LEE: You know, here at Marvel I've got Spider-man and all these characters and super villians like Dr. Doom to worry about.

I can't waste time worrying about things like shaving.

This guy calls me and he says

"try a Personna Double II." And I said "OK, I'll try it."

This Personna is beautifully designed.

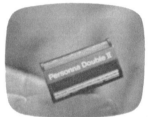

Twin blades on each side. It's clean, it's got quality.

Like they told me,

"There's no finer shaving system made." I may create a whole new character . . .

Personna Man!

Lee starring in Personna Double II razor commercial, 1976–1977. *Stan Lee Papers, Box 7, American Heritage Center, University of Wyoming*

Lee standing in front of a bookcase displaying *The Incredible Hulk* (1978) and *Marvel's Greatest Superhero Battles* (1978). *Stan Lee Papers, Box 6, American Heritage Center, University of Wyoming*

Lee with filmmaker and comic book store owner Kevin Smith, circa 1990s. In the background are some of the most iconic Marvel comics, including the first issues of *The Fantastic Four*, *The Amazing Spider-Man*, and Captain America's modern debut in *The Avengers*. *Photofest*

Lee with Spider-Man, 1994. *Stan Lee Papers, Box 138, American Heritage Center, University of Wyoming*

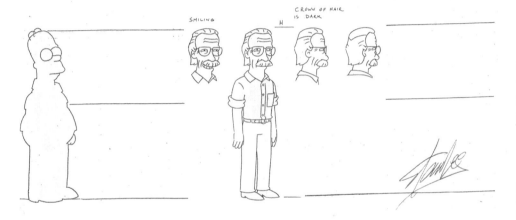

SMILING   CROWN OF HAIR
           IS DARK
           H

Artist sketch of Lee as a character on *The Simpsons* episode "I Am Furious Yellow" (2002). *Stan Lee Papers, Box 125, American Heritage Center, University of Wyoming*

Cameo as mailman Willie Lumpkin in *Fantastic Four* (2005). *20th Century Fox/Photofest*

Lee with contestants on reality show *Who Wants to Be a Superhero?* (Syfy) Season 2, 2007. *Syfy/Photofest*

Cameo as himself on hit TV show *The Big Bang Theory* (CBS), Season 3, 2009–2010. From left: Lee, Kaley Cuoco, Jim Parsons. *CBS/Photofest*

Cameo on *The Simpsons*, Season 25, 2013–2014, in the episode "Married to the Blob." From left: Comic Book Guy (voice: Hank Azaria), Lee (as himself). *Fox Network/Photofest*

Cameo in *The Amazing Spider-Man 2* (2014). *Columbia Pictures/Photofest*

Lee at the Cincinnati Comic Expo, September 24, 2016. *Courtesy of Suzette Percival*

CHAPTER 9

MARKETING THE MARVEL UNIVERSE

"**F**ACE FRONT!"

Not subtle or paternal, Stan Lee's demand that readers snap to attention kicked off the "Marvel Bullpen Bulletins" a feature page that ran in the back of all the December 1965 issues. It replaced the "Merry Marvel Bullpen Page," which had debuted earlier in August. Filled with "news" and "gossip," along with a checklist of current issues for sale with synopses, the yellow shadowboxes quickly became a familiar mainstay for Marvel readers.

No matter where comic book readers lived or whether they could even envision what the Marvel headquarters might look like, the bulletins made them feel like a part of the family. Some readers might gravitate to the insider perspective to see who inked a particular magazine or to find out the latest scoop on an artist's personal life. Others yearned for the merchandise offers, like the Spider-Man or Dr. Strange T-shirt that a kid could get by mail for just $1.50. Certainly more than a few young readers viewed the missives as personal letters from Lee, the coolest guy in the country.

Regardless of why comic book buyers loved the Bullpen Bulletins, the page showed off Lee in all his glory. On one hand, the notes gave him a place to really craft his voice as the main Marvelite. At the same time, the columns demonstrated his savvy strategic sense—Lee knew that deepening audience engagement would result in greater dedication to Marvel's books. From reading thousands of letters, the editor knew that his interaction, which seemed personal, increased sales.

The voice that emerged became a hallmark of Marvel Comics in the 1960s. "It was a little thing," Lee said, "but it was trying to give a feeling of warmth, a feeling of friendliness. . . . It seemed to work."[1] For teens and college-aged fans, the wink-wink, tongue-in-cheek tone spoke to their antiestablishment notions and seemed discernibly different from the voice they were used to hearing from adults. "It was all spontaneous," Lee remembered. "When I was writing a story, I'd think of something. So I'd throw it in."[2] His success with superheroes and their angst-ridden personas proved that if he trusted his instincts, good things would happen.

The chance to buy Marvel merchandise drew other readers to the Soapbox page. The cost was pretty meager at a buck or so, which seemed just within (or maybe outside) their reach. Just how many days of lunch money did a kid need to secret away in order to afford that Dr. Strange shirt? Others gravitated to the list of new members of the Merry Marvel Marching Society fan club to see kids from all over the country who shared their same interest.

Most important, Lee's Bullpen Bulletin gave him a forum to speak directly to all Marvel readers. The insider perspective turned Lee into the comic book nation's favorite uncle. He described the thriving relationship with Marvel readers as "part of an 'in' thing" or that they were "sharing a big joke together and having a lot of fun with this crazy Marvel Universe."[3]

With this singsong, chatty style, Lee turned up the wattage on his own celebrity status. The "Stan the Man" voice and personality came through in the dialogue of the comics and in the editorial content: "If I got a kick out of it, maybe a reader would, too," he reasoned. "Even in writing the credits, I'd try to make them humorous, because I enjoyed doing that."[4] Lee also awarded select fans who wrote intriguing letters or otherwise caught his fancy a "Marvel No-Prize," literally no prize for their effort. He sent them an empty envelope, even mockingly stamping "Handle with Care" on the outside. The sillier he acted, the more fans gobbled up the shtick. More importantly, sales continued to climb.

Over time, however, Lee also introduced the bullpen members on a first-name basis and gave them personalities, which translated into a familial feeling for fans. Lee is always "Smilin' Stan Lee" in the updates, a slightly whacky, permanently over-worked editor, who is keeping the whole place running by the seat of his pants. He explained the goal:

> Give our fans personal stuff, make them feel they were part of Marvel, make them feel as though they were on a first-name basis with the whole screwy staff. In a way, I wanted it to be as though they were getting a personal letter from a friend who was away at camp.[5]

More importantly, the page provided readers with a mental image of themselves sitting down next to the famed comic book chief as he regaled them with stories of Jack (King) Kirby or (Jolly) Joe Sinnott. Marvel filled readers' dreams with visions of the Hulk and Iron Man, and the news from the bullpen made readers and creative staff seem like long-lost friends. That tone gave kids in small towns across the nation the feeling that Lee was their comrade and that Marvel's superheroes—despite a reader's better judgment—might just be real.

Lee's mad dash over the previous four years resulted in a superhero frenzy and total repositioning of Marvel in the comic book industry. The company—as well as its editor—stood at the epicenter of cool. Superheroes were the hottest thing in American popular culture and increasingly for audiences around the globe. Other publishers jumped onboard the superhero wave, from Charlton Comics (who hired Steve Ditko after he left Marvel and granted him almost complete editorial control over his conservative Ayn Randian creations) and Tower Comics (which doled out work to high-profile artists, such as Wally Wood and Gil Kane) to the venerable Archie Comics (which launched its own group, called the *Mighty Crusaders*). The new entries into the marketplace attempted to capitalize on Marvel's popularity, often producing derivative content and cover art. They might try to emulate Lee and Kirby, but without the real thing, many of the publishers seemed simply eager to make a fast buck.

In 1965, Lee and his creative gang began a series of changes and slight modifications to the hero genre, which enabled them to build a more cohesive, unified cosmos, while simultaneously solidifying their growing fan base. For the next several years, the goal would not be to expand the universe by leaps and bounds, but to increase depth, nuance, and context. Lee believed that intensifying the relationships between characters and intertwining the superhero worlds would enable future growth, and, more importantly, create stronger bonds between the characters and readers.

Marvel's existential heart continued to center on the authentic, daily challenges presented as ordinary people gained larger-than-life powers. It did not take Lee long to utilize the most human of human problems—the trials and tribulations of romantic relationships—and such an approach was relatively organic to the creative staff, at least at the upper level. Both Lee and Kirby had long histories in teen romance comics. Kirby and partner Joe Simon basically invented the genre in 1947, creating *Young Romance*, a title DC was still publishing in the 1960s. Lee also had deep experience, serving as the primary writer for *Millie the Model*, as well as its many offshoots that were aimed to attract female readers. Indeed, *Millie* quite possibly stood as the most successful nonsuperhero title Marvel ever produced.

The romantic interlude that drew the most interest was the marriage of Reed Richards and Susan Storm in *Fantastic Four Annual #3*. Kirby dazzled readers with the oversized issue, which also contained reprints of two popular past issues. The cover featured a free-for-all: Almost every hero from the Marvel cosmos attended the star-studded event, which also drew countless villains who hoped to crash the festivities. While the two sides battled, a glum Sub-Mariner watches over the proceedings, his heart clearly broken. Inside, Lee called the issue: "The most sensational super-spectacle ever witnessed by human eyes!!"

The Baxter Building is surrounded by adoring fans (including teen beauty Patsy Walker, another longtime Marvel character), but also under constant attack. The Thing tries to ward off the bad guys, but needs the help of Nick Fury, the X-Men, Dr. Strange, and a host of others. After Richards saves the day, the episode ends with the wedding kiss. ("No mere words of ours can truly describe the tenderness of this moment . . . so we won't even try," Lee wrote.) Then, two interlopers in top hats and stylish overcoats attempt to crash the reception, but are stopped by Fury and his men. The trespassers are Lee and Kirby, only seen from the back. Not even the Fantastic Four creators could get into such a lavish celebration.

Also that year, Mary Jane Watson first appeared in *The Amazing Spider-Man #25*, but Ditko strategically hid her face, only allowing other characters to exclaim: "She's a friend of Peter's? She looks like a screen star!" Readers wouldn't actually see her for years. At the end of 1965, blonde beauty Gwen Stacy debuted. As with M.J., it would take the hapless Peter Parker years to begin dating her. When they initially met, Parker was so wrapped up with Aunt May and keeping his Spider-Man persona secret that he basically ignored Gwen.

The Marvel team used tactics that resembled the ones used by soap operas and other storytelling methods to create stronger ties between the characters and fans. Since Lee's superheroes were purposely more realistic and like regular people, the notion that they were entangled in difficult relationships and other real-world challenges deepened the connection.

In addition to guiding Marvel's art, writing, and production with a small team of full-time staffers and a growing cadre of freelancers, Lee also had to spend more time working to expand the company's brand. There were simply too many competing things to grab people's attention, ranging from the overtly commercial, like the national sensation caused by the arrival of the Beatles, to the wholly political, like Market Luther King's 1965 civil rights march in Alabama and the growing presence of American troops in Vietnam. Comic books might have a difficult time competing with these enormous issues, but the flipside was that they could be marketed as a pleasant diversion from the real-life hardships.

Given the growing sophistication of marketing, advertising, and public relations in the mid-1960s, Marvel pushed to increase profitability. A 1965 flyer aimed at comic book distributors used Lee's amped-up patter in a direct appeal to prospective dealers, exclaiming: "When fans EYE them, they BUY them!" While probably few newsstand owners bought the exaggerated language, none of them could have missed the dramatic sales growth. In 1960, Marvel sold about 16.1 million copies, but that number grew to 27.7 million in 1964, and the company expected to top 35 million the next year.[6]

The marketing brochure underscored pretty much what company insiders knew about Marvel's successes: the superhero "secret formula" that Lee and his team created vastly expanded the Marvel audience, thus reaching a greater number of older readers, including college students and adults. One of the critical aspects of Marvel's reach, according to the flyer, centered on superheroes "bringing in a brand new breed of reader. . . . Marvel Fan Clubs are springing up at every COLLEGE and UNIVERSITY from coast-to-coast." Although Marvel's marketers assumed that newsstand operators would be duly impressed with that information, the company boasted of already having 50,000 members within the handful of months since its launch.[7]

With sales booming and the end of restrictions on how many titles Marvel could publish each month, Lee sat atop a company with dozens of titles coming out on a monthly or bimonthly schedule. When the lineup expanded, editorial director Lee had to commit to writing a new series or find someone to take it over when there really wasn't a university pipeline of young talent. Consequently, Lee tapped into alternative sources—writers from fan magazines, talented journalists, and some people who were Marvel readers and just persisted in pushing until they got the editor's attention.

All along, however, Lee continued to refine and hone the unique scripting style that had become a Marvel trademark, because he had so much to write himself and he was responsible for controlling the editorial and artistic direction from his editor's perch. The relentless pace and increased number of titles forced the development of new processes to cope with the pressure.

Writer Denny O'Neil discussed how the combination of the company style and tight deadlines came together in July 1966, when Marvel upped production to take advantage of the surge in superhero popularity based on the *Batman* television series. He explained: "I did *Daredevil* #18 because Stan got into a deadline bind. Romita had done the art and put notes in the margins, but Stan didn't have time to do the script."[8] According to O'Neil, Lee worked harder than the writers he hired, putting in countless hours writing to bring the Marvel universe to its eager fans.

Lee's work effort and persistence became company lore and inspired the writers he hired to put in similar grueling hours. For example, even a citywide blackout could not stop Lee from completing his allotted pages. During the first significant power outage in New York City in 1965, O'Neil and assistant editor Roy Thomas gave themselves the night off, but Lee was at home writing by candlelight. "The pages had candle wax dripped on them," O'Neil says, though it's difficult to know whether we should take him at his word or if this is yet another Stan legend.[9]

For Lee, plotting took little time. He charted the different magazines out—perhaps ten to twelve a month—then gave them to the artists to draw. When the artist delivered the work, Lee sat down and put the words down. However, Lee's various roles necessitated that he also keep an eye on the art and covers. "While I was putting the copy in," he explained, "I'd be making notes on changes that the artist should make in the artwork." Sometimes, Lee said, he had to deviate from the original plot, because the artist took the story in a different direction. Kirby, for example, would change the plot to suit his needs and Lee would piece together the dialogue, which he likened to completing a "crossword puzzle."[10]

The popularity of Marvel's offbeat superheroes turned it into the hip 1960s comic book house, but DC still controlled the industry if sales figures were the principal measure. The ongoing competition between the publishers loomed large and focused each on outdoing the other. DC counted on the long-standing heroes in its stable—Batman, Superman, and Wonder Woman, while Lee and Marvel countered with the hip Spider-Man, Thor, and the Fantastic Four. The popular current seemed to tip toward Marvel, but then the ABC television series *Batman* debuted in January 1966. In a unique programming move, the show aired two nights a week—Wednesday and Thursday—in half-hour segments.

The instant success of the series made an immediate impact on the comic book industry and enabled DC to regain some of its swagger. With actor Adam West as the Caped Crusader and Burt Ward as the youthful sidekick, Robin, the series perfectly mixed camp and action in a way that appealed to contemporary audiences. It served up a steady stream of one-liners and plenty of "POW," "BAM," and "ZONK" to delight audiences across age groups. The music alone propelled the show, a mix of 1960s pop-infused soundtrack mixed with Batman-specific tunes that were catchy and stuck in listeners' heads like an earworm. *Batman* also took advantage of the color television craze, using bright color schemes to bring the comic book characters to life.

After half a decade of searching for the magic decoder ring that would open an inroad to Marvel readers, DC seemed to finally capture the voice that Lee brought to comics. *Batman* captured the nation's growing fascination with superheroes, especially in its satirical tone, which Lee had brought to the medium. In many respects, the snarky banter of the two heroes seemed closer in alignment to Spider-Man or the Fantastic Four than anything DC had recently produced.

Television grew so pervasive during the mid-1960s that DC benefited, but its popularity really raised sales across the board. All the major publishers saw sales increase, with Harvey Comics introducing superheroes *Spyman* and *Jigsaw*, while Tower Comics brought out *Dynamo* and *Noman*. Marvel attempted to counter *Batman* to some degree by beginning Thor's solo run in March 1966 and then debuting the Black Panther, the first African American superhero, in *Fantastic Four* #52 (July 1966).

Lee and Kirby did not let the Batmania thwart their efforts to further round out the Marvel Universe. As a kind of counterbalance, they introduced a three-part trilogy in *Fantastic Four* #48–50 (March–May 1966) that had the original supergroup battling Galactus, an omnipotent superbeing who sustained life by devouring the energy from entire planets. The epic trilogy pitted Marvel's most powerful villain against Earth's powerful superhero team. A comic book arc would have trouble competing head-to-head against a popular television series, but Marvel hoped to at least increase sales and entice more readers to pick up the comic.

Lee's aggressive antics to expand the comic book marketplace started to draw in a broader range of readers, but the change took place gradually. As late as July 1967, almost six years after *The Fantastic Four* debuted, *New York Times* reporter Leonard Sloane, who covered the advertising industry, correctly deduced that millions of people read comic books, but still most did not respect the medium. Sloane referenced the way advertisers thought of the average comic book reader, comprised mainly of "special audiences . . . children, servicemen and semi-adults (. . . those over 18 who may not always think at the same level as their chronological age)."[11] Yet, Marvel letter pages and the mail stacks were filled with articulate, passionate messages from educated readers from across the nation.

The mainstream media seemed a little slow to catch on to the comic book craze, as did advertisers, which created the strange mix of products for offer in the back pages, as well as Marvel's desire to sell its own licensed goods. In the mid- to late 1960s, comics, unlike other consumer-focused magazines, still generated most of their revenue from circulation, rather than advertising, but the latter was still significant. Sloane cited the still-number-one-ranked National Periodical, which published forty-eight titles a month that led to about seven million in monthly circulation. Advertising income, however, remained relatively small, only growing from $250,000 to $500,000 between 1962 and 1966. Comic book executives usually claimed that their selectivity kept the ad revenue down. Many companies, however, including Marvel, decided to run small-print ads for a variety of products, from novelty toys and mail-order gimmicks to hobby kits.[12] Many large corporations would not run ads in comic books, so publishers attempted to make up for the lack of direct advertising revenues by licensing the characters to other companies.

In contrast to DC, Marvel's monthly circulation hit about six million, according to Sloane, but the company initiated a campaign to run ads for products targeted at older audiences, like shaving cream. Lee equated the quality of the stories and the artwork with the class its audiences expected, explaining, "We editorialize. We try to back the soldiers and try to tell the kids not to drop out of school. We stand for the good virtues."[13] The decision to intentionally target older readers had been Lee's primary concern for years. A little more than midway through the decade, his determination started to pay dividends.

Lee also considered merchandising opportunities for Marvel. The latter grew in importance after *Batman* debuted on television. Reportedly, DC licensed the character to ninety companies, which would pull in about $75 million in sales; some tagged it as high as $150 million.[14] As the popularity of the books grew, Lee's tasks multiplied, but Goodman was determined to keep a relatively small staff around his star chief editor/art director.

Although he grew up in the film and radio era, Lee clearly understood the growing significance of television and believed that superhero sagas would be a perfect fit with that medium. Martin Goodman had stumbled and bumbled with Marvel licensing in the past, so it did not really surprise anyone when he basically gave away the company's animation rights. Figuring that the production part of the company should be run by someone young, the publisher turned over that aspect to his son Charles (Chip) Goodman to use as a proving ground for the heir's eventual taking over of the family business.

Audited circulation figures revealed that Marvel comic books jumped from eighteen million in 1961 to about thirty-two million in 1965. The surge in popularity attracted television executives, who attempted to figure out the company's secret appeal to young audiences. No one could put their finger on it exactly, usually pointing to the combination of the antihero themes and Lee's ability to correctly gauge the pulse of the youth market.

In September 1966, *Marvel Super Heroes* debuted, featuring a rotating set of stories based on the heroics of Captain America, Thor, Iron Man, Sub-Mariner, and the Hulk. Ads for the show ran in all the company's comic book titles the next month, listing the twenty stations carrying the cartoon, including stations in New York City, Chicago, and Los Angeles. In total, close to fifty stations carried the show, including overseas channels in Brazil, Puerto Rico, and Venezuela.

Produced by Grantray-Lawrence Animation, the cartoon version used color photostat reproductions of the actual comic books—rather than original animation—which created a seven-minute chapter that could then be played back-to-back or chopped up and fitted into other children's television programming. In total, the company generated 195 segments for the initial syndication effort stretching from September to December 1966.

The crude method of using the comic book panels reduced the animation aspect of *Marvel Super Heroes*, but did showcase the exquisite artwork of Kirby, Ditko, and the rest of Lee's talented team. In each shot, there is usually only one object animated. Sometimes it is Captain America's shield looping through the air, while other times it is the character's eyes blinking or lips moving as they speak. The *Marvel Super Heroes* theme song provided a brief overview of each character and then led into the next segment, with voices merrily singing, "the Marvel superheroes have arrived."

Hanna-Barbera Productions launched a second animated television series—*The Fantastic Four*—which first aired on ABC in the fall of 1967. The show began with a bang: a signal arcing into the nighttime sky and then bursting into a vibrant "4" that called the superheroes to their New York City headquarters. The minute-long introduction took the viewer through a condensed version of the group's origin story and then showed them battling a variety of bad guys. Aimed at an audience of young viewers, the series emphasized the super strength of the heroes and turned the villains into dangerous, but somewhat campy, versions of how they appeared in comic books. The writers aped some of Lee's style, showing its early infiltration into mainstream popular culture, as well as the sustained influence of Adam West's gonzo Batman.

The inevitable boom-and-bust mentality that seemed to plague comic books continued, however. Although the Marvel cartoons were popular, sales nosedived in 1967 when the televised *Batman* show sputtered and limped through a final year, more or less pulling all comic books sales down in its wake. DC remained on top, but total circulation across the industry decreased. *Spider-Man* was Marvel's highest-selling comic, but only placed fourteenth on the year-end list of top sellers.[15] Overall, Marvel did better than most of its competitors. Its books basically stayed even with the previous year's sales or showed slim increases. Surprisingly, in a down year for the industry, the fact that Marvel circulation remained consistent revealed how hipness and good marketing could overcome market forces.

The late 1960s were full of changes for Lee. After he rented his teenage daughter a place in the city so that she could study acting, Lee realized that perhaps he and Joanie should move back. The house in Hewlett Harbor seemed too big for just two people. Lee convinced the production company that bought the Spider-Man animation rights to rent him an apartment in the city so that he could serve as a consultant on the series. The year-long tryout convinced the couple that they would enjoy city life. They got an apartment at Sixtieth Street, where they stayed during the week. Then, shortly thereafter, they sold the house and bought an apartment on Sixty-Third with a large terrace, which had been Joanie's condition. After about two decades of suburban life, Lee and Joanie found their new home in the heart of the Big Apple.[16]

Lee's popularity continued to grow among college students, both as a speaker and de facto leader of the one hundred or so campus chapters of the Merry Marvel Marching Society fan club. The spotlight, however, caused tension with Goodman. "I began to think he almost resented the success of our comics line," Lee remembered. "I felt it wouldn't displease him to see sales slip and have my confidence taken down a peg." For Lee, it seemed that Goodman viewed him as a competitor, just as much as the fledgling publishers and DC, which still dominated the field.[17] The situation turned into a double-edged sword: Lee was too valuable and popular to fire, but his fame caused resentments. It didn't really matter if Lee was toned down or thoughtful in the many newspaper and magazine articles or interviews on the radio, his sound bites fueled the public's fascination. At the same time, Marvel benefited from Lee's willingness to be the face of the superhero genre.

One of Lee's highest-profile appearances took place on the popular *Dick Cavett Show*. Realizing that many nonreaders were tuned in—and facing a doubting Cavett, who seemed less than enthusiastic about the idea that comic books were important—the Marvel writer contextualized comics as a significant part of "the age of the offbeat." In this era, Marvel superheroes specifically represented the decade (perhaps despite their powers and seeming invincibility), because they had human feelings and problems even as they were saving the world from all-powerful aliens, supervillains, and other crises. Lee explained to Cavett—at the time one of the nation's great promoters of both high- and lowbrow culture—that in Marvel fandom, "our most popular heroes are the most wackiest." He singled out Hulk ("a green-skinned monster") and Spider-Man as representative of the quirky era.[18]

While Cavett and Pat McCormick, his erstwhile comedian sidekick poked fun at Lee and comics in general, the Marvel chief kept his cool, explaining that Spider-Man's popularity rested on his status as an "anti-hero hero" who "gets sinus attacks, he gets acne, and allergy attacks while he's fighting." Prior to a commercial break, McCormick fired the kind of zinger that Lee had been fighting against his entire career. The jokester snickered, "One thing I like about those comic books is that they're easy to turn while you're sucking your thumb with the other hand."[19]

A comedian like McCormick might have been able to play the dumbed-down nature of comic books for gags on television, but Lee stood at the center of a new comic book universe—one that he mainly created. When Jenette Kahn, later the head of rival DC, was asked what she considered the "most significant event" in the post-1950 comic book world, she pointed to Lee, explaining:

> Comic book characters pick up the unconscious trends of the time and become the spokesmen for those trends. That's why people can identify so fully that the characters can become part of the mythology. Stan Lee's characters did that in the sixties. He picked up on anti-Establishment feelings, on alienation and self-deprecation. . . . Stan came in with characters with bad breath and acne, punkier, younger, when young people needed symbols to replace many of the things they were rejecting.[20]

Not a bad tribute from Marvel's primary competitor and rival or considering the lowbrow roots the industry fought to overcome. In a flurry of creativity over a few short years, Lee upended American popular culture and forever changed the way people looked at heroes.

While Lee fixated on art, word balloons, continuing storylines, and the countless other responsibilities he faced, Goodman searched for an exit strategy. By the late 1960s large corporations started to gobble each other up in a series of mergers and acquisitions. And for Goodman, who had built Marvel from scratch, the wholesale corporate merger-mania provided a long-awaited opportunity to cash out. Martin could finally turn over the business to his son Chip, who had been apprenticing under his father's tutelage, which would allow the elder Goodman to walk away from the constant upheaval in magazine and comic book publishing,

At the midpoint of 1968, a budding corporate mogul and lawyer named Martin Ackerman approached Goodman about selling his whole company—both the men's magazines and the comic book division. Ackerman ran a handful of photo stores, pharmacies, and other concerns under the banner Perfect Film & Chemical Corporation. He fancied himself a major business figure, chomping away on cigars and pushing around staff and underlings, despite his diminutive stature. In a recent deal, Ackerman had extended a $5 million loan to Curtis Publishing, under the stipulation that he serve as president. What Ackerman really wanted out of the transaction was to control the distribution firm Curtis Circulation. Buying Goodman's Magazine Management collection of periodicals and comic books ensured Ackerman that he would have the content necessary to distribute, a kind of double-dipping that gave him more revenue and control within the publishing industry.

Goodman, though wracked with internal strife over the thought of selling, ultimately demanded a cash deal and sold the entire business to Ackerman for about $15 million. When Goodman made the sale, however, he pulled Lee aside and promised his longtime writer/editor "warrants," which he said were like stock options. Not only would Goodman get rich, but he explained that Lee would, too. "My pot of gold had arrived," Lee thought, "and I didn't even have to ask!"[21] As the deal got closer to fruition, however, Goodman not only didn't give Lee options, but never mentioned them again. Goodman signed a deal to remain publisher of Magazine Management, while Chip became editorial director, with the assumption he would eventually replace his father.

Ackerman and his underlings, according to Lee, "told Martin they wouldn't buy the company unless I signed a contract to stay on."[22] Ackerman saw Lee as the essential element in the purchase, but Stan didn't press Goodman for a big raise or other long-term financial gains, because he trusted his boss to take care of him. The three-year deal he eventually inked bumped Lee's salary up, but he started having lingering doubts about Goodman's backslapping and assurances.

Lee joined the many Marvel employees who believed that they should also have profited in the sale. "I'll see to it that you and Joanie will never have to want for anything as long as you live," Goodman told Lee over at the publisher's house for dinner the night after the sale.[23] Joanie Lee and Stan's cousin Jean were close friends. The sale called for a party. Ackerman celebrated too—he bought a $1.5 million private jet and a snazzy Park Avenue apartment to conduct business. Lee continued to worry about what might have been if Goodman had fulfilled his promises. Yet, he didn't press or threaten to leave Marvel, potentially at a time when he could have demanded a hefty fortune to not go running to DC.

Although Ackerman's Curtis Circulation took over Marvel's distribution, erasing the disastrous deal Goodman had been forced to sign ten years earlier, the entire industry reset somewhat as sales flattened. In response, Goodman took a heavy-handed approach with Marvel, threatening layoffs and canceling titles outright, including Lee's beloved *Doctor Strange*. The publisher even demanded that comics drop a page (from 20 to 19) in an effort to save money. All the interference boiled Lee's blood and again got him thinking about quitting the business. Chip Goodman also took the insane step of shutting down the Merry Marvel Marching Society fan club, which Lee felt energized the company's most loyal readers.[24]

Once again, Lee felt trapped. He had done everything in his power to build Marvel into the biggest comic book publisher in the industry, yet the sales slump put him right back in a vulnerable position. Goodman had not come through on his promises and, as a matter of fact, began hinting at another round of mass layoffs, which Lee would have to orchestrate. The writer yearned for a way out but couldn't figure which way to turn. "It's time I started thinking of other things," he said, considering a range of options, from writing a play or film treatment to just creating poems.[25] Film seemed the most logical avenue. He even dreamed of taking Kirby and artist John Buscema to Hollywood with him where they could work on set designs or storyboards while he crafted scripts.

While Lee considered his options, the company's new owner felt its first trembles. Perfect's board of directors ousted Ackerman. The combination of pressure from running Curtis and his flamboyant, decadent spending habits was too much for the company to bear. They replaced Ackerman with Sheldon Feinberg, another aggressive young executive with a law background. Feinberg led the charge to start fresh, changing the company name to Cadence Industries. He instituted a tight-fisted campaign to reduce the company's enormous debt. No longer the captain of the ship, Goodman fell in line. He ordered Lee to publish reprints of certain comic lines so that he didn't have to pay freelancers for creating new pages while Marvel attempted to weather the bleak sales outlook. Inching ever closer to the end of the decade, Feinberg and his young, bellicose team had quite a task ahead. Lee tried to keep the Marvel bullpen in high spirits, but the business side of the corporation controlled decision making.

The early 1960s hinged on creating new characters and establishing the Marvel Universe as readers took notice of the revolution occurring in the industry at the hands of the perennial second-tier company. In the latter part of the decade, Lee and his crew shifted their emphasis to solidifying Marvel's standing, as well as deepening and broadening the storylines. Lee also gave some heroes their own solo titles, including *Captain America*, *Hulk*, and *Iron Man*.

While many publishers watched sales drop, Marvel's stayed consistent during the downturn. When it upped monthly production, the additional revenue staved off mass layoffs, thus keeping Lee from having to eliminate coworkers and staff members that he considered almost as close as family members. At least the good cheer and hipness factor remained with Marvel. DC went through tougher times, being sold to Kinney National, yet another corporate conglomerate, and still unable to figure out how to compete with its smaller competitor.

As 1968 unfolded, Lee and Marvel would get increasingly caught up in world events. No one could ignore Vietnam, campus unrest, civil rights protests, or the growing women's rights campaigns. On the *Dick Cavett Show*, Lee discussed an earlier *Thor* issue that had the Norse god criticizing college students who drop out, rather than "plunge in." At the time of the interview, however, the significance of the protests had changed, as had the world in general. Lee could no longer use a superhero story to write "a good little sermon" in response. "Youth today," he told Cavett, "seem to be so much more activist, which I think is a very healthy thing."[26]

In 1968, the comic book business stood almost unrecognizable compared to the start of the decade, when *The Fantastic Four* launched a series of new villains, heroes, and monsters in 1961. All the new solo titles necessitated an increased universe of intricately woven plots and new characters to fill the superhero books. Lee feared that Cadence executives could close down Marvel at any moment, yet he soldiered on, hoping that the superhero universe he created would endure the bumps and blips of the chaotic era.

CHAPTER 10

CREATING AN ICON

What Stan Lee understood better than anyone else associated with Marvel—from his boss Martin Goodman and the Cadence executives overseeing the company to the newest assistant editor or freelance letterer—was that if the company had a spokesperson with stories as large-as-life as the Marvel superheroes, then that person could be almost as significant as the creations. Regardless of the artist, Lee had already put words into Spider-Man, Thor, and the others for years. His voice was the sound of Marvel Comics.

When journalists began sniffing around the company in an attempt to experience the hubbub firsthand, Lee seized a crucial opening. Reporters may have scratched their heads, expecting to come across someone younger, but they recognized that the enthusiastic, witty, quote-a-minute Lee had tapped into youth culture. For decades he had survived Goodman's downsizing and financial whims, repeatedly serving as a de facto one-man publishing company. So, when the press looked for a spokesman to contextualize the company's rampant success, Lee jumped at the chance. The new role not only played to his ego, but also allowed him to try out some of the acting chops that he not-so-secretly harbored, dating all the way back to his teen stage aspirations with the WPA.

Lee also grasped the monetary and branding value of serving as the company face. From one perspective, he grew up in the midst of the Great Depression and remembered listening to his parents shout at one another, usually about having no money. How would they manage to pay the rent without groveling to her relatives, who were better off than the Liebers? The challenge for Lee's father was joblessness, which the son could not abide. If he stepped into a role that made him essentially indispensible, then that position equaled job security. He carried a deep aversion for unemployment or even the hint of being underutilized. With his father's humiliation a painful memory, the idea shook Lee to the core.

In addition, the spokesperson role from a branding viewpoint ensured that Marvel remained in the public eye as new opportunities developed. Lee did not have to be a supergenius like Reed Richards to realize that the superhero craze would lead to an increased number of entertainment options that would build on Marvel's reputation—*and* Lee's. The public reaction to the superhero characters he helped create stacked up on his desk in the form of three hundred to four hundred fan letters each day. In some sense, Lee realized, he could become a real-life "Mr. Fantastic" just by capitalizing on his natural strengths and gregarious personality.[1]

The public role made Lee virtually indispensible. Ironically, as Lee's position expanded, he subsequently became further entrenched as a company man. He realized that his fate—as always—remained deeply entwined with Marvel comics. Although many comic book insiders would accuse Lee of self-aggrandizement for assuming this self-created mantle, he smartly moved in a direction that played on his natural talents. He was never going to be an inspirational chief executive—he never fully engaged with the business side of the organization—but he could rally crowds and fans. In addition to engaging with enthusiastic college students, he could just as effectively talk up comic books to worried parents or curious journalists.

After spending decades toiling in virtual obscurity and chagrined when people learned of his occupation, the tables turned when Marvel found itself at the center of the cultural zeitgeist. Lee leaped at the prospect of establishing himself as a brand both within and outside the company.

Goodman remained the prototypical business leader, keen on revenue and profit. He lacked the sense of pure creativity needed to appreciate the work being done by Lee, Kirby, Ditko, and the Marvel bullpen, but he created a financial infrastructure that enabled the artists and writers to flourish. And he continued to serve as a foil to Lee, even as the latter's power increased and Goodman's power lessened. Lee may have bristled at the financial maneuverings necessary for running a company, but he understood that Goodman and the Cadence management team played a critical role in the company's success.

Keeping the comic book division running, Lee had developed broad insight and experience with finances, but it never moved him the way the creative pieces did. He understood the need to build on the momentum of the new breed of superheroes Marvel created, but he remained somewhat removed from the corporate business decision making and the obsession with numbers that fueled middle management. Plus, he had no real time to get too intricately involved with finances. The expansion of titles per month meant that Lee had to corral a growing team of staffers and free-lancers. Titles had to hit publication deadlines. Missing the mark cost the company money in penalty fees and potential sales. The ironic aspect of Lee's concentration on marketing Marvel was that it took place after so many years. "I had to write just about everything," he recalled. "I was the editor. I was the art director. I was the head writer. So because of that, for better or worse, I had my personality stamped on those comics." It is important to remember, though, that the front-end creation—from writing to artwork and production—was the glitzy outcome that required a great deal of behind-the-scenes effort. "I was designing covers, writing cover blurbs, writing ads, the soapbox column, the Bullpen page," Lee explained.[2] The culmination of Lee's many creative roles over decades prepared him for the spotlight, which he had been yearning for from his earliest days in comic books and certainly at least dating back to his 1947 *Writer's Digest* article about making money writing comic books.

The persona Lee fashioned, with part sarcasm and large dollops of self-deprecation, created a voice that permeated Marvel. The popularity of Spider-Man, Hulk, Iron Man, and the others went beyond mere fandom to a kind of cult status that established Marvel as a major cultural influence. Yet, even though it became the hip comic book company, Marvel still trailed DC Comics in total sales. In 1968, for example, DC Comics published forty-seven titles with sales of approximately seventy-five million, while Marvel had twenty-two titles and fifty million (although in an August 1968 interview, Lee claimed sixty million). Even though Marvel published fewer than half the titles DC did, its sales were at least two-thirds as much, making the company in some ways more successful.

In countless speaking engagements and interviews, Lee continued to hone his public persona. Simultaneously, though, he never missed a chance to recognize Marvel fans and his creative team (then numbering around thirty-five staff and free-lancers). "Marvel readers must be among the most fanatical in the land," he claimed. "They ask questions, find mistakes, [and] make suggestions."[3] The thousands of letters Lee received and the interaction with fans at comic industry gatherings gave him direct insight into his target demographic, from the obsessed diehards who chided Lee for every *Spider-Man* frame that left out some minor detail to the casual observers attempting to understand how comic books got so popular.[4]

Lee never shied from telling the world how innovative or creative Marvel's new work (and by extension, his writing) stood in comparison to past characters and comic book publishers, particularly DC, which he constantly chided as a monument to an outdated era.

Lee sincerely believed in the educational and cultural value of comic books, so his basic earnestness led to an authenticity that people accepted, particularly when delivered in the corny, self-deprecating style that he perfected as the speaking engagements piled up. Lee understood that fans wanted Marvel books to engage with real-life socioeconomic and political topics. Staying flexible and listening to fans, Lee responded, explaining, "they want a whole ethos, a philosophy, within the framework of the comic character. They seem desperate for someone to believe in. . . . I don't want to let them down."[5] In the late 1960s much of the editorializing expressed via Spider-Man, Thor, and others addressing pertinent issues helped legitimize comic books for a wider audience.

Although Lee could be criticized for not taking a more progressive tone, given that he had the youth market at his feet, he often dropped his self-deprecating mask and spoke to readers about serious topics. In late 1968, for example, he used a "Stan's Soapbox" column to speak out against bigotry and racism, which he labeled the "deadliest social ills plaguing the world today." Lee said it was "totally irrational, patently insane to condemn an entire race—to despise an entire nation—to vilify an entire religion." Instead, he urged Marvelites to be tolerant.[6]

Similar thinking about societal concerns prevalent in the chaotic era led Marvel to create several African American characters, including Robbie Robertson, a city editor at the *Daily Bugle* in Spider-Man books and, more centrally, the Black Panther, the superhero guise of T'Challa, the prince of a mythical African country. Around the same time, Marvel introduced the Falcon, another black superhero, but this time an American. After debating what to do with the Black Panther, Lee confessed to hoping that the fan mail would provide him with insight about how to carry on. In 1970, Lee claimed that he wanted to offer black heroes earlier, but "the powers-that-be" were "very cautious" and would not let him.[7] Whether this finger wagging was aimed directly at Goodman or the Cadence bosses, Lee did not feel that he had to hold back.

In March 1970, Lee again turned to the Soapbox to lay out Marvel's policy on "moralizing." Some readers simply wanted escapist reading, but Lee countered: "I can't see it that way." He compared a story without a message to a person without a soul. Giving the reader insight into his world, Lee explained that his visits to college campuses led to "as much discussion of war and peace, civil rights, and the so-called youth rebellion as . . . of our Marvel mags." All these ideas, Lee said, shape our lives. No one should run from them or think that reading comic books might insulate someone from important societal topics.[8]

Despite all the attention he received and the outpouring of fan affection bordering on cult-like devotion, Lee couldn't shake feelings of inadequacy. He continued to receive off-putting reactions from other adults who worked in more mainstream jobs. As a result, Lee searched for legitimacy. No accolades seemed enough to erase those initial negative perceptions of being "just a comic book writer."

Often, when Lee faced challenges, he turned to Spider-Man. From a literary standpoint, Spider-Man tapped into the era's existentialism—an average person who fell victim to an accident that changed his life in every way imaginable. The radioactive spider that injected its venom directly into Peter Parker's bloodstream enabled the boy to transform into a superhero, but the venom did not cast aside Peter's insecurities, anxieties, or basic humanity. As a matter of fact, a moment of indecision and hubris led to the death of his beloved Uncle Ben and left the boy reeling and reflective. The dichotomy between hubris and humility made the character compelling to legions of Marvel fans.

As a symbol of the 1960s and its collective unrest, which resulted in a kind of split personality between protest and conservatism, Spider-Man was another iteration of the figures populating books, film, and celebrity tabloids during the era. Peter Parker occupies the same city that drove young Holden Caulfield to the brink in J. D. Salinger's *The Catcher in the Rye* (1951). Similarly to Caulfield, Parker questions his place in the world. While Lee knew the character resonated with younger audiences, he also believed that more mature readers and adults would connect with the character as well, which he had seen in his lectures on college campuses. He just needed to get the superhero in front of this expanded audience. The growing college-aged population gobbled up *Catcher*, just as it devoured Marvel comics.

In July 1968, in hopes of thwarting some of the criticisms he faced about being in an inferior industry, Lee launched *The Spectacular Spider-Man*, which was not only magazine-sized, but its interior art was in black and white, a trend mirrored in underground comics. The fifty-plus-page magazine debuted for thirty-five cents, nearly triple the newsstand price of regular comic books at twelve cents.

The first issue featured a rewritten and redrawn origin story and a Lee original, "Lo, This Monster." The covers were distinctive as well. Harry Rosenbaum, an artist who did cover art for men's adventure magazines, painted an image of the hero in acrylic, which gave it a deeply textured and mature look. The second issue presented a striking cover by artist John Romita that showed the Green Goblin zapping Spidey with a colorful yellow burst. The energy of the Romita cover exploded from the page and quickly became a fan favorite.

Lee revealed his hopes for the magazine in a general Soapbox update, calling the magazine "a real, glitzy, status-drenched, slick-paper publication" that readers could find "amongst the so-called 'better' magazines at your newsstand." In his "Stan's Soapbox" call-out, Lee declared the magazine, "possibly Marvel's finest achievement to date" and a "Marvel milestone" that would go down in comic book history. The

editor-in-chief saw the magazine as an opportunity to create a bridge to adult readers, featuring more mature themes and topics. He also felt it would provide him
some gravitas among adults and win them over to his viewpoint regarding comics.

What Lee didn't anticipate was that the new adult-oriented comic seemed to oc-
cupy a no-man's land between kids and older readers. No amount of bluster or hype
on Lee's part could save the title from bombing. For average fans, *The Spectacular
Spider-Man* cost too much. The foray into black and white did not help either. The
second issue went back to interior color, but it was already too late. That second issue with the beautiful cover would be the last, though Marvel rehashed the Lee story
later in 1973 in *The Amazing Spider-Man* #116–118, with revisions by writer Gerry
Conway. Another story from the second issue, featuring the Green Goblin, would
later be repurposed (as Marvel so frequently did) in *The Amazing Spider-Man Annual* #9 (1973).

Although the failure of the adult version delivered a blow to Lee's notions of
crossing into a more traditional form of mainstream success, the magazine didn't
diminish Spider-Man's overall popularity among comic book fans. Nonetheless, Lee
still reeled with career frustration. Since the late 1940s, he had attempted to gain a
sense of legitimacy by self-publishing material for older readers or moonlighting for
Goodman's adult-oriented magazines. On the outside, Lee seemed upbeat and passionate about comic books and his superhero creations. Throughout his long career
in comics, though, he had internalized the negativity, hiding deep fears about working in an industry that others deemed unacceptable.

In early 1970, Lee faced another challenge. Kirby's contract had expired around
the time Goodman sold the company to Perfect Film. The corporate leaders who
ran the business had little interest in re-signing Kirby for the big money the artist
expected, and Goodman didn't back him, either. Kirby correctly gauged that it was
his turn to get paid for all that he had done to build Marvel into the industry leader,
but according to Mark Evanier, no one would talk to him or his lawyer about a new
contract.[9] Eventually, he turned to Lee for help, incorrectly assuming that the editor had the power to help. Though Kirby thought Lee sandbagged him, there is no
evidence that he could have swayed Goodman or the corporate management team
to give Kirby what he wanted.

The contract impasse drove another wedge between Lee and Kirby—in hind-
sight, one that seemed based on misjudgment rather than malice. The irony of the
relationship between Kirby and Lee is that the two are tied together forever in comic
book lore, yet their complexities turned the relationship at times indifferent, or be-
grudgingly cordial, sour, and even hostile.

Kirby seemed to care less about the fame that came with creating successful
superheroes and comic books. He loved his craft. His desire centered on earning

a living and getting treated with equity—receiving a fair share of the money that corporations were making off his art, ideas, and reputation. With Kirby, the feeling emerges that no matter how financially sound he might have been, the haunting recollections of his youth in the Lower East Side slums would never be far from his mind. "All of Kirby's work in the '60s was for Marvel, and he was always terrified that he would stop getting assignments," Joe Simon explained. "It was a big deal for him."[10]

Both Kirby and Simon, like Lee, had lived through the hardscrabble times of the Great Depression, which fundamentally colored the way they viewed work and money. According to Simon, Kirby put a lot of pressure on himself to provide for his family, at least in part because his own parents had been so poor. "He had to bring the money home for Roz, put food on the table for the kids."[11] This kind of intimate relationship with poverty never leaves a person. Kirby's demons regarding money hovered ominously over his worldview. His $35,000 freelance salary in 1970 (about $220,000 in current buying power) allowed him to make a decent living, but one could certainly argue that he should have been making multiples more than that, perhaps in the millions of dollars.

Despite their shared history of growing up poor, for Lee, recognition was a far greater desire than the financial compensation that Kirby sought. He also drew from important lessons bestowed on him as a child—a mother who demanded perfection and success and the toll that financial hardship had taken on his family. Adulation was the check Lee needed to cash.

Though forever linked as a creative tandem, Lee and Kirby's complex relationship suffered from different desires, one for fame, the other for financial security. Thus, Kirby's frustration with Goodman's penny-pinching and reneged-on promises, as well as lingering exasperation with Lee, led him to turn down a new contract with Marvel in 1970. Instead he boarded DC, where Carmine Infantino ran the editorial ship. Kirby was given free rein to develop a new superhero universe, called "The Fourth World." At DC, he created three new titles that enabled the artist/writer to tackle the biblical, existential, and science fiction machine-driven questions that were at the center of his mythical worldview.

Comic books were big business and had been a hit in other mediums, demonstrating how central superhero narratives were in contemporary American culture. Envious of the way Superman and Batman had moved from radio to film and television, Marvel made similar plans. Historically, the emphasis had been on creating demand for comic books by crossing platforms. During this era, publishing executives realized how television and film would drive licensing.

For Lee and the corporate honchos in New York, the ultimate dream for Marvel's superheroes centered on a series of movies and television shows. Moving into these mediums had two primary objectives. First, increasing the overall size of the audience would establish the characters for successive generations of fans. Next, the increased exposure would lead to greater demand, thereby generating a catalog of profitable licensing deals. Despite some early successes the company had getting the figures into animated series, most attempts at adapting them for live-action floundered, often stuck somewhere in the jumble of the Hollywood process that took an idea to script, then development and casting.

The early *Marvel Super Heroes* animated program produced by Grantray-Lawrence proved that even a crudely done series featuring the company's main superheroes would find an audience. The next logical step, based on the ever-growing popularity of Spider-Man, was that the web slinger would get a show. Grantray-Lawrence led production efforts in late 1967 and worked on the series into 1968. The struggling studio went into bankruptcy, however, enabling famed animator Ralph Bakshi to take over the reins. The series aired on ABC and proved a hit, running until 1970.

Animation juggernaut Hanna-Barbera Productions produced another series for ABC—the first series for *The Fantastic Four*—that ran from 1967 to 1970. The new program ran alongside *Spider-Man*, giving audiences an extended dose of superhero stories. Lee and Kirby's original comic books were truncated to fit into the thirty-minute time slot and watered down so that children could easily follow the stories. Considered one of the first Saturday morning educational cartoons, each episode had a segment dedicated to Mister Fantastic explaining a scientific term or concept to viewers.

Producers downplayed Kirby's ominous depiction of Doctor Doom and made Galactus less imposing, but these stylistic changes were offset to a degree by the enthusiasm of the voice actors, including film and television star Gerald Mohr voicing Reed Richards. This formula—making some characters more generic and operating within the technology boundaries (in this case, clunky animation)—seemed to hinder how production companies brought Marvel characters to the screen. Publicly, Lee supported the show, but had little to do with it otherwise. The lack of control irritated him. He believed that if Marvel created its own programming, like Disney, that its superheroes would rival Walt's famous mouse and princesses. The urge to start a production company began to gnaw at Lee.

In 1971, a *New York Times* reporter estimated that about 300 million comic books were printed each year.[12] Considering even a conservative pass-through rate equating to four others reading each comic sold, that means around 1.2 billion comic books were read at a time when the total world population stood near 3.7 billion. Despite lingering questions about its negative effects on young readers, the medium had grown into a central component of mainstream culture. And Lee was its pivotal figure. In the eyes of many, the name "Stan Lee" was synonymous with comic books, a kind of Johnny Appleseed who toured the nation to spread the joy and significance of comic books.

In May of that year, Lee showed how comic books could be used for good with *The Amazing Spider-Man* #96. In that issue, Spidey saves a young black kid who mistakenly jumps off a rooftop, because, as the superhero explains, "The poor guy's stoned right out of his mind." After the rescue, other characters exchange words about drug use and Spider-Man thinks: "My life as Spider-Man is probably as dangerous as any—but I'd rather face a hundred super-villains than toss it away by getting hooked on hard drugs." Peter Parker's African American friend Randy later gets into a heated exchange with Norman Osborn, explaining that blacks hate drugs the most, because young people "got no hope," which makes them "easier pickin's for the pushers."

Casual readers may have regarded the antidrug message as yet another aspect of their favorite comic book's approach to realism. Marvel fans probably didn't know that Lee had received a letter asking for his help from an official at the National Institute of Mental Health, a division of the Department of Health, Education and Welfare. The executive implored Lee to use Spidey's popularity to fight drug abuse by directly confronting the issue in comic book form. Government officials believed that the character's esteem among high school and college students would enable the agency to get factual information to this key demographic.

Although Lee realized that mentioning drug use would be a violation of the Comics Code, he decided to fulfill the request. Understanding the broader implications, he explained, "We can't keep our heads in the sand. . . . If this story would help one kid anywhere in the world not to try drugs or to lay off drugs one day earlier, then it's worth it rather than waiting for the code authority to give permission."[13]

Most comic book publishers and editors set internal rules about dealing with the Code of the Comics Magazine Association. Despite regulations about dealing with sex and the depiction of government officials in a bad light, the Code did not include information about drug abuse. No publisher could release a story featuring a werewolf or vampire, those tales were clearly outlawed by the Code. Drugs, though, were a hazy subject for regulators. *The Amazing Spider-Man* #96 did not bear the Comic Code seal of approval, which represented a bold step for Marvel and Lee. He continued the drug plot for the next two issues, revealing that Harry Osborn had a pill addiction. Parker chalks Harry's habit up to him being "so weak." Later, Osborn obtains pills from a dealer (resembling a blond version of Stan Lee in comic book form), who promises the pills are "just what the doctor ordered." Back at the apartment he shares with Parker, Osborn passes out after taking a handful of pills. When Peter finds him, they are interrupted by Harry's father, the Green Goblin, who wants to kill Spider-Man. After battling the villain above the high-rises and apartment buildings of New York, Spidey eventually convinces the Goblin to see his hospitalized son. The trauma causes the Goblin to black out, which seems to put an end to his villainous ways.

While government officials were happy to have Spider-Man and Lee on their side in the fight against drug use, not everyone agreed. John Goldwater, the publisher of Archie Comics and founding president of the Comics Magazine Association in 1954, publicly announced his disapproval, including declaring topical use of drugs or drug abuse in comic books "still taboo."[14] Yet, the far-reaching positive publicity Marvel received handcuffed Goldwater and the CMA. The organization issued no sanctions against Marvel or Lee.

In addition to bringing the Comics Code Authority into modern times, Lee's decision to publish the special *Spider-Man* issues put Marvel out ahead of DC, which had been rumored to be working on its own issues based on the same topic. Carmine Infantino, the editorial director at DC, also railed against Marvel, implying that the move should be considered potentially harmful, particularly to children who might read it.[15]

Rejecting the code enabled Lee and Marvel to push harder on other social issues, and allowed them to take a stab at appealing to more college-aged readers. One method for proving the relevancy of comics focused on introducing nonwhite and ethnically diverse superheroes into the lineups. Marvel launched *Hero for Hire* in June 1972, featuring a black superhero, Luke, who fights crime in Harlem. Two years later, the Cage became *Power Man* and had a successful run teaming up with white martial arts legend Iron Fist.

Following these pioneering efforts and after the company introduced Black Panther, using the character in a series of titles, Marvel published *Red Wolf* (1972–1973), a Native American superhero. Shortly after, when the television show *Kung Fu*, starring David Carradine, hit the air in 1972, Marvel picked up on the martial arts wave (which included the work of Bruce Lee and others using karate as the driving force on film). The company developed *Master of Kung Fu*, featuring Asian superhero Shang-Chi, who first appeared in *Special Marvel Edition* #15 (December 1973). By April 1974, the title changed to *The Hands of Shang-Chi: Master of Kung Fu* and began a long, popular run, eventually appearing in crossovers with Marvel's top superheroes.

Lee always harbored ambitions to be more than "just" a comic book writer and editor. When he was a boy, his mother showered him with praise and joked almost daily that Hollywood talent scouts would soon take him from her. He acted out scripts for artists and other writers and enjoyed the constant bustle of hustling from campus to campus as a one-man Marvel marketing machine. Most of these efforts paid dividends in terms of growing fan loyalty or spreading the comic book gospel. Sometimes, however, Lee's willingness to take chances backfired.

In early December 1971, a distinctive ad ran in the hip NYC paper the *Village Voice* announcing "Stan Lee at Carnegie Hall!" in January. For $3.50 in advance or $4.50 at the door, fans could attend the show, which promised "All Live! Music! Magic! and Myth!" The advertisement didn't feature many details, but Thor, Spider-Man, and Hulk were crammed into the image, with Spidey (in characteristic Lee style) promising: "An erudite evening of cataclysmic culture with your friendly neighborhood bullpen gang."[16] Later, the official name of the event changed to "A Marvelous Evening with Stan Lee."

Whether the evening was "marvelous" or not most likely depended on the viewer's feelings about Marvel and its band of superheroes. Most adults, particularly those reviewing the shindig for metropolitan newspapers, found the evening anything but amazing, likening it to an "employer at his own Christmas party" and "a company revue."[17] Lee served as host and ringleader, which is an apt description, since the night devolved into a chaotic mess. There were second-rate music acts, some vague discussions of comic book art with Romita and Buscema, and an appearance by new journalism star Tom Wolfe, who completed his white suit ensemble with an Uncle Sam top hat. Other oddities included the world's tallest man, nine-foot-eight Eddie Carmel, reading a poem about the Hulk, and Geoff Crozier, an Australian illusionist, performing a strange magic act.[18] The highlight for Lee was reading parts of the poem "God Woke" from the stage with his wife Joanie and daughter J.C. Fans really didn't know what to make of the show and made paper airplanes to lob at the stage in mockery and frustration.

Continually trying to establish Marvel as different, Lee started calling the company the "House of Ideas," which stuck with journalists and became part of the company's cachet. If a downside existed in the surge of Marvel comics into the public consciousness it is that Lee and his bullpen teammates had to balance between entertainment, taking a stance on social issues, and maintaining profitability. He placed value in the joy people derived from reading comics, but he wanted them to be useful as well, explaining, "hopefully I can make them enjoyable and also beneficial. . . . This is a difficult trick, but I try within the limits of my own talent."[19] Lee wanted to have it both ways—for people to read the books as entertainment, but also to be taken seriously.

At the same time, Marvel had to sell comics, which meant that little kids and young teenagers drove a sizeable chunk of the market. In 1970, Lee estimated that 60 percent of Marvel's readers were under sixteen. The remaining adult readership was enormous, in historical numbers, but kept Lee focused on the larger demographic. "We're still a business," he told an interviewer. "It doesn't do us any good to put out stuff we like if the books don't sell. . . . I would gain nothing by not doing things to reach the kids, because I would lose my job and we'd go out of business."[20]

As Lee's position as the voice and face of Marvel Comics solidified, it rankled Goodman and created a rift between the publisher and his star employee. On one hand, the industry moved so quickly that Lee and his creative teams constantly fought to get issues out on time. The number of titles Marvel put out meant that everyone had to be constantly producing. So, when Lee was in the office or working from home, he committed to getting content out. Roy Thomas recalls, "Stan and I were editing everything, and the writers were editing what they did, and we had a few assistant editors that didn't really have any authority . . . that was about it."[21] However, that chaotic atmosphere made it easy for animosities to form or fester. Lee needed content out the door and Goodman tried to maintain control over cover artwork and other details that inevitably slowed down the process.

"Stan and Goodman were increasingly on different wavelengths as the time came near the end of their relationship," explained Thomas, who had a front row seat watching the acrimony build. "Goodman and his son, Chip, were still making those decisions at that time. Chip, in that last year or less before Stan took over, was the official publisher as Martin withdrew from the business more. I don't know if Goodman was even in the office then, because I never saw him very much anyway. His office was way at the other end of the hall."[22]

In 1972, Goodman finally made good on his wish to retire, four long years after Cadence took over the company. He expected Cadence executives to make his son Chip the new publisher. Instead, shortly after Goodman left, the new owners showed his son the door—so much for handshake agreements and family ties. Instead, Cadence CEO Sheldon Feinberg named Lee Marvel's publisher and president.

The new post meant that Lee would have to step down as editorial director. After some internal wrangling and indecision regarding who would replace him, Lee handed over the duties to Roy Thomas, his handpicked successor.

"Now I'll be able to do things the way I want them," Lee thought, but he was wrong. Instead, he attended a dizzying succession of meetings and strategy sessions to discuss the financial status of all the company's publications, including the men's magazines. "I suddenly realized that I am doing something that millions of people can do better than I can do. The thing I enjoy doing—the creative stuff—I'm not doing anymore." This realization led Lee to soon give up the president position to concentrate on the publisher's duties.[23]

In the meantime, Goodman didn't stay retired for long. Angered by his son's termination, Goodman retaliated by founding Atlas Comics. He put Chip in charge and began an aggressive poaching program, even hiring away Lee's younger brother Larry to serve as editor. Many other Marvel freelancers and artists also left because Goodman paid more. The desertions grew so prevalent that Lee had to issue a memo reminding staffers and freelancers of Marvel's commitment to them. Although a negative blip for Lee, the industry had changed, and Goodman's maneuverings were outdated. Atlas soon folded.

There were additional growing pains for Lee as publisher and Thomas as editor. Lee had a looser vibe with people, but also was a legendary figure. "He sent them off feeling very enthused about doing something new," says writer Mark Evanier, who worked with both Lee and Kirby. "They didn't operate for him out of fear, as they did for some editors."[24] Thomas inherited a staff loyal to Lee, but they still had to churn out some forty titles a month. The production schedule remained king. "I knew I didn't have the power Stan had had as editor-in-chief, because he was right there, and I wasn't looking for that," Thomas recalled. "I wasn't threatened by anybody, and who's going to have a better rapport with Stan than I did? It was very good, most of the time, so I didn't feel that insecure."[25]

Thomas's ascension and Lee's pull toward management did shift the editorial direction, if for no other reason than that Stan wouldn't be writing full-time any longer. "It was time to kind of branch out a little bit," Thomas explained. "We wanted to keep some of that Marvel magic, and at the same time, there had to be room for other art styles and other writing styles."[26] The most overt change came when Lee turned in the copy for *The Amazing Spider-Man* #110. The late 1971 issue was the last Lee wrote for the character. Writer Gerry Conway succeeded Lee and the next books in the series would be cocreated by Conway and star artist John Romita.

While many adults looked down on Lee for writing comic books, especially early in his career, he developed a masterful style that rivals or mirrors those of contemporary novelists. Lee explained:

Every character I write is really me, in some way or other. Even the villains. Now I'm not implying that I'm in any way a villainous person. Oh, perish forbid! But how can anyone write a believable villain without thinking, "How would I act if he (or she) were me? What would I do if I were trying to conquer the world, or jaywalk across the street? . . . What would I say if I were the one threatening Spider-Man? See what I mean? No other way to do it."[27]

Lee's distinctive voice captured the essence of his chosen medium.

Lee also understood that the meaning of success in contemporary pop culture necessitated that he embrace the burgeoning celebrity culture. If a generation of teen and college-aged readers hoped to shape him into their leader, Lee would gladly accept the mantle and be their gonzo king. Fashioning this image in a lecture circuit that took him around the nation, as well as within the pages of Marvel's books, Lee created a persona larger than his publisher or employer. As a result, he transformed the comic book industry.

CHAPTER 11

MARVEL'S MULTITUDE OF MALADIES

Although it might have been difficult to put downbeat words in the mouth of the company's most important promoter, the 1970s were troubling times for Lee and the company. Everyone at Marvel—including Lee, the creative teams responsible for putting out the books, the accountants struggling to make sense of internal spending, and corporate managers determined to rein in the comics division—seemed at war with one another, desperate to address the sagging sales.

Like so much of the national scene, the comic book industry faced years of uncertainty, slippery footing, and ultimately a struggle to survive. Marvel's per-comic sales dropped, so the company attempted to offset the decrease by publishing more titles. For example, there were ten comics with "Marvel" in the title (ranging from *Mighty Marvel Western* and *Marvel Triple Action* to *Special Marvel Edition*).[1]

By January 1973, Lee oversaw the annual production of some sixty-nine titles, including twenty-eight superhero books, sixteen mystery/monsters, and ten westerns. Total sales rose, but the fact that Marvel published so many comics actually concealed weaknesses internally and revealed stagnation across the industry.[2] Flooding the marketplace had been a Martin Goodman trick from the early days. The practice boosted the overall financial picture but also increased pressure on the creative teams who put pen and ink to paper.

Yet, in front of a microphone or with a reporter nearby, Lee remained positive, trumpeting the company's successes. Reading the Stan's Soapbox essays, no one would have guessed at the troubles that dogged Marvel, particularly after it achieved its primary goal, which was to knock DC off as the industry leader. When that happened, Marvel had to change. It was no longer the scrappy underdog and perennial also-ran. For some organizations, that drive to the top defines its culture. Once Marvel became the top comic book producer, the company had to find a new path.

Amid the chaotic climate of the early 1970s and Marvel's struggles to find its footing, Lee's transition from writer, art director, and editorial lead to publisher proved jarring. In the office, he shifted from creative force to company man, serving as a kind of conduit between the intransigent figures running the corporation at the top of the executive food chain and the chaos of the creative bullpen filled with artists and writers who—like the 1970s as a decade—wanted to buck the system.

Lee struggled to find his place in this unfamiliar corporate system, never fully understanding his fellow "suits," but also constantly worried about the status of the artists and writers, who thumbed their noses at conformity and economic realities. He had to be the boss, for example, creating an approval process for cover art and copy for all domestic comics, plus the British titles, while balancing storylines and juggling the workloads of the creative teams.[3] The operation grew too large for one person to control everything, but the publisher role demanded his attention across the business and creative functions.

Unlike his friends and protégés in the bullpen (many of the them younger writers or artists who grew up inspired by his work), Lee knew the intricacies of the financial situation and recognized just how precarious the future looked. In an interview, he discussed his role, explaining, "What I do mainly is worry about the product we are turning out. . . . I'm really like an over-all executive editor."[4] He worked with Cadence leaders to get approvals for new magazines and comics, each decision having significant consequences, since the profit margins in the comic book division were so thin.

Lee and many other industry insiders expected the superhero craze to eventually fizzle. If Marvel faltered, the best-case scenario for Lee would send him back to his editor's desk, writing multiple books for whatever the next fad might be, again relying on freelance artists to keep the company afloat. He shuddered at this thought, having no desire to return to his former role as a one-man comic book operation. Such fear drove him to keep up a relentless pace—at any given moment, Lee could be found overseeing strategic editorial decisions, managing the expectations and meddling of his corporate bosses, launching new magazines, or flying from college campus to campus to fulfill his marketing and lecturing role.

Marvel needed a boost. Superhero popularity skyrocketed, yet sales dropped. Demographics worked against Marvel. Readers skewed younger, buying titles such as *Archie Comics*, the bestselling comic of 1970 at 515,000 sold per issue versus *The Amazing Spider-Man* at about 373,000.[5] At the end of 1971, the official Audit Bureau of Circulation (ABC) audit revealed that paid circulation per month had dropped over the preceding three years. Marvel sold about 96 million comic books in 1968, but the figure fell to 91.8 in 1971, despite more total books on sale.[6] Over the following year and a half, the number would plummet to just over 5.8 million per month or just under 70 million annually for 1972 and 1973. In comparison, DC dipped from about 6.3 million per month in 1968 to just 4.7 million five years later.[7]

Hoping to reverse course, the comic book division spent the early 1970s jumping from fad to fad. Marvel rushed headlong into the fantasy and horror market, publishing *The Tomb of Dracula*, *The Monster of Frankenstein*, and *Man-Thing*, among others. Lee urged fans to accept the new direction in Soapbox columns, calling the new *Monster Madness* title, "the most frantic, far-out, fabulously frenzied monster mag you've ever goose-pimpled over!" In his carnival barker cadence, he implored readers to obey the first Marvel Commandment in his faux biblical exhortation: "thou shall not miss it!"[8]

The move into horror came after the Comics Code adapted to shifting cultural norms after Lee pushed through the *Amazing Spider-Man* #96 issue that tackled drug use at the behest of the U.S. Department of Health, Education, and Welfare. In 1972, Code regulators officially eliminated restrictions prohibiting horror comics, particularly ones featuring werewolves and vampires.

Cadence executives did not really understand the comic book division, so they had a difficult time comprehending the wildly fluctuating sales numbers or how to stop the decline. Historically, comic books garnered a high pass-through rate, which meant that for every comic purchased, about three to five additional people read it—three to five people who had no reason to buy a copy for themselves. These discouraging numbers forced Cadence officials to tighten down on editorial, including Lee and protégé Roy Thomas, who had become a kind of mini-Lee, both writing original content and editing the other titles in the lineup.

Thomas played an instrumental role in getting Marvel focused and pointed in new directions post-Lee's editorship. For example, he convinced a skeptical Lee to take a shot on the sword-wielding *Conan the Barbarian* in late 1970, and the title became a hit.

In late 1972, Lee's role took on an official strategic component when he became publisher of Marvel Comics. "I was deciding what books we would publish and what to concentrate on," he explained. "I worked with the editor and oversaw most of what we did."[9] With Thomas as the new editor in chief, they began charting a different path for Marvel, but at a time when the softness in the marketplace became clearer. Thomas pushed the comic book division into new areas, less reliant on traditional superheroes, including Man-Thing, Ghost Rider, and Dracula. The entire 1970s seemed a topsy-turvy mix of innovative new characters trying to survive in a faltering market, while Lee mixed his publisher duties with promoting and marketing Marvel at a time when his personal celebrity skyrocketed but decreasing sales rocked Cadence corporate leaders.

Merchandising and licensing had been a kind of afterthought back when Goodman ran the company. That changed when Cadence took over and caused schisms between the corporate leadership and the comic book creators. Some critics of the new regime argued that Cadence simply wanted to turn Marvel into a marketing machine, ignoring superheroes and comic books unless they had licensing potential. In 1973 and 1974, the marketing work resulted in deals with numerous toy companies and publishers, as well as Columbia Records, Hostess, Mattel, and others.[10] The merchandising deals grew in significance as circulation declined. No one expected 1971 to be a trendsetter, but Marvel did not reach that 7.4 million copies per month threshold again until 1987.

As editor, Lee had some distance from licensing, often as bemused as the next person when he saw a Spider-Man or Hulk tchotchke. In his publisher role, though, Lee became a conduit between Marvel and potential advertisers, particularly young salesmen who had grown up reading his comics. Lee's celebrity status made him an attraction at trade shows and other venues where Cadence hobnobbed with corporate execs. Thus, Lee's importance actually increased as circulation plummeted and the corporate bosses exerted pressure to squeeze revenues wherever they could find them. Even somewhat meager advertising and licensing money meant something when comic books were priced at twenty cents a copy.

Despite the softness in the marketplace, the exterior Lee, the public face of Marvel, remained as joyful and exuberant as ever. Legions of fans still flocked to see their leader as Lee barnstormed the nation spreading the gospel of comic books. In mid-1975, his fame grew when a reporter at the *Chicago Tribune* dubbed Lee "the creator of a modern mythology" and, more blatantly, "the Homer of pop culture" (a moniker given to Lee by Princeton students in 1966).[11]

Giving up the day-to-day editorial duties, he increased lecture time, averaging one a week and expanded his trips to include Europe, Canada, and Latin America.[12] In the first two months of 1975, for example, Lee spoke at seven colleges, from Sir George Williams College in Montreal to Augustana College in Rock Island, Illinois. During that stretch, he also conducted numerous radio interviews, spoke to print journalists, appeared on a Canadian television show, and served as featured speaker at Creation Con in New York City.[13] As Lee's celebrity status swelled, his schedule soon had to be booked about a year in advance.

Demographics weren't the only obstacle for Marvel. Attempting to fill Lee's shoes as editor-in-chief turned into a nightmare position. Trying to learn on the job and in Lee's shadow created too much pressure. Adding to the challenge, sales bottomed out and the Cadence management team increasingly meddled in the division. The friction proved too much for a series of editors that began with Thomas (who left Marvel in 1974, contending that he would rather write comics than worry about climbing corporate ladders and managing staffers) and ended with the promotion of Jim Shooter in 1978.

The revolving door of post-Lee editors shook up the creative staff and spooked freelancers. For example, when Archie Goodwin took over in 1976, he came to the role with a great deal of authority, since many people considered him one of the best writers in the business. Yet, Goodwin only lasted until late 1977; the strain of Cadence president Jim Galton's cutbacks and penny-pinching simply took the joy out of the work for him.

While both Thomas and Goodwin bristled at the business and strategy aspects of Lee's former role, both were instrumental in pulling the company out of the plummeting sales cycle. Before Thomas left, he met with a little-known filmmaker named George Lucas who had a science fiction movie coming out called *Star Wars*. Thomas first heard about the film and urged Lee to OK a comic book version. Lee was lukewarm about the film and turned down the request. Thomas, however, continued to pester his editor, telling him that Alec Guinness was one of the film's stars. When Lee heard about the esteemed actor's role, he relented.[14]

Once Thomas got Lee's approval, they worked out a deal with Lucas that would be mutually beneficial. The director cut a sweetheart deal with Marvel because he wanted to use the illustrated comic book as a lead-in to the film.[15]

When *Star Wars* eventually took the world by storm, Marvel basked in the demand for anything related to the surprise blockbuster. Its six-issue adaptation, written by Thomas (even though Goodwin was then editor), sold more than a million copies per issue, the first comics to reach that peak since the 1940s, even taking into account the Batmania that swept the nation in the mid-1960s. When *Star Wars* became a monthly title, Goodwin took over the writing duties, gladly vacating the editor's chair that he held so briefly.[16] Some company insiders, particularly Jim Shooter, feel that the *Star Wars* adaptation saved Marvel from certain bankruptcy and maybe even folding.

Although Lee had relinquished his primary writing duties at Marvel, he never really stopped producing. He couldn't help coming up with new ideas and getting them down on paper. He even carried tiny spiral notepads that fit in his front pocket to jot down thoughts and placed a tape recorder by his bed, in case inspiration struck in the middle of the night.

The publisher title meant that Lee had more control over the non–comic book publications, essentially the stragglers left over from Goodman's pulp and girlie magazine empire. Whether it was his own feelings of inadequacy or the fear that the superhero craze would end, Lee poured a lot of effort into the magazine work. He always felt like people working on magazines were a step or two above comic book writers and gave them outsized appreciation.

Looking at the magazine landscape, it seems as if Lee had a particularly difficult time with the success and influence of *Mad* magazine. Perhaps he envied the ability of *Mad*'s publisher, William Gaines, to get out of comics after the Wertham mess, or maybe it was that he knew and worked with so many of the writers and artists that gave *Mad* its unique voice, such as Al Jaffee, Wally Wood, and others. Lee attempted to duplicate the zany humor and satirical wit using basically the same staff that produced Marvel comics, creating his own version, *Crazy*, which debuted in October 1973. Although it seemed new, *Crazy* had been one of Goodman's attempts to mimic *Mad* in the early 1950s—a venture that failed.

Like Marvel comics, *Crazy* featured the "Stan Lee presents" banner. Marv Wolfman, who wrote *The Tomb of Dracula* comic and later created African American vampire hunter Blade, edited the magazine. Thomas served as executive editor. *Crazy* featured a mix of black and white illustrations and photographs, the latter captioned with puns and satirical quips. Like *Mad*, the magazine took on popular culture topics, parodying films and fads, such as the James Bond thriller *Live and Let Die*, which they changed to *Live and Let Spy*, featuring Agent 07-11 and a series of scantily clad females. In addition to overseeing the magazine, Lee contributed, often adding puns to campy photos, such as a piece on the campus streaking craze that swept the nation during that era. A photo of two officers carrying a naked man by the shoulders and feet featured Lee's typical humor: "Wait'll they find out I'm the Dean!"[17] The magazine lampooned everything, taking swipes at race relations, President Richard M. Nixon, and even Marvel, including a recurring feature on the challenges of Teen Hulk.

Growing up, Lee had loved newspaper comic strips, so once he got into comics, he developed ideas. Over the years, he created heartwarming strips such as *Mrs. Lyon's Cubs* and *Willy Lumpkin*, but they never lasted long. In October 1976, Lee teamed up with freelance artist Frank Springer to create *The Virtue of Vera Valiant*, a campy comic strip for newspaper syndication that satirized the melodrama of television soap operas. The title character earned her moniker because of her role in an odd love triangle—head over heels for a man whose wife fell asleep on their honeymoon and never woke up.

After serving in the Army during World War II and getting an art school education, Springer began his comic book career, but did not start with Marvel until the mid-1960s. Soon, though, like many of Lee's favored freelancers, the artist worked several different characters, honing each one's style under Lee's guidance. Eventually, Springer took over on *Spider-Man*, drawing the book from the mid-1970s into the 1980s. When he began working with Lee in the mid-1960s, Springer says that the writer had unwavering power, explaining, "At that time, Stan Lee was the guy you talked to about whether you did this book or not and how you did it and whether you did the next one."[18]

Vera Valiant featured Lee's madcap sass and dry wit. The strip opens on a macabre note, when Vera's brother Herbert botches a suicide attempt. Vera learns that he is flunking out of correspondence school and is distraught. When she turns to Winthrop, the dashing CPA, for comfort, she exclaims, "What will **become** of Herbert . . . if he's **expelled** from correspondence school?" Winthrop deadpans: "We won't let that happen! The world **needs** podiatrists!" Later, when the accountant confronts the deadbeat sibling regarding all his sister has given, he explains, "She's always **dreamed** of a podiatrist in the family!"[19] In three panels per day and eight on Sundays, Lee and Springer presented a zany adventure featuring podiatry, space alien real estate agents, and a wife suffering from "sleeping disease" for fourteen years.

Much closer to his heart, in 1977 Lee debuted a *Spider-Man* comic strip for syndication. At the time, *Spider-Man* sold millions of comic books a year, giving Marvel and Lee a great deal of cachet with newspaper editors. Initially appearing in about one hundred newspapers nationwide, the *Spider-Man* strip—penned by Lee and drawn by John Romita—gave newspapers a shot at attracting a younger readership. By mid-1978, about four hundred newspapers had picked it up, which provided Lee with an entrée to a new demographic of adult readers.

Lee had some difficulty adjusting to the constraints of a daily cartoon strip. No matter how much background and subplot he hoped to put into the effort, he still had a limited number of panels per day. How could a writer used to filling page after page boil a plot down to three frames when, according to Lee, the first box had to recap, the next box moved the story ahead, and the third box left the reader with a cliffhanger?[20] Steadily, he adapted to the minimalist style and grew to love the daily strip. The work gave him interaction with readers who wrote detailed letters about plot points, character motivations, and other topics. He explained, "At least I know someone's out there—someone's really reading the stuff!"[21] For Lee, the excitement readers had for the strip led to a wealth of ideas, so many, in fact, that he had difficulty paring them down.

The popularity of the *Spider-Man* daily comic led the Tribune syndicate to launch a full frontal assault. The company asked DC to create one for the Justice

League of America, dubbed *The World's Greatest Superheroes*. Veteran *Superman* writer Martin Pasko initially authored the strip. George Tuska, who had previously been the writer/artist on the *Buck Rogers* strip over its last decade (1959–1967), as well as drawing *Iron Man* and *The Hulk* for Marvel, penciled the DC comic, and Julius Schwartz edited it. Initially the strip centered on the adventures of all the JLA heroes, including Wonder Woman, Batman, and the Flash, but eventually focused primarily on Superman. The competing cartoon strip also found its way into newspapers nationwide.[22]

Discussing his creative process for the web-crawler strip, Lee explained: "I first try to come up with a unique human interest angle, or a compelling subplot, some problem for Peter that seems virtually unsolvable. And one of the best ways to do that is to say 'What If?'"[23] What Lee liked to do was load his stories up with complicated plots and obstacles that created a momentum to push the story toward a conclusion. At one point, he admitted: "The formula for the Spidey strip should be to treat it almost like a soap opera."[24] Lee faced an inherent challenge—entice younger readers to daily comic strips while simultaneously keeping older readers interested.

Cadence executives had more experience in book publishing than comic books, so naturally they moved in that direction. Lee had always wanted to write a novel and had dabbled in self-publishing earlier in his career, so the idea of writing a series of Marvel books, which were really more like edited collections with brief new introductions and essays, appealed to his vanity and the ever-pressing time constraints.

Working with the venerable New York publishing firm Simon and Schuster, Marvel published a series called "Marvel Fireside Books" that were written or edited by Lee and comprised of short essays and reprints of many superhero and villain origin stories. Between 1974 and the end of 1979, some eleven Fireside Books were published, ranging from the launch of *Origins of Marvel Comics* (September 1974) to *Marvel's Greatest Superhero Battles* (November 1978).

Readers delighted in the Fireside series because it gave them a relatively inexpensive and convenient method for digging into the birth of the Marvel Universe (*Origins* cost $11.95 in hardcover, while a book on Silver Surfer ran $7.95). Until that time, they had to rely on reprint issues or tracking down old copies. According to a Marvel internal document from May 1978, the series sold well, listing the following sales figures: *Origins* (one hundred sixty thousand sold), *Son of Origins of Marvel Comics* (one hundred thousand), *Bring on the Bad Guys: Origins of Marvel Comics Villains* (seventy thousand), and 1978's *How to Draw Comics the Marvel Way*, coauthored with artist John Buscema (twenty thousand hardcover alone).[25] Lee worked on these titles in the evenings, after he finished the *Spider-Man* and *Vera Valiant* newspaper work and his many other writing commitments.[26]

In 1977, Lee edited one of the titles in the Fireside series, *The Superhero Women*, a book of essays and reprints of comics featuring female heroines and villains, including Wasp, Red Sonja, and Medusa. The book addressed the issues regarding women in superhero comics, a mounting concern during the era. Lee explained that Marvel never had a policy about creating books for male versus female readers, instead crafting stories "savored by anyone who loves fantasy and adventure."[27] Yet, over the years, Lee had attempted to build readership for female superheroes and kept a close eye on subsequent sales figures. His interest seemed to go beyond circulation numbers to a genuine concern for attracting female readers.

Although not considered revolutionary when it came to writing and publishing books for female readers, Lee had great success writing *Millie the Model* and its many offshoots, as well as other titles aimed at girls and young women. When he and Kirby brought back superheroes to the Marvel line, he had made the Fantastic Four's Susan Storm an interesting character with real power, not just a weak sidekick or stereotypical girlfriend figure. Still, female superheroes were not always progressive. Wasp, for example, spent most of her time in early *Avengers* comics gushing over the dreamy Thor and basically flirting with all the male stars, despite her seemingly serious relationship with Henry Pym.

In response to criticisms about the role of heroines, what Lee might explain is that the comic book industry was almost exclusively driven by sales figures in the 1960s and 1970s. Circulation numbers determined which titles were published and those that stuck around, particularly when Marvel's primary competitor controlled its entire distribution cycle. Books that didn't sell could not take up a valuable spot on the limited roster.

The Fireside books were one part of the Cadence strategy in the decade, but it also pursued another lineup of books designed to entice younger readers, such as *The Mighty Marvel Superheroes Fun Book* (1976) and *Marvel Mazes to Drive You Mad* (1978). These included a series of coloring books, activity pads, and even a Marvel cookbook, along with a number of calendars that booksellers could use to entice readers to buy more products. Marvel even constructed special sales racks designed specifically for its books and collections. The 1977 display featured a three-sided, color riser card designed by Lee. The launch of the Spider-Man and Hulk books was timed to the release of the live-action television series featuring the Marvel heroes.[28]

Lee's writing schedule as publisher juggled the Fireside books along with the daily efforts centered on approving merchandise and advertising copy, as well as the comic books themselves. In addition, he wrote a "Publisher's Perspective" column each month for Cadence's *Celebrity* magazine and continued to author the Soapbox essays. As outside production companies worked on the live-action adaptations, Lee also had a hand in the process as "consulting editor or associate producer," mainly to "read all those scripts and give opinions."[29]

Other writing projects also took up time as Lee worked on books outside the Marvel Universe. In 1979, *Stan Lee Presents the Best of the Worst* came out. An odd conglomeration of illustrations, pithy facts, and Lee's irreverent humor, *Best of the Worst* drew from Lee's previous work on Goodman's humor and men's magazine lines. For example, Lee identified Australian William Gold as "The Worst Writer," who wrote fifteen books over eighteen years, but only sold one article to a Canberra newspaper, earning a whopping fifty cents. Lee's primary contribution was a sentence after the narrative, joking: "Probably after lengthy negotiations."[30]

After relinquishing the editor-in-chief position at Marvel, Lee was still spreading himself thin. Yet, from another perspective, he enjoyed the freedom from being chained to the editor's desk. Plus, like other celebrities, Lee had to maximize his efforts at monetizing his fame. He explained: "People feel comic books make millions and millions of dollars, but there are many years when the companies have literally lost money . . . it's not a case of everybody's pocketing millions and just trampling on the poor artists and writers."[31] Given the freedom to take on additional work outside the strictures of Marvel, Lee jumped at the chance.

The animation work that had kicked off in the late 1960s and come together in the early 1970s continued later in the decade. In 1978, an animated series called *The New Fantastic Four* appeared. Both Lee and Thomas wrote many of the scripts. However, the show was the final nail in the coffin of the Lee-Kirby relationship and the King's days at Marvel. Although Lee had been able to lure Kirby back to Marvel in 1975, the artist had an uneasy relationship with Goodman and still held a grudge against his cocreator for numerous slights (many real and many imagined). According to Kirby biographer Mark Evanier, "He was sick of the business" and wanted out, if only he could think of a different way to earn a living.[32]

Perhaps the magic had ended for Lee and Kirby, or maybe the King couldn't stomach any additional snubs, but his final stint at Marvel seemed more or less doomed from the start. He decided against renewing his contract, which would have limited his rights of ownership to past work under copyright and failed to address other issues he had with Goodman. Instead, in 1978, he accepted an offer to serve as an artist for the new animated *Fantastic Four* series. First with Hanna-Barbera, then with the DePatie-Freleng studio, which ultimately made the *FF* show, Kirby found colleagues who deeply respected his work, bosses that cared for him, and enough money to get him away from the comic book publishers.

Jack and Stan had a notoriously rocky relationship, but their combined legacy of successes enabled them to cover the animosity with a patchwork of excuses. Once the final schism occurred, they would never really mend it. They ignored the issues that caused the fallout and got along well enough on the *FF* animated series to actually team up on one more go at *Silver Surfer*, a graphic novel version released in 1978.

Kirby spent a great deal of his later years blaming Lee for the problems he had with Marvel executives and others, just as he had insinuated back in 1941 that Lee had squealed on him and Simon when they were moonlighting for DC. It is not difficult to imagine Kirby nursing that wound for more than thirty years. Though loving and kind to those around him and his family, the King had a long memory for professional slights and constant feelings that his work was underappreciated.

Certainly Kirby could be cantankerous, and no one doubted his amazing work ethic, but there is also another side to the artist that is rarely highlighted: his quarrels with artistic partners and subsequent feuds or minifeuds that would ensue. Kirby and Lee both developed acolytes and critics over their long careers. Some insiders with little or no skin in Kirby's long-term reputation, however, have weighed in on the topic. George Kashdan, a longtime DC writer and editor, explains, "Kirby always had fallouts with friends." He remembers, "Once, we were having lunch together, and he talked about his falling out with Joe Simon."[33] He and Simon would later politely disagree about much of Captain America's origin and who deserved credit for the character. Later, Kirby would unleash on Lee, essentially attempting to diminish or remove him completely from the creative process and take all the credit for the Marvel lineup.

The time Kirby spent in Hollywood seemed to rejuvenate him. He worked with young artists who were admirers of his art or had grown up emulating him. And he received a salary and benefits that were commensurate with his status as one of the industry's titans. Kirby later hooked up with Ruby-Spears Productions, which enabled him to do work on the animated *Thundarr the Barbarian* (1980–1981). They loved his work and gave him the title "Producer," which he cherished.[34]

Where Marvel could have used more Lee-Kirby magic in the era was in live-action programming. Reporters salivated in 1975 when Lee announced that a *Spider-Man* movie was imminent, though one wire service didn't take comic books or Lee all that seriously, calling him "the man behind Spidey and a horde of other weirdos found in Marvel Comics." Later, the writer dubs comics "flaky," and filled with "kinky dialogue." Lee, always working to expand the idea that comic books crossed age boundaries, told the reporter: "The books combine humor for college kids with action and adventure for the little ones." Despite the publicity and media response, however, the proposed *Spider-Man* flick never materialized.[35]

In 1977, when *Spider-Man* debuted as a live-action television series, Lee was horrified. "It was so juvenile. Spider-Man had no personality and no humor," the character's cocreator explained. "It was one-dimensional." The challenge for anyone hoping to adapt Marvel characters using actors was that the technology did not really exist that enabled them to really seem larger than life. Lee found the adaptations bland and far less sophisticated than the comic books themselves.[36]

Live-action *Spider-Man* seemed to work, however, in "Spidey Super Stories" on the PBS children's television program *The Electric Company*. Designed to help kids learn to read (dancer Danny Seagren donned the iconic costume), the short skits first aired in the 1974–1975 season and made the program a "must see" for kids who couldn't get enough of the superhero. The writing mimicked Lee's, but Spider-Man never actually spoke. His words appeared in comic-like word balloons, which served as the hook for getting children to practice reading.

Most of the web slinger's stories on *The Electric Company* were silly romps. The show's mainstay actors, such as Morgan Freeman and Luis Avalos, played a variety of odd villains and supporting characters, as well as narrating the action, since the hero remained silent. Running about a dozen skits each season for three years, a typical encounter had Spidey battling the Birthday Bandit, a villain who talks in a rhyming, sing-song voice (the narrator calls him "that foe of fun and festivity") in a playfully colored suit adorned with a cummerbund and top hat who steals from children's birthday parties. After a cake-smashing episode and some fisticuffs that gets cake smeared on Spider-Man's costume, the hero fights off the villain, eventually snaring the bandit in a web, and thus saving the day. In keeping with the Lee playfulness, the final panel is a drawing of Spidey at a laundromat covered with a blanket while sitting in a chair, waiting for his costume to wash. The skit theme song ends with a brassy horn section. The singer wails: "Nobody knows who you are."

As 1979 drew to a close, Marvel's internal woes were played out in the pages of the *New York Times*. Drawing on anonymous interviews and extensive insider perspectives, writer N. R. Kleinfield presented the comic book division as a dysfunctional outfit that pitted editors against writers and artists against management. The days of Lee's Merry Marvel Bullpen and the singsong nicknames seemed like a distant past.

The reporter placed much of the blame at the doorstep of Jim Shooter, labeling him "power-thirsty." Shooter, who began his comic book career at the precocious age of thirteen, writing for DC, was either loved or hated by the Marvel staff. Some accused the imposing six-foot, eight-inch writer/editor of having an ego even larger than he was. A group of Marvel staffers harbored jealousies because he took the reins as a twenty-something when they believed an insider with more seniority should inherit the role.

Other unnamed company executives were considered, who were "more interested in coining money from licensing deals than they are in the superheroes."[37] Roy Thomas sided with the creative teams, calling Marvel both "callous" and "inhuman."[38] The article revealed the deep mistrust between the comic book editorial side of the operations and the rest of the company, many of whom simply wanted to exploit the characters for licensing and all the product marketing they could muster. While creative teams wanted to focus on craft, the corporate heads demanded profits. The age-old battle between inspiration and capitalism waged on at Marvel.

All of Lee's stored-up goodwill with the public and the other artists and writers kept him out of the direct firing line. In the article, Kleinfield called Lee a "creative genius" made famous by "inventing heroes" that had realistic life challenges. But, an anonymous writer pointed out some sour grapes at Marvel HQ directed at the old boss, chiding Lee because he "wants to be like Walt Disney" and views comic books as "sort of beneath him."[39]

Even as revered as he remained, Lee could not deflect all the heat stirred up in the late 1970s, as the comic book industry felt the squeeze from television and a smaller target demographic. Baby boomers had carried the industry in the early and mid-1960s, but were aging out of their fascination with the medium. In addition, many longtime fans thought that the comics simply weren't as good.

In response, the industry's two heavy-hitters—DC Comics and Marvel—both cut back on monthly titles (Marvel from more than forty down to thirty-two). Each brought in more money via licensing deals than in the comics that its heroes appeared in. Lee told the *Times* that he felt the new in-house licensing division might have ruffled feathers, since some artists and writers had to turn their attention to that part of the business. "It used to be that the only artists in the place were drawing the strips," he explained. "Now we have artists who have to draw box tops."[40] The nightmare scenario for comic book purists had come true—the Spider-Man lunchboxes and bath towels were now more important to the corporation that owned Marvel than the comic books that ran the superhero stories.

Both DC and Marvel faced declining circulation across the decade, so each determined that quantity would make up for the losses. Overall sales grew, but the standing of the entire industry seemed less stable. Prior to the cutbacks, the two market leaders published dozens of new titles in a vain attempt at profitability. In 1979, Marvel's operating income was a measly $1.5 million after sales that exceeded $23 million.[41] In this kind of tight financial pinch, Lee's Hollywood deal making held endless potential if the company could deliver a hit or build up its licensing business. The traditional notion that comic books drove licensing deals was flipped on its head. Clearly, the big two of Marvel and DC were licensing agencies first, because that drove profits.

Depending on one's perspective, the end of the 1970s could have been a total downer or the beginning of something big for Lee. The era contained elements of both sentiments for him. On one hand, as Marvel publisher, he earned over $150,000 a year and had steady added income from college lectures and working on television projects (he was paid separately for this work). Fans mobbed him at comic book conventions and college students cheered thunderously when he appeared on campus. They packed tightly around him, just to inch a little closer to the man who created their heroes and essentially provided a central narrative of their young lives.

Even with so many avenues going in his direction, however, Lee chafed at the thought that he couldn't get out of comic books. He really wanted to make it in Hollywood. Although the superhero craze had lasted more than a decade and Lee delighted in the characters he cocreated, he fully expected the genre to fade into oblivion. Increasingly, he faced more than a little regret when he spoke about his career, explaining to a reporter: "I would have liked to make movies, to be a director or a screenwriter, to have a job like Norm Lear or Freddie Silverman. I'd like to be doing what I'm doing here, but in a bigger arena."[42] Although a celebrity in his own right and a downright hero to fans globally, Lee couldn't shake the notion that he could be doing more.

As Lee searched for additional outlets for his superheroes, the effort increasingly brought him to Hollywood, the great American dream factory. As he envisioned the next phase of his career, he looked West to California's golden shores.

CHAPTER 12

LURE OF HOLLYWOOD

Whether it was hearing the Lone Ranger cry "Hi-Yo, Silver! Away!" or the sound of air rushing by as Superman flew through the skies, the early history of television is intimately entwined with superheroes and comic books. While comics could take readers inside the minds of the characters in ways that film couldn't, something about actually seeing the live-action superhero on the screen gave fans a different kind of thrill.

The popularity of televised superheroes often pushed the comic book trade into boom and bust cycles that usually had little to do with the quality of the comics or who produced them. The volatility would drive most people batty. Both the *Superman* and *Batman* television shows caused surges in comic book sales in the 1950s and late 1960s. Looking at the television landscape and recalling those two phenomenally popular programs, Marvel executives, including Cadence president Jim Galton, wondered why their company couldn't replicate these successes in the 1970s, particularly given that it had replaced longtime rival DC as the industry leader in sales.

The fight for sales supremacy between the comic book giants had taken decades to win. Galton and other leaders wanted to capitalize on the victory by establishing a stronger foothold on the West Coast. They also wanted to use the television momentum to show film studios that superheroes could carry feature films. These endeavors would be more lucrative for Cadence and counterbalance the cyclical nature of the print division.

The timing for Lee neared perfection. Searching for new ways to attract audiences, he did what so many Americans had done before him: looked across the country to the golden shores of California.

By the end of the 1970s, he had been in comic book publishing for forty years. Now in his late fifties, he hoped to reinvigorate his career, just as he had a decade before when he faced throngs of college readers on campuses across the nation. Galton, who had a great relationship with his publisher, schemed with Lee to propose that the company buy a Hollywood production studio. When the television networks started showing interest in Marvel's superheroes in animation and live-action, Lee was sent west to plot their course.

Although Lee's superheroes revolutionized popular culture and were read by fanatics worldwide, he left for Los Angeles in an odd position. He was already a big name, a celebrity in his own right, which made it difficult (if not impossible) for him to learn the business from the ground up. Lee had the mighty Marvel content behind him, which would open many doors, but it simultaneously raised expectations on the part of his bosses that the path to success would be straightforward. Lee also was used to calling the shots, as he had with Marvel since his teen years. Hollywood simply did not work that way. Lee had to convince skeptical television executives that Marvel's heroes would translate to live-action programming and that adult viewers would tune in.

Yet the winds of change were already set in motion. In addition to Marvel's ascension to the top of the comic book world and Lee's pervasive influence on popular culture as a result, science fiction and fantasy films and television shows had become incredibly popular. On the small screen, *The Six Million Dollar Man* (1974–1978) proved that audiences would respond to a superhero-like lead character. Steve Austin (played by Lee Majors) developed into a pop culture phenomenon, spawning comic books (featuring artwork by Lee's friends Howard Chaykin and Neal Adams), albums, and action figures. The spinoff *The Bionic Woman* (1976–1978) expanded the cyborg adventures, this time featuring the lead female Jaime Sommers (actress Lindsay Wagner). Her popularity also meant a merchandise line, ranging from an action figure to a board game to a lunchbox, which became a must-have item for elementary school kids.

The late 1960s had also helped pave the way for superhero and science fiction narratives among mainstream audiences. In 1968, for example, the films *2001: A Space Odyssey* and *Planet of the Apes* thrilled audiences and generated strong box-office returns. These films reinforced the new style of storytelling that audiences demanded, as well as set the stage for science fiction and fantasy aimed at adults. Later, a film like *Logan's Run* (1976) demonstrated how fantasy content could be enhanced by innovative technology and special effects. In 1977, George Lucas's *Star Wars* showed film and television executives, as well as people around the world, the vitality of science fiction and fantasy. Didn't Luke Skywalker, after all, seem like a futuristic version of Spider-Man, an outsider who must deal with possessing extraordinary powers? A year later, the mighty *Superman* would fly into theaters, also blowing audiences' minds. Movies like these proved that innovative filmmaking technology could power fantastic plots and characters. Special effects were finally catching up with the imaginations of writers and artists, opening doors for science fiction and fantasy projects on screens both large and small. The time was ripe for comic book characters to make the transition.

Lee spent time crisscrossing the nation, attempting to keep his fingers on the pulse of the comic book division, but increasingly focusing on getting Marvel further established in television and film. He viewed Los Angeles as "Nirvana," a celestial utopia that would enable him to launch a new career path in his late-fifties without having to discard all that he had done to that point.[1] The trepidation of leaving New York City, basically his home for his entire life, got swept away in a sea of excitement about the work he would be doing and the sheer magnificence of the West Coast: the warm breezes blowing off the Pacific Ocean and the hidden enclaves surrounded by thick woods and hillsides.

The move from print to television seemed natural in a world increasingly dominated by images and movement. Lee called the Marvel style "a very cinematic approach" that married dialogue and art.[2] A flurry of activity in Los Angeles and deals with several networks and production companies gave Marvel a lift. However, some of the resulting television shows did not live up to Lee's standards. Others didn't quite catch on with viewers. Hollywood studio executives and the teams of writers, directors, and producers underestimated the importance of Lee's style and voice in making Marvel superheroes iconic. Honestly, they felt that they could get it right themselves, since they were the experts, or could at least duplicate what they understood as pithy banter and human pathos. For movie and television leaders, Marvel characters were "properties" to be turned into content that would sell. The soul of the superheroes and what turned fans into rapid consumers of Marvel content often died in the translation.

On the surface, many of Lee's characters seemed a natural fit for live-action television. However, it was one of the least likely—the green-skinned, raging behemoth Hulk—that made it to the screen. Former Mr. Universe Lou Ferrigno, a six-foot, five-inch, 285-pound mass of rippling muscles, played the lead character. Veteran television actor Bill Bixby played mild-mannered physician and scientist David Banner (series writers changed his first name from Lee's original "Bruce"). Critics speculated about the show's popularity, usually deducing that it was a mix of women gawking at Ferrigno and the overall tenor that played to adult sensibilities, rather than a youth audience. Producer Ken Johnson explained the tone to a reporter, saying, "We've tried to make it an adult show that kids are allowed to watch." The writers purposely played down the "camp" elements, Johnson said. We "try to keep it as straight and honest as possible."[3] For his part, Lee enjoyed the adaptation, noting the quality of the acting and story changes the television team made so that the superhero would appeal to an older audience.

Some commentators speculated that many adult viewers took pleasure in seeing a character let loose when angered and go into a rage. Lee identified with the cathartic impulse, saying, "We'd all like to 'Hulk out' sometimes. Nobody pushed the Hulk around, and people can identify with that."[4] The show was a surprise hit in the United States, but even bigger in the United Kingdom, where it reached number one. Perhaps in the 1970s the British had a stronger desire to "Hulk out" than Americans. Ultimately, it would be the most successful live-action Marvel property for decades to come.

CBS also brought Spider-Man, Doctor Strange (changed to "Dr. Strange"), and Captain America to the small screen. *The Amazing Spider-Man* starred Nicholas Hammond as Peter Parker, running sporadically on CBS for two seasons. *Dr. Strange*, featuring Peter Hooten, debuted as a television film/pilot in September 1978, while *Captain America* also came out as a TV film, starring Reb Brown as the title hero.

Of the three productions, *Spider-Man* had the greatest success in terms of viewers. Demonstrating how pervasive Spidey was in popular culture, the pilot earned a 30-share Nielsen rating, the network's highest rating for 1978. CBS execs worried, though, that the movie did not do well in the important eighteen-to-forty-nine-year-old demographic. They hedged their bet on the superhero and only picked up a five-episode run to gauge if it might garner more viewers from that group (running in April and May 1978). The series debut also did well in the ratings, winning the week for CBS and placing in the top ten overall. Although it eventually placed in the top twenty for the season, network officials perceived it as a show aimed at younger audiences.

Fans tuned into the live-action *Spider-Man*, but Lee hated it, criticizing the series because it "looked silly . . . juvenile, comic-booky." He had run-ins with producer Daniel R. Goodman, claiming that the series should be aimed at adults. "Spider-Man was a TV series for a while, and it was terrible. Just dreadful. It had no personality. No humor. None of the ingredients it should have had."[5] In a bind, CBS ordered seven episodes for the next season, and then aired them in mishmash fashion, usually against ratings juggernauts on the competing networks. New producer Lionel Siegel took over and made changes, downplaying Spidey's superpowers and adding a female love interest. Despite solid ratings, CBS officials axed the show after the second season. They feared the network was being typecast for having so many superhero programs.

Lee disliked the *Spider-Man* series, calling it "terrible" because it didn't have the "Marvel pacing" that had made the comic book a best seller for decades. The aspects of the superhero's life as Peter Parker and Spider-Man just weren't captured in the CBS show, and then the network more or less gave up on it. But when it came to the *Captain America* movie, Lee could barely contain himself, declaring it an "abomination."[6] Each of the television shows that made it to air deviated widely from the overriding concept that Lee and his cocreators had established when they constructed the Marvel Universe.

Shuttling back and forth between the coasts, Lee shuddered at the way Hollywood fiddled with the superheroes as if they were afterthoughts to plug into the network lineups. Many creative types on the West Coast carried the same elitist ideas that Lee had encountered most of his career—thinking that superheroes were kid stuff and that adults wouldn't respond unless there were heavy doses of romantic intrigue added to the story lines. The countless issues sold over the last two decades and the billions of times Marvel comic books had been read and passed around by a generation and a half of readers could not convince Hollywood that superheroes would succeed as adult fare. While the studio heads and creative teams wanted to meet the famous creator of the Marvel Universe, securing contracts with the studios was another matter altogether.

Lee's carnival-barker banter in his Soapbox columns and college lectures helped promote Marvel, but this over-the-top approach didn't translate well in Los Angeles. Lee made it a habit of announcing deals and hyping his production work, which drove anticipation, but backfired when a project became mired in preproduction or later fizzled completely.

Lee had to answer to many people, including his bosses back at Cadence, as well as work to establish himself as an independent entity apart from his famous characters. All the while, he had to separate the genuine meetings from the ones that took place simply because a director or producer who had grown up reading Marvel books wanted to meet a childhood hero.

Marvel's West Coast operation needed to demonstrate progress, so Lee and his team started piecing together deals. They worked with NBC to bring the *Silver Surfer* graphic novel he did with Kirby to television. Then ABC made noise about developing a Spider-Woman show. Soon, another twelve characters, including Thor, Daredevil, and Doctor Strange, were optioned to Universal.

But as the announcements about new projects piled up, they also served as a kind of ball and chain, because many deals—like so many in Hollywood—simply dissolved. Lee's frustrations with the Hollywood process mounted. Deal after deal fell through, which left him deflated: "We've been working with other production companies, and I have to go along with what they want to do. It's just taking forever to come up with a story that everyone agrees on."[7]

Lee's perpetual challenge during his early years in Hollywood circled back to the same encounter over and over again. He could not close the kind of deal that would make him and Marvel major players on the Hollywood scene. Almost cyclically, it seemed, Lee would draw media attention and then list a plethora of potential projects, but few ever saw the light of day. Even worse, some that did bombed horribly because the script had problems, the production company did not understand the character's appeal, or the technology did not exist to make the hero seem heroic or powerful enough. "There is no way of ever predicting which the networks will buy and which they won't," Lee lamented.[8]

The never-ending series of meetings also severely disrupted Lee's time to actually write. "Out here, you get an idea for a movie and years later, you're still trying to get it on the screen," Lee explained. "Here, it is much more big business. There are contracts and negotiations and turnarounds. I find that a little frustrating, because I like to move fast and write fast."[9] Movie studios and publishing companies approached him about writing scripts and novels, he recalls, but he couldn't find the "few months off" that this kind of work required. Life in L.A. seemed a kind of vicious cycle of meetings, talks, deals, and waiting around. Lee spent more time talking about creativity than producing anything creative.

Despite his general frustration with the Hollywood process, the idea of physically moving to Hollywood appealed to Lee. Ironically, DC's film success helped him and Joanie get to Los Angeles on a full-time basis. In 1978, the Warner Bros. *Superman* film starring Christopher Reeve as the Man of Steel thrilled audiences and influential film critic Roger Ebert gave the movie a strong review. Viewers responded—the film earned $300 million in its initial release. The hit movie, combined with the popularity of *The Incredible Hulk* on television, seemed to make the time ripe for more superhero programming. Lee convinced his bosses at Marvel to allow him to set up an office on the West Coast.

In a May 1979 letter to his friend, eminent French New Wave filmmaker Alain Resnais, Lee wrote about his "love" for Los Angeles and his hope that he might "be able to infiltrate into the TV and movie business." He also mentioned a potential deal with Lee Kramer, a producer and the manager/boyfriend of popular singer and actress Olivia Newton-John, to make a big budget Silver Surfer movie.[10]

Lee spent most of the year working in Los Angeles, while dreaming about moving there permanently. "The fact was that I had fallen in love with L.A. during my many trips," he explained.[11] But he hadn't fully convinced Joanie that it was the right move. Later, she warmed to the idea, chiefly after the Lee's apartment in New York was robbed and all of her jewelry and other valuables were stolen. Lee called it, "the most depressing and distressing thing imaginable." They both viewed Hollywood as a new start. Lee did try to put on a brave face for his friend, joking in the letter that Alain and his wife, Flo, should "Lock up your jewelry!"[12]

By July 1979, Lee's work to get to L.A. picked up steam. Attempting to adapt the Marvel Method to movies, he dictated the plot for a film about a witch who only kills bad guys, called *The Night of the Witch*, into a tape machine. Independent filmmaker Lloyd Kaufman (who would later score with the hit cult film *The Toxic Avenger*) transcribed the tapes and then worked the material into a full script. Kaufman had met Lee while a Marvel-obsessed student at Yale University. The young man later cofounded Troma Entertainment, a low-budget studio that mixed comedy, screwball antics, and horror into reasonably successful, midnight movies. The two continued to collaborate for years. *The Night of the Witch* got picked up for a meager $500, but never went into development.[13] Later, they put together another Lee idea, pitching it directly to Resnais. Titled *The Man Who Talked to God*, the director did not option the treatment.

Despite his legendary status as the cocreator of iconic superheroes, Lee was really just a fledgling scriptwriter and he didn't really have the time to write full scripts himself, which put him at the mercy of other writers who would craft a full treatment from his ideas. In the early 1970s, he had teamed with Resnais to option a couple of scripts, but in the intervening years he couldn't find the time.

It made sense for Lee to work with other writers to piece together his ideas. The process fit his frenetic style. What often emerged, though, remained a level removed and did not really capture Lee's Marvel voice or style. It seemed as if he became too committed to the Marvel Method without finding a writer the equivalent of a Kirby or Ditko to fulfill his vision.

When Lee finally convinced his Cadence bosses that he needed to be in California full time, he opened a little shop in the San Fernando Valley. Announced in mid-1980, Lee set up Marvel Productions in a little flat building at 4610 Van Nuys Boulevard in Sherman Oaks, which Lee described as a "mini-Pentagon built around a lush garden atrium."[14] In true Lee spirit, he established an aggressive pace and worked hard, attempting to live up to the "Excelsior" sign hanging on the office door. A lifelong New Yorker, Lee relished the sunshine of L.A. People thought he was crazy because he would go out into the atrium and work in the sunlight. What a difference from cold, gray New York City and Marvel's Madison Avenue office.

A handful of executives who had experience in television and film joined Lee in the new venture, thus balancing his relative newcomer status. David H. DePatie, a longtime animation veteran who had worked on several Dr. Seuss specials and won an Oscar for a Pink Panther short, served as president of Marvel Productions. DePatie brought along Lee Gunther as vice president of production. When the company announced the studio's formation, it noted that the group already had begun a number of animated and live-action projects, including commercials for Oscar Mayer and Owens-Corning.[15]

Lee yearned to land a blockbuster film deal, but his initial mission centered on expanding the Marvel universe and following up with other potential opportunities, like the commercials and new licensing agreements. Under Cadence's new management structure, Lee added the formal title of "vice president, creative affairs" to his publisher role. The rather nebulous title fit Lee's vague duties on the West Coast.

Galton discussed how each piece strengthened the whole, explaining that the studio would "contribute to the success of our licensees, our wholesalers, our advertisers." He recognized that the "future for Marvel has never looked better," particularly given "all the benefits to be reaped from the formation."[16] Lee's marching orders included pursuing numerous projects, while also continuing to champion Marvel in person and via the press.

In 1979, *Time* magazine speculated that Lee deserved most of the kudos for turning television into "one big electronic comic book," declaring he was "chiefly responsible" for the trend. The reporter speculated that CBS had so many comic book shows on the air that the company name might be changed to "Comic Book Supplier."[17] The hype for the shows outlived the quality, however, and all the live-action programs outside of the Bixby/Ferrigno *Hulk* gave Lee headaches.

Marvel Productions had actually been established to focus on animation, particularly with DePatie at the helm. The company believed that animated Saturday morning cartoons were a better fit for Marvel at the time. Lee's negotiations with the networks focused on "ability, the capability, the know-how and the dependability," he explained, while DePatie's credentials helped overcome the networks' reticence.[18]

Within a couple years, Marvel Productions teamed with other producers, such as Fred Silverman, to get shows created, particularly on subjects outside the Marvel Universe. The partnership resulted in *Meatballs and Spaghetti*, which ran in the CBS Saturday morning programming block. The series featured the escapades of a married singing duo who wander around the country in a mobile home. CBS also picked up *Dungeons and Dragons*, a Marvel production based on the popular dice role-playing game.[19]

In the early 1980s, Lee expanded his participation in the *Spider-Man* and *Hulk* animated series by serving as script consultant and narrator. Fans loved hearing Lee's actual voice, but he found the experience somewhat frustrating, because he couldn't change what he said based on timing. Still, he tried to "make the bits of narration sound like my own style."[20] The *Hulk* show did not last as long, because although the green giant remained popular with boys, the program couldn't generate interest among young girls.

While the ups-and-downs of the television and film industries bedeviled Lee, particularly when his career producing comic books had centered on speed and teamwork, he had greater inroads and success in merchandising and licensing Marvel's superheroes. This area may not have been the most glamorous part of Lee's Hollywood work, but the kinds of deals he spearheaded were essential in broadening the Marvel brand. Creating tie-in opportunities pushed the characters deeper into the consumer psyche, while also giving Lee a chance to discuss his favorite cause— getting audiences aware of the benefits of comic books in literacy education.

To get corporate leaders excited about Marvel, Lee unleashed demographic information that revealed that the nation's two hundred twenty-five million comics appealed to an audience ranging from ages six to seventeen, comprising about 40 percent girls and 60 percent boys. Some 60 percent of comic book readers were from middle- and upper-income families. Lee boasted that 92 percent of the youngsters in this age bracket read comic books. Moreover, while Lee spoke at industry conferences, actors dressed up as Marvel superheroes, which the company also offered on rental for mall openings, parades, conventions, and state and county fairs.[21]

The attempt to lure female readers led to the introduction of She-Hulk, followed by the Dazzler and plans for additional super-powered heroines. The first issue of the *Savage She-Hulk* #1 (February 1980) sold a quarter of a million copies. Lee told a reporter, "We've always wanted to do books about females," yet he admitted that profits drove editorial decisions, saying, "But for years, we were never able to make any of our female characters sell well."[22] Unfortunately, like so many other attempts at female superheroes, *She-Hulk* only lasted two years, ending its run in February 1982.

By the mid- to late 1980s, Lee had completely distanced himself from the day-to-day events back in New York, despite several fancy titles, like "vice-president of creative affairs for Marvel Productions," that made it seem like he was still in the loop. Actually, Michael Z. Hobson, Cadence vice president in charge of publishing took over most of Lee's publisher responsibilities. Lee spent time writing scripts and treatments, keeping an eye on the work created for Marvel's animated productions, and shepherding potential deals with numerous production companies. He barely even read the company's comics, admitting, "Sometimes they stack up so high, I only have a chance to flip through them."[23]

Although purposely staying at arm's length from the print division, Lee never backed off his role as Marvel's full-time spokesman, though he did up his speaking fee to $3,000 to give colleges less incentive to book him.[24] When the Hollywood efforts forced him off the college campus lecture circuit, he upped his attendance at big-ticket events, like comic conventions, as well as his appearances on television and radio programs. The influx of cable television channels and the growing radio industry gave Lee more opportunities to reach audiences. For talk show hosts and radio deejays, Lee was routinely a stellar guest. Years of practice had honed his skills, so he offered great sound bites, as well as the tried-and-true, seemingly timeless stories about superhero origins. Lee had a knack for making each host or caller feel as if no one had ever asked him which superhero he liked best or if he had a single favorite comic book issue.

In 1984, prior to appearing at the New York City Dimension Convention, Lee did a radio interview, boasting that comic books were at that time "far bigger than they've ever been," citing Marvel's role in creating "a fan following for comic books, that never existed twenty or thirty years ago."[25] He also noted the connection between the collecting craze, the rise of independent comic book shops, and the intense fandom that Marvel had created over the years.

While Lee entertained fans that called in to the radio show with questions about changes in Spider-Man's costume and how much old comics might be worth, the episode also revealed why many people grew angry with Lee over the years regarding the origins of the superhero characters. In the frenzied pace of television and radio programming, hosts and others who were not experts in comic book history and had no stake in it would take shortcuts to save time, like calling Lee the "creator of such characters as . . ." without attributing the cocreator status to the artists. The interviewers simply did not have the background to understand, but what about Lee's responses? Should he have corrected or added information within the context of the appearance or let it slide? Sometimes he did and sometimes not. On the one hand, correcting the interviewer diverted time and attention, potentially leading to an awkward situation. But not mentioning the artists generated animosity among those in the know. Lee constantly balanced an on-air role that mixed spokesperson, provocateur, pitchman, historian, and actor—and in doing so, may have sacrificed truth for the sake of showmanship and audience entertainment.

In 1986, Lee wrote a long essay, "Spidey and Me," for a book that collected a number of his *Spider-Man* newspaper strips: *The Best of Spider-Man*. While the piece describes the character and revisits the origin story, it is also a kind of mini-autobiography. Lee admitted that his own ideas slipped into the strip, explaining, "I feel that it's as difficult for writers to keep their own personal convictions out of what they write as it is for people in general to keep their personal thoughts . . . out of what they say in conversation."[26] Moreover, Lee wrote at length that each character "is really me. . . . I'm every single one of them . . . [but] Spider-Man is practically my autobiography."[27]

Lee dedicated three days a week—Saturday, Sunday, and Wednesday—to writing projects, while leaving the other four days for business meetings and strategy sessions. Just as he did in New York, he wrote outside, covering his word processor with a cardboard contraption of his own devising so that the glare didn't blind him and the West Coast sun didn't melt the various moving parts. Lee kept up his seven-days-a-week schedule, feeling that the move to Los Angeles "served to keep the creative juices flowing." In an environment where everyone is dedicated to creativity, "I find myself 'thinking story' almost twenty-four hours a day."[28]

As Lee settled into his Hollywood role, Cadence Industries sold Marvel for $46 million in November 1986 to New World Pictures, a film production company and distributor that wanted to pair its TV and film efforts with Marvel characters. Harry Sloan, one of the partners who had purchased New World from director Roger Corman and his brother for $16.5 million three years earlier, told everyone who would listen that he believed the Marvel purchase would turn the company into a "mini-Disney."[29] Many at Marvel might have loved hearing such aspirational language, but Disney made its mark through film and merchandising, not publishing. What seemed like happy days might actually be a little portentous.

New World leaders, including chief executive Robert Rehme, welcomed Lee to the company and relocated him to a fancy new office in its Westwood headquarters. On the surface, they respected Lee. Several members of the board of directors asked for his autograph for themselves or their children. It seemed that he finally would get some of the admiration that he earned through his dedication to Marvel and the superhero genre, as well as creative control over them in the transition to television and film.[30] At the same time, though, there were conflicting reports that Rehme didn't really know Marvel from DC or the comic book business in general, confusing the two publishers (and their respective superheroes) when discussing the purchase with New World employees. Supposedly, when Rehme realized that New World bought Spider-Man, not Superman, he yelled: "Holy shit. We gotta stop this. Cannon has the Spider-Man movie."[31] Rehme didn't know the characters that well or read the comic books to find out, but he did push the company to pursue new ideas.

New World quickly sought to use superheroes in attention-grabbing ways, especially Spider-Man. The web slinger would soon be turned into a 9,522-cubic-foot helium balloon for the Macy's Thanksgiving Day Parade at a cost of $300,000.

Officials estimated that about eighty million viewers would see the televised parade each year, along with two million in person, so that marketing push would offset the initial expense. Next, company marketers decided to bring the character to life in the summer of 1987, having Spidey marry longtime sweetheart Mary Jane Watson at home plate in Shea Stadium before a sellout crowd of fifty-five thousand on hand to watch the world champion New York Mets.[32]

At the center of the spectacle, Lee played the role of justice of the peace presiding over the wedding ceremony. The event parlayed Lee's celebrity status and more or less rewarded him for coming up with the idea of having the pair wed in the daily newspaper strip (also replicated in the comic books). New World created a branding campaign for the live-action nuptials, getting Lee a morning television interview with popular newscasters Maria Shriver and Forrest Sawyer on *Good Morning America* and coverage on the nightly tabloid *Entertainment Tonight*. Countless newspapers around the country covered the marriage, getting the iconic character back into the national spotlight, not to mention its human creator. Lee worked tirelessly to provide a voice for the character to the myriad of journalists and broadcasters who wanted to chat about the event.

Despite the public relations successes and Marvel's ability to generate profits, New World limped along on a financial shoestring. The stock market collapse in late 1987 and the lackluster performance of its big-budget films left the company deeply in debt and exceedingly vulnerable in an age of corporate raiders who liked to buy up struggling companies and profit off the juiciest pieces of the carcass.

Lee, fixated on pitching superheroes to New World producers, was once again pushed to the sidelines. A New World insider reported: "Stan's not in the loop, because he's not a player; he's not a partner. He wasn't a vote. But he was like a pit bull. He just didn't want to walk away."[33] The internal politics took a turn for the worse for Lee, but no one realized how the company teetered on the edge of bankruptcy.

Gradually, the whole story would be revealed as a series of financial manipulations that led to New World putting Marvel on the chopping block. Many suitors took immediate interest, as long as Lee signed a deal to stay onboard. Eventually, Ronald O. Perelman, one of the biggest sharks in the capitalist seas, won the bid, putting up $82.5 million via a series of shell corporations.

Celebrating fifty years as a Marvel employee in 1989, Lee once more faced a new scenario, with chaos perhaps being the most consistent theme of those five decades. But, Stan had endured all the upheaval, based on a mix of tenacity and enthusiasm and his trump card—he symbolized the Marvel Universe for generations of fans. Lee was Marvel, no matter who actually owned the company, just as he became the father of superheroes to generations of readers and viewers, regardless of his actual role.

CHAPTER 13

MARVEL MANIPULATIONS

In 1989, as President Ronald Reagan and wife Nancy prepared to return to civilian life after eight long years in the White House, CBS *60 Minutes* reporter Mike Wallace interviewed the first couple just days before they left for their California ranch. The conversation touched on numerous topics, ranging from the strength of the Reagan's long marriage to the trying times they spent in the nation's capital. At one point, Wallace turned the discussion to an interesting but unrelated topic to give viewers a flavor of how the president lived a regular life, even while serving as the leader of the free world.

Wallace asked the president, "You read the comics in the morning?" Reagan then spoke about his morning routine, explaining that he first turned to the comics section, and then read the "serious stuff" to prepare for the day. Wallace revealed that *Spider-Man* was Reagan's favorite comic strip, while the president spoke about how much he loved to read and couldn't stand to be without a book at all times.[1] Reagan's critics may have joked that the syndicated *Spider-Man* comic may have been as much as Reagan could handle intellectually, but knowing that the president read his work gratified Lee, who had readily committed Spidey to a series of public service campaigns over the character's long history.

Reagan's admission that he read *Spider-Man* as he enjoyed his breakfast symbolized how influential the character, Marvel Comics, and Stan Lee had grown over the preceding decades. The leader of the free world started his day reading Lee's words! That kind of news could get just about anyone through another boring meeting with a film production company or the idea that yet another big-name Hollywood actor wanted to play a Marvel superhero. When the world found out that the president read Lee's strip, the writer had just turned sixty-six years old, but his exuberance matched that of someone half his age.

In the 1980s, Philadelphia native Ronald O. Perelman stood as one of the richest men in New York. Many considered him a leader with a King Midas touch, turning everything around him into gold. In an era characterized by financial jockeying, leveraged buyouts, and hostile takeovers, Perelman waged economic and corporate warfare with other tycoons in high-stakes chess matches with hundreds of millions of dollars hanging in the balance.

In early 1989, when New World Entertainment searched for a company to buy Marvel so that it could finance of fresh wave of television and film expansion, Perelman responded with an $82.5 million offer through MacAndrews & Forbes, a shell company that he owned in an intricate web of holding companies and parent firms that were all controlled by the billionaire. While Perelman served as the public face of the deal and put up about $10.5 million of his own money to finance the purchase, Chase Manhattan Bank actually took on most of the debt, a typical setup in the go-go capitalist takeover era.

Securing Marvel—including its iconic superhero characters and licensing rights—for less than $100 million seemed like a steal to many observers. The transaction seemed financially sound and potentially lucrative. "It is a mini-Disney in terms of intellectual property," Perelman explained. "We are now in the business of the creation and marketing of characters."[2] On paper, the mogul seemed potentially the right leader to turn Marvel into an international media powerhouse. He had a solid plan to push the company toward a global audience and build off some of the world's most recognizable characters. More importantly, Perelman had the resources and financial backing to build a team that could accomplish this goal.

Perelman took a chance on Marvel, because the comic book industry was riding a wave of resurgence in the late 1980s. But the financier knew the real money would come when he sold stocks in the company. Several factors merged to make its impending IPO (initial public offering) rewarding, ranging from a growing comic book store expansion to several aggressive price increases that seemed to push sales higher, rather than drive readers away. Simultaneously, comic books had transformed from cheap magazines to glossy, foil-covered collector's items. Subsequently, Marvel's sales per copy jumped over 30 percent year-over-year from the last half of 1989 to 1990.[3]

Overall, Marvel's sales in 1990 eclipsed $70 million, with an addition $11 million from licensing. While insiders like Perelman stood to get even richer at the IPO, outside investors had to determine the risk involved, given that profits stood at a meager $5.4 million in 1990. The figure rose as sales increased, but as recently as two years before they had only been $2.4 million.[4] Circulation and store sales were only one part of the Marvel puzzle, however. There were eighty companies that licensed Marvel characters and added to the earnings potential. The influx of technology at the time led to even more deals, including superhero-based video games and television and film productions on VHS.

For a financier like Perelman, turning a part of his far-reaching empire into the next Disney would create a legacy unmatched in the entertainment business. Critics, however, thought that he really meant to just hype his new purchase, gussying it up as a way of prepping parts of it for sale or other forms of financial exploitation. Certainly, Perelman's primary interest was fixed on making money, not reading *Spider-Man* comic books. In the quest to emulate Disney, corporate America's master empire builder, the company needed a strong film division, which it created with Marvel Films.

Bill Bevins, Perelman's top manager and former chief financial officer at Turner Broadcasting would run Marvel. He named Lee to head the new Marvel Films entity and surprised him by immediately tripling his salary. The move obviously pleased Lee, particularly after being marginalized by the Hollywood sharks at New World. In his view, Lee felt that he had received insufficient pay over the years. When Bevins announced the increase, it caught Lee off-guard. He even thought that he must have misheard his new boss. That evening he told Joanie about the exchange and admitted to her that he certainly must have been hearing things. The two of them spent the rest of the night trying to figure out what Bevins might have actually muttered. A couple weeks later, however, Joanie checked the mail. There was Stan's paycheck. When Joanie ripped it open and saw the figure, she nearly fell over. Lee's former salary had indeed been tripled. From that point forward, Lee had nothing but kind words for Bevins. More important than his own improved financial standing, though, Lee believed that the raise symbolized the way the new owners wanted to build Marvel into the kind of efficient corporation that could compete with any entertainment company in the world.

Lee's future looked bright. Once again he had the power to oversee Marvel's film and television expansion. He had long shared the notion that Marvel could transform into a modern Disney-like empire. Perhaps Perelman had the money and cachet to pull it off. Lee had never felt comfortable with the staff at New World. Perelman, ever on the prowl, would exact a bit of revenge several months later, buying New World outright when the company continued to slip. Now Lee had a larger playground to operate in as he attempted to build Marvel's live-action and animated business.

Lee's long relationship with Spider-Man never waned, even decades after he and Ditko had created the teen superhero with a mountain of real-life problems. Over the years, whenever Spider-Man would zip back to the top of the pop culture radar, there Lee would be, ready with a story and sound bite, whether providing comments about Gwen Stacy's death in June 1973 or marrying the character to Mary Jane Watson in a live-action wedding before fifty-five thousand screaming fans at Shea Stadium in June 1987. Lee's marketing mirrored Marvel's efforts at keeping the web crawler at the heart of the company. Most observers felt that Spider-Man had become the most popular superhero in the world, displacing the competitor's invincible strongman in the red cape and the scowling guy in the black mask.

In August 1990, Marvel released Todd McFarlane's *Spider-Man* #1, a highly stylized and visually stunning reboot, with a variety of colorful covers, meant to spark media attention and sing to the hearts of comic book collectors. The combination of the national exposure and cover variants led to the issue becoming the best-selling comic in history with about 2.85 million copies getting into readers' hands. McFarlane focused on the character's visual identity, as he explained, "to break people of reading a comic book the way they've been used to for the last twenty years."[5] In other words, McFarlane hoped to start a new conversation with Spider-Man, the way Lee had been able to do at the dawn of the Marvel Universe.

Lee never gave up hope that someone in Hollywood would turn Spider-Man into a big screen hero. But in the early 1990s, he had to look to other characters first. Lee had become a fixture in Hollywood. Among his many tasks, he often served as a story consultant for Marvel-related media, like the 1990 NBC television film *The Death of the Incredible Hulk*, with Lou Ferrigno and Bill Bixby. Although it had been years since the original series aired, the live-action Hulk grew in popularity over time as fans looked back at the program with nostalgic longing. There was something magical and thoughtful about the Bixby/Ferrigno team that audiences coveted, particularly Bixby's tortured loner persona and existence as a stranger in his own life.[6] Several years later, when superhero comics in general were marked by extreme violence and action, the *Hulk* television series and its spin-off films seemed almost quaint.

In 1994, Lee edited *The Ultimate Spider-Man*, a collection of short stories by a number of important comic book veteran writers and illustrators. His introduction provided readers with an insider's glimpse into how the character came about, as well as Lee's thinking at the time. He divulged, "no one at Marvel expected Spidey to become a cultural icon. . . . At that time, he was just one of many, many characters that were being continuously hatched, published, abandoned, and forgotten if they didn't catch on."[7] So, instead of disappointing fans and journalists who asked about Spider-Man's origins and expected a big, triumphant story, Lee admits that he "cooked up" a vision of the day in which he saw a spider on the window that hatched the idea. He later came up with "Amazing" for Spider-Man, just because he liked the way it sounded.[8] Lee constantly moved between downplaying his own efforts and an overly confident guise that readers understood was (at least partially) tongue-in-cheek.

The straightforward, yet lighthearted and personal banter between Lee and the reader had been developed over decades and dates back to his initial stories in *Captain America* in the early 1940s. The consistent—some might say relentless—patter between Lee and comic book readers had a major upside: the bond of trust that resulted. Whether Lee's story about seeing the spider at his desk on the fourteenth floor of the Empire State Building is true or an utter falsehood, readers lapped it up. They fully believed in "Stan the Man," no matter the increasing criticism of hardcore fan-boys and comic book historians. *Spider-Man* newspaper strip fan (and eminent novelist) John Updike caused a national stir when he wrote a letter to the editor of the *Boston Globe* for canceling the series (which the paper later rescinded). Lee sent Updike a Spider-Man sweatshirt for his wife and a framed, autographed copy of the strip—another satisfied fan.[9]

The centerpiece of the 1994 book was a novella by Lee that revised and expanded Spider-Man's origin story. Peter Parker's Uncle Ben and Aunt May are further explored and humanized. Lee's playfulness is on display in the piece—Aunt May whacks a spider that gets in the way of her cleaning, exclaiming "I just can't stand spiders, that's all. Disgusting creatures." She looks at the tiny dead arachnid to make sure it "was good and squished."[10]

Lee's new story is significant, because it reveals how he and later Marvel writers were willing to expand and revise a character's origin story to develop with time. For example, Lee puts the infamous radioactive spider in Dr. Octopus's lab at Empire State University and infuses it with thoughts and feelings, particularly after it is shot through with radiation. The spider later causes the scientist to set off a nuclear explosion and then, seconds after, land the bite that transforms Peter Parker forever. The accident not only leads to Spider-Man, but to Dr. Octopus having the metallic arms fused to his body. Spider-Man ultimately defeats the villain, but Uncle Ben still dies, and Parker battles with Flash Thompson. The final famous line is changed slightly to conform to the new origin story: "that with great power . . . comes great responsibility."[11]

The Ultimate Spider-Man collection also played an additional role in Lee's mythmaking. The biography section did not mention Kirby or Ditko, but stressed

Lee's role, explaining, "Hundreds of legendary characters, such as Spider-Man, the Incredible Hulk, the Fantastic Four, Iron Man, Daredevil, and Dr. Strange, all grew out of his fertile imagination."[12] Certainly, the bio is a form of publicity for Lee and the book, but these kinds of winner-take-all statements also alienated the comic book "true believers" who worshipped at the altar of the two great artists and co-creators. Granted, from Lee's perspective, he didn't directly make these choices, but since his name is on the book as editor, readers and comic book fans expected that he might demonstrate some level of modesty. A careful reader, though, may have noticed the Lee dedication: "To Steve Ditko, who was there at the beginning."[13]

Under the leadership of Bevins and the strategic direction of Perelman, Marvel increased revenue and profitability. The mogul's next move focused on taking the company public. That decision enabled him to extract more money from the company as investors bought up shares. The IPO resulted in about $82 million coming into Perelman's coffers. He poured $50 million of that money back into a number of his parent companies, essentially guaranteeing himself a 500 percent return on his initial investment and a 60 percent stake in Marvel. As part of the public relations campaign, an actor dressed as Spider-Man appeared on the floor of the New York Stock Exchange, waving and shaking hands with the traders.[14]

The stock market valued momentum, and Perelman fed the beast with news of director James Cameron (having recent successes with *The Terminator* and *Aliens*) writing and directing a *Spider-Man* film (which made Lee's heart sing and started a long friendship between the two). The stock price more than doubled, trading at $35 per share by the end of 1993 when the company reported revenues of $415 million and earnings at $56 million. On paper, Perelman's stake in Marvel reached $2.7 billion.[15] It seemed another enormous success for the financial raider.

While the future looked promising at Marvel, the boom market showed signs of cracking, and simultaneously Perelman's purchase of trading card company Fleer in mid-1992 for $286 million took place at a shaky moment in professional sports. Fans responded by staying away. Then, Marvel gave toy maker Toy Biz, which specialized in action figures, a royalty-free license to its characters in exchange for a 46 percent stake in the New York-based company led by Ike Perlmutter and Avi Arad.

Neither Perelman nor his management team realized how the collector craze artificially propped up store sales. The 1989 *Batman* film, starring Michael Keaton, and the 1992 *Death of Superman* comic book, which had sold six million copies, had reinvigorated comic books, but that mania soon fizzled. The decline left Marvel vulnerable, despite its recent successes, especially when Perelman concentrated on profits, not reinvesting money into product development. His team attempted to correct the slide by buying a sticker company, another trading card company, and two small publishers: Welsh Publishing Group, which published children's magazines, and Malibu Publishing, a small West Coast comic book company that DC had been courting (the directive at Marvel was to buy Malibu regardless of cost, because DC would have become the market share leader with the acquisition). The bloat from these acquisitions actually rocked the delicate infrastructure even more. By 1995, Marvel reported its first loss under Perelman's control, losing $48 million, despite sales of $829 million. The debt swelled to about $600 million, which forced the company's banks to put the company on watch. There wouldn't be any money for new developments, like a much-needed Internet division or other projects that might help the company generate revenues.

Perelman had issued a number of junk bonds to continue the shopping spree. Fellow corporate raider Carl Icahn, even richer than Perelman, saw the company ripe for a hostile takeover and gobbled up the bonds, about $40 million worth. Eventually, when Marvel had trouble paying its debt obligations, Perelman offered to grant $350 million in exchange for more shares, but Icahn owned 25 percent of the company and refused the deal. Suddenly, in the midst of a downturn in the comic book market, two of America's richest men went to war over the future of the company. Though Icahn seemed to want to save Marvel, few believed that he wouldn't just buy it as cheaply as possible and then later sell it off piecemeal.[16]

On December 27, 1996, just a day prior to Lee's seventy-fourth birthday, Perelman took the only step available and plunged Marvel into bankruptcy in a last-ditch effort to thwart Icahn's takeover attempt. "The news release was short and not so sweet," said Shirrel Rhoades, a Marvel executive during the tumultuous period. The comic book world shuddered: "It sent ripples of fear throughout the comics industry."[17] The two sides swapped reorganization plans, neither acceptable to the other. Ironically, the publishing part of the company held Marvel afloat after the bankruptcy announcement, while the trading cards continued to strain the budget, as well as advertising and licensing deals that disappeared.

In February 1997, the bankruptcy court allowed Icahn to take control of Marvel, and then in June, he won control over the company's board of directors, thus enabling him to oust Perelman and his crew for good. Various estimates place Perelman's profit during his ownership of Marvel at $200 to $400 million. While Icahn started to put a management team in place, suddenly, little Toy Biz, led by Perlmutter and Arad, jumped into the negotiations and put forth its own plan for rescuing Marvel. The company wanted to protect its no-royalty license agreement, particularly since more than half its toys were based on Marvel characters.

In December 1997, Marvel's fate was in the hands of a trustee named John J. Gibbons, appointed by Delaware U.S. District Court Judge Roderick McKelvie. Marvel execs questioned the Toy Biz deal, which lit a fire under Perlmutter and Arad. They put together a group of investors and made a $400 million offer to purchase Marvel outright. Over Icahn's objections, Judge McKelvie approved the Toy Biz proposal. The newly merged company would pay creditors a portion of the debt and offer equity claims.[18] Arad convinced many of the financial leaders involved in the proceedings that Marvel's future as a film company warranted a gamble on its future. His impassioned overture would later prove prophetic.

While business titans and corporate raiders battled to control Marvel in the late 1990s, Lee played good company soldier and continued to weave his way through Hollywood and a variety of animation, television, and film deals. The only time the bankruptcy hurt Lee was when production companies grew leery about working with Marvel when the future seemed undetermined. Previously, Bevins generally let him work independently, only interfering once when Lee had different networks approve animated shows for Black Widow and Daredevil. The overall uncertainty regarding Marvel's fate caused Bevins to squash the deal.[19] A portion of Lee's efforts also harkened back to his editorial days, primarily ensuring that writers for the animated programs understood Marvel standards for character development and plot. "I spend most of my time in the office working on movies, television shows and animation," Lee said.

The fate of Marvel seemed to hang in the balance as courts and judges determined who would own the company after it emerged from bankruptcy. The outcome had little personal consequence for Lee, who was too valuable a property to be discarded, no matter who won control. He more or less stood above the fray. "I stay out of all that business stuff because my area of concern is the creative ends of things," he said.[20] And, the company saw a payoff for Lee's supervision of the production line: *Spider-Man*, *X-Men*, and *The Incredible Hulk* drew significant viewers as part of the children's television lineup. "Our shows generally do very well. . . . That's the most important thing as far as I'm concerned," Lee explained.[21]

Although often overlooked as part of a larger Marvel strategy, Lee's work in building the animation arm of the company vastly expanded the fan base. For a lifelong movie buff like Lee, however, the real glitz and glamour came from the big screen. While a *Spider-Man* feature film seemed less likely, because of legal wrangling and disputes over who controlled the character's film rights, other characters moved closer to production, including the X-Men and Hulk.

Surprisingly, the first Marvel feature to really break out of the pack turned out to be based on a lesser-known, supporting character: the vampire hunter *Blade*, created by Marv Wolfman and artist Gene Colan. The film version, starring Wesley Snipes, was released in late summer 1998 to mixed reviews, but fan acclaim. After opening strongly in the United States and abroad, the film eventually brought in about $70 million domestically and $131 million worldwide. Although Lee's brief cameo ended up on the cutting-room floor, *Blade* confirmed his long-standing notion that Marvel characters would do well on-screen.

As the 1990s closed, Lee wrapped up an odd decade for him. His aspirations for bringing Marvel superheroes to life on film or television had either happened or appeared on the near horizon. Yet, Marvel itself seemed to tread on shaky ground. The company had a seemingly endless supply of characters, and its core superheroes were among the most well-known properties in the world, but the various corporate conglomerates that acquired it didn't have a sense of how to make it work or a strategy that took advantage of its assets. Only Perlmutter and Arad at Toy Biz seemed to comprehend how to turn Marvel superheroes into cash, capitalizing first on the royalty-free agreement and later parlaying that into taking full control of the company.

Although in his seventies, Lee kept his eyes on how technology began to change the comic book industry. He investigated a whole range of options, from video games to electronic comic books delivered via CD-ROM or the burgeoning Internet. Lee starred in some of Marvel's earliest Web work, answering fan questions on an AOL homepage in the late 1990s. He didn't understand how the Web worked, but Lee knew that it presented the next significant entertainment channel for surfers around the world.

Few writers, musicians, artists, or other creative icons remained relevant at Lee's age, but he refused to retire, imagining that the lack of work would sap his will to live. The constant buzz that followed him at comic conventions, media opportunities, and celebrity interactions in Los Angeles seemed like a magic elixir for the iconic writer. It wasn't that Lee simply didn't want to stop—he genuinely couldn't.

CHAPTER 14

RISE AND FALL OF STAN LEE MEDIA

In January 1999, news of Stan Lee's new Internet company Stan Lee Media Inc. (SLM) exploded across the Web. Journalists rushed to cover the story. An interview with Lee gave reporters a chance to hear about the start-up, as well as listen to the man himself spin yarns about the fabled creation of his Marvel superheroes. The marriage of the world's most exciting storytelling channel and the world's most interesting storyteller seemed to promise a surefire success.

Lee launched SLM with Peter F. Paul, an entrepreneurial Hollywood gadfly who had started a nonprofit foundation with legendary screen star Jimmy Stewart and led several high-profile fund-raising campaigns. SLM marketing documents called Paul a "new media producer," touting his experience as founder of Digicon Entertainment, which created a Marilyn Monroe artificial intelligence/virtual reality animation for Sony.[1] More recently, Paul had successfully boosted heartthrob Fabio's career and displayed a keen knack for making friends with the rich and powerful, like President Bill Clinton and wife Hillary.

The rise of the Internet and its global significance provided Lee with yet another opportunity to show that he could master a new media form, even at seventy-six years old. "When Peter Paul suggested we start an Internet company, the only thing I really knew about the web was that it was going to be the biggest force for entertainment and communications that the world has ever known. So, naturally, I was excited about getting involved in it," Lee explained.[2] Paul estimated that Lee's name alone accounted for about $30 million in brand value. SLM could not use the superheroes that Lee created or cocreated, since Marvel owned the copyrights, but the old master could launch an entirely new superhero universe that the start-up venture would own outright.

The idea of showing Marvel and the world that he could unleash a rival super-hero collection fueled Lee, his competitive streak sparked by the recent woes Marvel had faced and the slights he felt in the battle over his lifetime contract, despite the "Chairman Emeritus" title Marvel bestowed on him. He chafed at the notion that after a lifetime of service he was little more than a figurehead.

Lee also felt hurt and angry that he had to grovel with new Marvel head Ike Perlmutter to renegotiate a new deal after he had been working under a lifetime contract that provided financial security and acknowledged his role in building the company. Lee found Perlmutter's initial offer insulting, from a lifetime contract to a two-year deal at "exactly half what I had been earning." Lee wondered whether the ghost of Martin Goodman may have been guiding the new Marvel leadership team.[3]

Ultimately, Marvel executives realized Lee's value as spiritual head of comic books and couldn't risk a public relations nightmare if the legendary figure went off to DC or another publisher. Attorney Arthur Lieberman negotiated the final deal that gave Lee a raise (to more than $800,000 annually for life) and $125,000 a year for the *Spider-Man* newspaper strip, but more importantly a $500,000 annual pension for Joanie and a 10 percent stake in future Marvel film and TV profits.[4] The new contract also gave Lee an escape clause, essentially permitting him to work on any other projects he wanted, regardless of publisher or organization.

Now, with the launch of SLM, Lee could take a bit of a shot at Marvel, declaring that in contrast to his former outfit, SLM would produce online comic books and superheroes that were "edgy, high-concept, and surprising."[5] According to Lee, the new company would also partner with online production firms, create Web pages and virtual comic books, launch interactive games, and feature Web-based classes with the comic book legend for those who wanted to break into the business.

Stan Lee Media launched in early 1999 in a typically nondescript office building on Ventura Boulevard in Encino, California. Although on the outside the place looked just like all the other businesses in the sea of buildings twenty miles from Los Angeles, SLM issued glossy press kits in bright, almost garish colors, hyping Lee and his past successes as a way to draw in new investors and spring quickly toward a stock IPO, the route to riches that Internet companies had charted over the last several years. The press kit exclaimed that Lee had "exerted more influence over the comicbook industry than anyone in history" and that "more than 2 billion of his comicbooks have been published in 75 countries and in 25 languages."[6] SLM's centerpiece was www.stanlee.net, a hub for new characters and products.

The icon's move to the Web created headlines. People were curious about how printed materials would transition to the virtual world. Lee's earnestness and enthusiasm spilled out in countless interviews and profiles. In an interview on NPR, Lee explained that the Web-based comic books were "really miniature movies. We have actors reading the roles. There are no dialog balloons."[7] The idea of Lee creating a new superhero universe intrigued investors and excited fans. SLM had a jump on its competitors in moving online, another factor that led institutional investors to fund the enterprise. One reporter explained Paul's vision of SLM, explaining that the deal maker would trade on Lee's past accomplishments to create "a Stan who could be offered up piecemeal to fans and eager licensing partners from the virtual balcony of a new House of Old Ideas built on the fluid foundation of the Internet."[8]

In August 1999, eager to get on the stock exchange and unwilling to take the traditional IPO route, Paul and investment banker Stan Medley concocted a reverse merger with a public company called Boulder Capital Opportunities, Inc. The new entity would be traded as Stan Lee Media under the symbol SLEE. As creative lead and chairman, Lee received stock options for more than six million shares, as did Paul and others at the executive level. The options had little initial value, but promised to make Lee and the others extraordinarily wealthy (Lee's annual salary was $272,500). In its first year on the top floor of the Encino building (also the point of operations for many of Paul's other shadowy business endeavors), the company grew to 150 employees.

The flagship franchise would be *The 7th Portal*, a superhero team battling villains that could travel to Earth through a hidden gateway. Lee took a hands-on approach, according to Buzz Dixon, the vice president of creative affairs. Initially, Lee focused on six or seven projects, writing outlines and character sketches. "Everything I saw had Stan's creative imprint on it," Dixon said.[9] While Lee and a new bullpen of writers and artists worked through a multitude of ideas, company officials explained to the world what was really for sale—Lee himself, remarking, "The fact is that Stan is a recognized brand in the global marketplace."[10] Paul and other executives even considered starting a Lee clothing line based on his many catchphrases and new ones they might trademark. Interviewers noted that Lee routinely reported to work each morning in his black convertible Mercedes E320 around 9:30 and often stayed until 8:00 p.m.[11]

SLM debuted the *7th Portal* at a star-studded gala on February 29, 2000, that Paul orchestrated at Raleigh Studios in North Carolina. Television personality Dick Clark hosted the party, which featured performances by Jerry Lee Lewis, Ray Charles, and Chaka Khan. Three months later, SLM announced a deal with Paramount Parks to develop a 3-D ride based on the *7th Portal* franchise for its twelve million annual visitors.

SLM had plenty of brand recognition, but it didn't have enough content to capitalize on the multitude of deals Paul had negotiated. Lee backed the ideas of his writers and artists, but his cofounder kept the actual wheeling and dealing close to his chest, ultimately preventing Lee from exercising any significant decision-making authority. According to insiders, Lee, "would sit in business meetings and occasionally say something. But mainly he'd sit there and doodle, or fall asleep."[12] Paul kept Lee and the start-up in the news with the marketing machine operating at full speed. However, fewer and fewer of the deals amounted to any actual content or products.

Using Lee's involvement as a lure, other celebrities also jumped on the bandwagon. SLM announced high-profile ventures with a range of stars, including the Backstreet Boys and Mary J. Blige. Pundits saw the venture as the culmination of Lee's long career in comics and believed that given his supervision, SLM might become the Internet era's version of Disney. It was one thing for the general public to see the "Stan Lee" name attached to an entity and equate it with Marvel's successes or feel that such a company could become another Marvel, but it was another for the media, stock analysts, and others to climb aboard the same runaway train. The hysteria surrounding the New Economy bubble far outstripped the media's ability to recognize its farcical elements or anticipate the fated consequences.

Dot.com mania spread from San Jose and San Francisco across the United States to New York City's Silicon Alley and then around the world to burgeoning technology hubs like Dublin, Tel Aviv, and Moscow. In this overheated environment, when a simple idea for selling mundane consumer products on the Internet could lead to venture capitalists lining up to provide millions or tens of millions in funding, SLM seemed a surefire winner. In early 2000—at the height of the boom—Wall Street valued the company at $31 a share, which would have essentially given SLM enough paper wealth ($350 million) to buy Marvel Comics outright. Pop superstar Michael Jackson considered purchasing Marvel, personally asking Lee if he would run it if Jackson did so. Of course Lee agreed, but the acquisition never took place.

Lee excelled at doing what he always did so well—becoming the face of the organization, and even more importantly, the face of a new generation of online comic books and online media. The extraordinary level of hype and willingness to believe in it with little or no validation created the perfect environment for Lee's longing "true believers" to truly believe (and get in on the ground floor of a Stan the Man enterprise). When Lee spoke at tech conferences and other events, he stood among his kind of people, a generation of self-anointed nerds who grew up on superhero stories and were avid comic book readers.

Although some SLM employees secretly questioned the legitimacy of the many partnerships and deals, no one outside Paul and a small number of coconspirators understood how fast the company was burning through its start-up and stock funds. Court documents later revealed that SLM had plowed through about $26 million from its earliest incorporation through September 2000. In contrast, the venture only brought in about $1 million in revenue during that span.[13]

Like many other dot.com "bombs," SLM was a house of cards—almost completely hype and marketing acumen built atop the good idea of bringing the comic book world online. While many dot.bombs were the outcome of excessive exuberance that capitalized on a pervasive stock market bubble and the notion that size mattered more than profitability, SLM engaged in actual fraud and stock manipulation.[14] The company's 150 workers lost their jobs when the company declared bankruptcy in December 2000. The SEC and FBI started investigations into Paul, Lee, and other SLM leaders. While authorities soon cleared Lee of financial wrongdoing, their efforts fixed on Paul. Soon, people around the world would know his name: he was the guy who caught Stan Lee up in one of the contemporary world's most egregious Ponzi schemes.[15]

Just two weeks before Lee's seventy-eighth birthday, staffers at SLM, despite their concern for their jobs and the ominous news stories about the company's demise, bought their leader a seven-foot-tall Spider-Man statue imported from Germany. They pieced together the birthday present and kept their fingers crossed that in superhero fashion, Lee would somehow save the day. Maybe the web slinger could magically come to life and lead the charge.

During a staff meeting, the remaining SLM executives entered the main conference room and announced that the company was shutting down and the entire staff would be laid off. Amid tears and stunned faces, the employees could not believe what they were hearing, even though many had begun to realize how the financial situation had deteriorated. In less than two years the company crashed and burned through tens of millions of dollars, another web venture left to history's dustbin. Lee physically collapsed after hearing the news and had to be helped out of the building. The memories of Goodman forcing him to deliver similar news to staffers and freelancers at Marvel still burned in his memory.[16]

If Paul really were a supervillain, one might imagine his slick, tuxedo-wearing exterior transforming into a slimy, super-snake or maybe an energy mass fueled to superhuman power by money and jewels. The list of iconic celebrities and political figures Paul duped is extensive. He also conned the business press as well. The *Los Angeles Business Journal*, for example, once dubbed him "Spider-Man's Business Brain" and suggested that his work would transform Lee's new characters "into a business empire." Paul boasted that SLM was "the Disney of the 21st century."[17]

Paul obviously had vast visions of grandeur. His web start-up scheme seemed simple and followed the same outline that other ventures had created during the dot. com craze. First, he would employ marketing and publicity tactics to hype the start-up and Lee. Then, despite limited products and revenue, he would lead the company to public status, even without much actual substance in terms of products or content. The public offering enabled Paul to essentially use the stock money to fund an escalating deficit (and simultaneously line his pockets). In the end, the financial losses would be outsourced to shareholders, while providing riches for Paul and his allies, who turned their self-granted stock options into countless millions.

What authorities would unravel was a stock swindle orchestrated by Paul and several well-placed henchmen, including SLM executive vice president Stephen M. Gordon, sentenced in 2003 to six and a half years in federal prison for his role in the check-kiting scheme.[18] Paul borrowed money from banks using the bloated SLM stock price as collateral, then sold shares illegally. The full scope of the Ponzi scheme would take investigators years to sort out, but Paul also had more straightforward illegal maneuverings, including reneging on paying back a $250,000 personal loan from Lee. He also forged Lee's signature on multiple contracts (handwriting experts later proved that Lee did not sign the documents).[19]

On February 16, 2001, SLM filed bankruptcy petitions in the United States Bankruptcy Court for the Central District of California. In August 2002, the Colorado Secretary of State dissolved the company and its case was dismissed for failure to pay U.S. Trustee fees.[20] While the legal machinations took time to unfurl, Paul had already fled the scene, turning up in Brazil in December 2000, hoping to avoid prosecution. However, in August 2001, Brazilian officials arrested the fugitive and imprisoned him for two years. U.S. authorities arranged for extradition, which took place in September 2003.

Although Paul would repeatedly attempt to wriggle out of legal troubles, the many complaints demonstrated that he bilked various parties out of at least $25 million.[21] In 2005, he pleaded guilty to these criminal charges and first spent four years under house arrest, then in 2009 began serving a ten-year prison term at a federal institution in Anthony, Texas. Officials paroled Paul in late 2014.

Several generations worth of goodwill helped Lee dodge a great deal of the fallout. Not only did Lee physically look the part of the eccentric grandpa in the early 2000s, but it became clear to investigators that he indeed had been duped by his business partners. Not all the revelations were kind, however. Stories circulated in the business press saying that Lee slept through meetings and generally steered clear of the financial side of the firm. He did not control the money, but no one could deny that he may have had some reason to stay more on top of events unfolding at a company bearing his name.

Perhaps the saving grace for Lee centered on just how corrupt and manipulative Paul had been. The list of those he conned ranged from powerful individuals, such as Bill and Hillary Clinton, to Muhammad Ali and iconic actor Jimmy Stewart. Labeled by one journalist as a "sometimes-mysterious figure with searing eyes and grand gestures," Paul became one of the more fantastical figures of the dot.com age, claiming at one point to have ties to secret government agencies, which necessitated federal officials to create the trumped-up charges in an effort to silence him.[22]

The SLM debacle virtually erased three years of Lee's life and changed his basic outlook. "No platitude will ever repair the harm that's been done, to me and countless others," Lee explained. "But one thing's for sure—I'll never be so stupidly trusting again."[23] After the dot.bomb debacle, most experts and observers figured that Lee's career would slowly fade to black. Perhaps the superhero industry's greatest showman would finally call it a day after four decades in the spotlight. Few thought that even the ever-resilient Lee could sidestep the scandal, despite government investigators clearing him from any wrongdoing in the SLM crash and burn.

From a broader perspective, though, the utter collapse of the dot.com boom caught countless corporate leaders asleep, including many who had worked at the upper echelons of the business world for decades. Their shortcomings put Lee's troubles in perspective. The widespread bust that shook the global economy made the SLM boondoggle seem like just another dot.com nightmare come true. Plus, as Peter Paul's criminal past, outlandish scheming to deceive Wall Street, and zany claims about working for secret military operations became public, it became apparent that the con man had swindled Lee, taking advantage of their friendship to set in motion a devious plot for personal gain.

The crash of Lee's self-titled venture ratcheted up his competitive resolve. Whatever the potential outcome, he would not ease up or retire with the SLM catastrophe as his enduring legacy. Working with *Batman* movie producer and industry insider Michael Uslan, Lee struck a deal with longtime competitor DC to reimagine the company's famous characters through his eyes. They called the series *Just Imagine Stan Lee*, which allowed Lee to rewrite and reconceptualize the major characters in the DC pantheon, including Superman, Batman, and Wonder Woman.

The series led to some private negotiations with DC and its parent company Time Warner to possibly expand its relationship with Lee. The talks included the creation of a boutique publishing operation, potentially as a way, according to one insider, to "remove that yoke of worry from Stan's shoulders." Within months of the bankruptcy, Lee and the people closest to him were definitely searching for ways to deflect the negative publicity from the SLM debacle.[24]

Despite turning seventy-nine years old at the end of 2001, Lee vowed to continue producing superheroes and work on new and exciting projects. As usual, he tapped into his seemingly endless supply of creativity to fashion a new image as pop culture's elder statesman and the godfather of comic books.

CHAPTER 15

MEANWHILE . . .

Before the first *X-Men* film hit the big screen in July 2000, Stan Lee had met with director Bryan Singer to discuss the characters and how the film might be brought to life. At that time, Singer explained, "There was no template for it. Comic book movies had died, there was no concept of one as anything but camp." The discussion with Lee took the proposed film in a new direction. He encouraged Singer to research the characters on his own, which led him to scrap earlier scripts Fox had commissioned and begin anew.[1]

After an extensive marketing campaign, *X-Men* set a record for comic book films at that time, earning $54.5 million its opening weekend. Lee appeared in the movie, playing a hot dog vendor. He didn't have any lines, but he and Senator Kelly stare at each other as the politician emerges from the ocean. The cameo merely provided a glimpse of Lee in his blue denim shirt and bright red apron, but the film's box office success relaunched superhero films and started Lee's string of appearances in films about characters he played a role in creating.

Lee's career renaissance began with *X-Men*, which eventually made $296 million worldwide. Long after the SLM debacle started to fade into history's dustbin, Lee grew into a familiar face for Marvel filmgoers. Lee explained that the movie work, even for a moment, ended up "elevating my career again." Soon, "it became tradition to see Stan the Man wandering through Marvel productions."[2] Lee would appear in eight other superhero films over the next seven years.

In November 2001, Lee joined with attorney Arthur Lieberman and producer Gill Champion to form POW! Entertainment. Lee served as chief creative officer.

Certainly part of his rationale for starting POW! had to do with pride. "I just wanted to show that I can succeed," Lee explained, especially, he continued, when "working with people who are honorable and competent." He and his partners repudiated the ostentation of Stan Lee Media. Instead, they hired a small staff and kept the operation manageable. Much of the work, however, remained the same as SLM. The team focused on creating characters based on Lee's ideas. Most importantly, the new company would not concentrate entirely on Web-based products and characters.[3]

The hyperbole that always came with anything Lee touched continued with the new company. An early press release announcing a three-film deal with the Sci-Fi Channel touted Lee as the "creator and inventor of the modern superhero," who "revolutionized the comic book industry" via characters that had superpowers but were "none the less plagued by the same doubts and difficulties experienced by ordinary people."[4] The document accentuates Lee's role in creating Marvel's most popular heroes, calling them "his most enduring characters" and then naming Spider-Man, the Hulk, and X-Men. Since most of the characters had been around since the 1960s, POW! communicators made an effort to contextualize and remind readers of Lee's central role.

Subsequently, POW! ran up a string of media deals and new projects designed to take advantage of Lee's status as one of pop culture's elder statesmen. However, the constant embellishment and lack of completed products left some observers shaking their heads. Inevitably, critics questioned the new company's viability when so much of its potential required Lee's creativity and oversight.

The shifting winds of pop culture helped Lee recalibrate. Just as he and his colleagues at Marvel had caught the cultural zeitgeist in the early 1960s, Lee did it again in the early 2000s. Something peculiar took place in the fusion of the Internet, cable television, and expanding film: geek culture took hold—and superheroes were at its epicenter.

Before long, the success of Marvel's films made the company and its characters as hip in the new century as they had been during Lee, Kirby, and Ditko's heyday. Fans lined up for hours to get a glimpse of Lee or his signature on their carefully plastic-sealed and cardboard-packaged comic books. Lee found himself surrounded and propped up by a generation of movie directors, screenwriters, artists, and studio heads, in addition to a generation of comic book writers, who paid homage to the work of the early masters. Time had paid Lee in dividends—the people who grew up reading his work and idolizing him came to power and authority across mass media channels and outlets.

In 2002, for example, hot indie filmmaker Kevin Smith (*Clerks*, *Dogma*), a lifelong comic book fan and comic book store owner, released *Stan Lee's Mutants,*

Monsters and Marvels, a collection of discussions between the two, along with additional Lee-centric material, heavy on his glory days and the consequences of superheroes on American culture. Lee and Smith had been friends over the years, particularly since the Marvel writer's extended role in Smith's 1995 film *Mallrats*. For Lee, Smith's stamp of approval both paved the way and demonstrated how Lee should be put on a pedestal by his pop culture offspring—a generation or two of creators, artists, filmmakers, and others who grew up gazing in wonder toward New York City and "Smilin' Stan."

That same year, Lee published his long-awaited autobiography, titled *Excelsior! The Amazing Life of Stan Lee* (with George Mair). The book presents Lee as a kind of heroic figure who achieved the American Dream through smarts, hard work, and quick wit. For Lee aficionados, it is a priceless examination of his career, supplying many details that the icon had never discussed.

Lee traded on his expanding fame and celebrity on the West Coast, purposely distancing himself from the Marvel comic book business. Instead, as he had with Stan Lee Media, he focused chiefly on multimedia projects. Lee could never tear himself away from the superheroes he helped birth. He rarely had time to read the new comics coming from Marvel, but he endured as the father of the superheroes. The public persona as popular culture's elder statesman helped him craft a new narrative in the post-SLM years.

At the same time, Lee and POW! concentrated on new technology and innovations. In late 2003, Lee served as a consultant for Activision, then one of the top video game production companies. Lee's job—the kind that seemed to suit him best—involved developing future superhero video games. When Marvel and Activision agreed to a new licensing deal, which included Spider-Man, Iron Man, X-Men, and the Fantastic Four, Lee provided input on game design, story ideas, and character development.

These types of consulting jobs played to Lee's strength as a creator and idea man, while letting others figure out the details and execute the larger grand vision he outlined. Within six months of signing the Activision video game contract, Lee made an agreement with Peak Entertainment Holdings, a United Kingdom–based multimedia company. Peak provided Lee and POW! with a production and distribution channel, while Lee could help Peak get its animated characters into live-action vehicles and films.

A substantial number of agreements and partnerships were in the works for Lee. However, the same challenges that had dogged him since the 1970s still existed—the deliberate pace of creating content and getting it produced. Sometimes it was POW! that overreached, while other agreements simply dissolved, which frequently happens in the entertainment world.

The challenge for Lee during the early and mid-2000s is that many deals would get signed, which sparked media interest. The news headlines spanned far and wide, yet little of substance seemed to later emerge. Some of the business leaders he made agreements with appeared shady, essentially bolstering the argument that Lee was selling his name and past successes for a quick buck.

One aspect of Lee's work that frustrated audiences and fueled his critics was his frequent involvement in projects that many observers found sordid or beneath someone of Lee's stature. In 2003, for example, he launched the adult-themed animated series *Stripperella* with *Playboy* pinup, *Baywatch* actor, and paparazzi provocateur Pamela Anderson. Jumping in bed with Anderson and other kinds of campy, adult content seemed tacky. A mercenary vibe surfaced, making it seem as if Lee worked on these topics simply to make money.

Lee had pitched the show to Anderson in person on the set of her television series *V.I.P.*, where she played a bumbling celebrity bodyguard. The two had more than a passing interest in working together, since they shared the same agent. Anderson found him "kooky" and "very eccentric," but grew to love the idea of an animated series of a stripper turned crime fighter.[5] Part of Spike TV's animated block of programming aimed to the station's tagline: the "first network for men," *Stripperella* certainly lived up to the adult theme, filled with double entendres and sexual overtones. The main character Anderson voiced, Erica Jones/Agent 0069, wore suggestive costumes, heavy on cleavage, with skimpy, skintight bottoms.

Lee did not write *Stripperella* but served as the show's coproducer, art director, and story editor. He didn't shy away from the cartoon's racy aspects. He explained, "It's not what I would call a dirty show. It's kind of funny-sexy, bad taste, as treated tastefully." Lee even compared it to a kind of "late-night version of *The Simpsons*."[6] Although the adult cartoon only lasted one season of thirteen episodes, stations around the world picked it up, often running it uncensored (Spike blurred out topless scenes), including Australia, the United Kingdom, Germany, Brazil, and Italy. One wonders how the clunky, ham-fisted villains, such as Klinko, who uses a copy machine to brainwash customers into becoming criminals, or the evil Queen Clitoris played to foreign audiences.

The success of the *Stripperella* series led to a series of deals with MTV and its sister networks, like Spike TV. Lee also served as an executive producer on MTV's animated *Spider-Man* show. The network needed content that appealed to a young demographic and Lee had that pedigree.

In late 2004, Lee began working with *Playboy* founder Hugh Hefner on an animated show called *Hef's Superbunnies*. Similarly to *Charlie's Angels*, the hit ABC show that launched Farrah Fawcett's career, Hefner would send out teams of playmates to save the world for democracy. In his distinctive overblown style, Lee praised Hefner and the project, explaining, "As a fan who bought and cherished the very first copy of *Playboy* in 1953, it is an enormous thrill for me to be partnering with a man who has done so much to shape the culture of the times we live in."[7]

The comic creator always seemed to have a soft spot for Hefner. The two men had a great deal in common, born in major American cities in the same decade (Hefner in Chicago on April 9, 1926). Hefner took a more traditional route than Lee, active in high school politics and journalism, he started the school newspaper and created a comic book. Neither saw combat in World War II, and both emerged from the global conflict full of vigor and optimism.

After a brief stint working for *Esquire*, Hefner borrowed heavily from dozens of investors to debut *Playboy* magazine with just $8,000. He even initially wanted to call the magazine *Stag Party*, but couldn't when Goodman had already copyrighted *Stag*. In December 1953, while Lee was editing and writing romance, western, and cuddly animal comic books, Hefner brought out the first issue of *Playboy*, featuring a color image of Marilyn Monroe in the centerfold. The magazine was an instant hit, its supporters viewing it as a fresh attack on the repressive postwar era. Hefner focused the magazine on urbane, sophisticated, intelligent readers, showcasing a lifestyle that would be both playful and aspirational. Before the decade ended, *Playboy* surpassed *Esquire*, and sold about one million copies a month.

Perhaps Lee sensed what life might have entailed for him if he had put all his efforts into one of Goodman's men's magazines, rather than toiling away in comic books. He certainly admired Hefner's ability to earn credibility in a part of the publishing industry that many people looked down on. *Playboy*'s critics constantly railed against the magazine, labeling it pornography. Lee had faced many conservative critics, such as Wertham and religious groups, before Marvel launched its iconic superheroes in the 1960s. Over the years, a friendship grew and they often considered working together, but while they both transformed popular culture in their own industries, none of the shared efforts ever appeared.

Decades later, Lee's praise for the *Playboy* tycoon went overboard, calling him "one of the great communicators in our society" and admitting, "I can't think of anyone I'd rather partner with." The release that accompanied the announcement heaped the praise on Lee as well, calling him "godfather of the modern comic book superhero," while Hefner claimed comic books were a lifelong passion for him and that he couldn't wait to work with "creative genius" Lee.[8] Although MTV announced that it would pick up the pilot, the program never aired.

In the wake of SLM and perhaps the ongoing desire to show fans, critics, and even Marvel itself that he remained a vibrant creator, Lee latched onto these shady projects. While he hid his true feelings behind his always-smiling carnival-barker routine, Lee had something to prove and hoped to finally create franchises that he owned, and thereby not have to watch as some new corporate overlord reaped massive profits on his ideas and hard work.

Lee clearly enjoyed signing deal after deal and the spotlight that came with the resulting media frenzy. What he didn't possess, in contrast to his Marvel years, was a team of creators, artists, and other visionaries that could assist him in transforming his ideas into completed projects and products.

Much of Stan Lee's effort to create new characters, companies, and heroic plots outside the Marvel Universe came about because he—like countless other artists and writers—did not own or hold the copyright on the characters he had created or cocreated. Right or wrong, this is the way the comic book industry ran during those early decades. The difference between Lee and the others like Superman creators Jerry Siegel and Joe Shuster, was Lee's role as Marvel's public face.

Despite his role as a self-avowed "company man," Lee resented that Marvel made so much from his ideas, particularly after the movie industry finally caught on to what he had been preaching in Hollywood for decades.

In late October 2002, the popular news program *60 Minutes II* aired a segment about the state of comic books and the tremendous popularity of superhero films. A large portion showcased Lee's potential skirmish with Marvel over the contract language and what payment Lee justly deserved. The show painted Marvel in an evil light—a greedy corporation making insane amounts of money off the backs of its writers and artists. Lee's contract seemed straightforward, but when it was inked no one expected the future to include such wildly successful films—*X-Men* (2000) earned nearly $300 million worldwide, while *Spider-Man* (2002) became a global phenomenon, drawing some $821 million. *60 Minutes II* correspondent Bob Simon, employing a bit of spicy language for the venerable CBS show, actually asked Lee if he felt "screwed" by Marvel. Lee toned down his usual bombast, though, and displayed remorse for having to sue his employer, saying, "I try not to think of it."[9] As a result, many Marvel fans sided with Lee in the dispute.

Mere days after the segment aired, Lee sued Marvel for not honoring a stipulation in his 1998 contract that promised to pay him 10 percent of the profits from Marvel Enterprise film and television productions. Despite his $1 million annual salary as chairman emeritus, Lee's attorney's argued that the provision be honored. The grand battle between Marvel and its most famous employee shocked observers and sparked news headlines around the globe. Summing up the public's general feeling about the controversy, one reporter said, "You can't blame the pitchman for standing firm and insisting on his due."[10]

The public nature of the contract and its terms (including his hefty salary for a mere fifteen hours of work each week, guaranteed first-class travel, and hefty pension payouts to Joanie and J.C.) led some comic book insiders to once again dredge up the argument regarding how the comic book artists and cocreators—most notably Jack Kirby—were treated by Marvel (and by extension Lee).[11] Rehashing this notion and the idea that Lee attempted to capitalize off the success of the films turned some people against Lee. To critics, Lee got rich, while Kirby and others didn't. The injustice had been done and they weren't going to change their opinions, regardless of what Lee's contract stipulated.

In early 2005, after the judge ruled in Lee's favor, he again appeared on *60 Minutes*. "It was very emotional," said Lee. "I guess what happened was I was really hurt. We had always had this great relationship, the company and me. I felt I was a part of it."[12] Despite the high-profile nature of the lawsuit and its apparent newsworthiness, Marvel attempted to bury the settlement agreement with Lee in a quarterly earnings press release.

In April 2005, Marvel announced that it had settled with Lee, suggesting that the payoff cost the company $10 million. Of course, the idea that Lee had to sue the company that he had spent his life working for and crisscrossing the globe promoting gave journalists the attention-grabbing headline they needed. And, while the settlement amount seemed grandiose, it was a pittance from the first *Spider-Man* film alone, which netted Marvel some $150 million in merchandising and licensing fees.

The upside for Marvel was that the settlement put in motion plans for it to produce its own movies, a major shift in policy. Since the early 1960s, Marvel and its predecessor companies had licensed its superheroes to other production companies. Back then, the strategy allowed Marvel to outsource the risk involved with making television shows and films, but it also severely hindered it from profiting from the creations. This move gave Marvel control, not only of the films themselves, but the future cable television and video products that would generate revenues.

Merrill Lynch & Co extended a $525 million credit line for Marvel to launch the venture (using limited rights to ten Marvel characters as collateral), and Paramount Pictures signed an eight-year deal to distribute up to ten films, including fronting marketing and advertising costs.[13] Interestingly, the details of the agreement shed light on the suspect Hollywood accounting practices that film companies use to artificially reduce profitability. For example, for all the successes Marvel films had in the early 2000s, raking in some $2 billion in revenues between 2000 and 2005, Marvel's cut for licensing equaled about $50 million. Despite his earlier contract with the company, Lee had received no royalties.[14]

Lee had always been a self-promoter, but what he realized in the midst of the legal battle with Marvel was that in a world driven by pop culture influences and hyperdedicated fans, he could market himself just as readily as the company and its superheroes. The idea to license himself as a character took shape in 2004 when Lee founded Stan Lee Collectibles with his personal assistant and event manager, Max Anderson, and entrepreneur Tony Carroll. Lee's familiar face became a product and collectors could purchase memorabilia signed by Lee and authenticated by the store. For Marvel comic book and film fans, Lee's image was almost as recognizable as Spider-Man or Iron Man. Through Stan Lee Collectibles, fans could own a piece of "the Man."

In 2006, in celebration of Lee's sixty-fifth anniversary with Marvel (which would have incorrectly put his start date in 1941 rather than 1938 or 1939), the company released a series of comic books called *Stan Lee Meets . . .*, which featured Lee as a character within the story who meets and interacts with his creations. Lee wrote the first adventure with the specific superhero, and other writers penned minitributes to him to fill out the book, including Joss Whedon and Jeph Loeb. Comically, most of the heroes and villains Lee meets don't actually like him much or at all.

The episodes Lee wrote were filled with inside jokes and plenty of Lee's corny humor. In the *Spider-Man* issue, for example, the story opens with Lee in the kitchen baking up some cookies, wearing a Fantastic Four apron. In the foreground, the reader sees an image on the television screen of Lou Ferrigno as the Hulk. Later, it turns out that the web crawler wants to live a "normal" life and approaches Lee for advice. When the hero reconsiders, Lee jokes: "The next time Spidey has a problem—I wish he'd take it to Ditko." In the issue where he meets the Thing, New York City is filled with billboards that make fun of past Marvel artists, such as Gene Colan and the Buscemas, as well as Lee's 1976 commercial for the Personna razor in which he declared himself "Personna Man."

Lee's "King of the Cameos" title pushed into other media, not just Marvel films. On April 28, 2002, Lee guest-starred as an animated version of himself on *The Simpsons* in an episode titled "I Am Furious (Yellow)." After a comic book craze blossoms in Bart's class, the students all rush to create their own heroes. Lee waltzes into the Comic Book Guy's shop, deftly placing an issue of *X-Men* in front of one of *Superman* on a countertop display rack. Then, he criticizes *Danger Dude*, a comic book created by Bart Simpson, but encourages him to keep trying. Lee jokes: "If you fail, you can always open a comic book store." Then, taking a Batmobile from another young patron, he attempts to jam The Thing into the car, breaking it into pieces. When the child cries that Lee destroyed it, he retorts: "Broke, or made it better?" Later, he is portrayed as a little crazy, ripping off his shirt and attempting to transform into the Hulk.

Joining the reality television craze, Lee created and hosted the Sci-Fi Channel show *Who Wants to Be a Superhero?* Season One debuted on July 27, 2006, featuring twelve contestants who created their own superhero personas, such as Ty'Veculus (thirty-four-year-old E. Quincy Sloan from Bakersfield, California) who possesses super-strength and the ability to detect when people are lying, since he could only hear when people are telling the truth.

Similarly to reality shows like *Big Brother* and *Survivor*, participants engaged in a series of contests designed to prove which of them could be most heroic. At the end of each episode, Lee evaluated the way the players contended with the challenge and then eliminated the player who displayed the least heroic qualities. The first season winner was Feedback (a.k.a. Matthew Atherton, a thirty-four-year-old computer whiz from New Mexico). His superpower consisted of absorbing limited power from video games and being able to disrupt electronics in a fifteen-foot radius. As the winner, Feedback was featured in a *Dark Horse Comics* issue written by Lee in July 2007 and appeared in the Sci-Fi original TV movie *Mega Snake* (August 25, 2007). Atherton also played the character at several subsequent comic conventions and fund-raisers. A second season debuted on July 26, 2007, and ran for eight episodes.

Lee's 1998 contract granted him exclusive rights to his likeness and certain catchphrases, like "Excelsior" and "Stan Lee Presents." POW! used the latter in a series of new superhero animated films released in 2007. *Mosaic* debuted on January 9 and the Cartoon Network later aired it on television in March. *Mosaic* starred Anna Paquin (who played Rogue in the X-Men film franchise) as Maggie Nelson, an aspiring actress who gains an array of superhero powers, but primarily shape shifting, superhuman strength, and invisibility. Returning to the formula he basically mastered during Marvel's 1960s heyday, Lee created the story lines, but would then turn them over to an industry veteran for scripting. *The Condor*, starring actor Wilmer Valderrama, debuted on Cartoon Network on March 24, 2007, after its direct-to-DVD release several days earlier.

After SLM failed, many thought Lee's career looked to be on the ropes. If that was ever really the case, he did not stay there long. Essentially a free agent, Lee attempted to build a new infrastructure that would give him the creative freedom to build superhero franchises that he owned.

With some taint regarding SLM lingering and its hype still hanging in the air, the natural question regarding POW! Entertainment projects focused simply on what was real and what was marketing fluff. That fine line is one that Lee and his people seemed to disregard. Perhaps Lee enjoyed the thrill of chasing new deals more than he liked executing the projects afterward. Another lingering question was exactly what might the pop culture world expect from a man in his eighties—even one as energetic as Lee. Without an extensive lineup of writers, artists, designers, and Web-savvy colleagues, could POW! fulfill the dizzying array of contracts being signed, consulting jobs negotiated, and a litter of half-completed projects on the drawing board.

As could be expected, some fans were disappointed in Lee's POW! work, given that the company had not produced any memorable characters, much less another blockbuster like Spider-Man or X-Men. In other words, Lee had not originated an important creation that might again redefine his career in the early years of the new century. Condemning Lee in this fashion seems disingenuous, though, when contemplating his long career. In comparison, few successful writers, actors, or artists generate much of anything of significance when they are in their eighties. Of those who live that long, most have retired or given up.

At eighty-five years old at the end of 2007, Lee could have stopped working and lived out his remaining years as a creative icon, an easy path that few would have faulted him for after the dot.com meltdown. Lee, though, worked earnestly on new projects for POW!, while also fulfilling his Marvel agreements, which included visiting comic book conventions, appearing in film and television cameos, and fulfilling numerous writing projects. Lee's longevity is part of his legend. His tenacity in the early and mid-2000s revealed the depth of his character.

CHAPTER 16

LARGER THAN LIFE

A debonair celebrity walks the red carpet, blowing off an attractive onlooker. He approaches a dapper older man being surrounded and hugged by three young blond beauties. Patting him on the shoulder, he says: "Looking great Hef!" The man spins around, not revealing *Playboy* founder and consummate cad Hugh Hefner, but a pipe-wielding Stan Lee doing his best Hef impression. Yet another Lee cameo—this time in *Iron Man* (2008), starring Robert Downey Jr. as Tony Stark/Iron Man. The film would eventually gross about $585 million worldwide.

Lee's momentary appearances in Marvel films brought him a new level of fame and recognition. The cameos, which moviegoers expect and anticipate, serve as a kind of nod to Marvel's past and Lee's role in the creation of the Marvel Universe. Suddenly moviegoers who knew little or nothing about Lee—and who had no idea what he looked like—had an image and face to put with the famous name (and in some of the highest-grossing films of all time). The appearances are musts for Marvel fans, many of whom await each one with nearly as much interest as they do the movies themselves.

The film cameos upped Lee's cool factor geometrically among fans, but also among other celebrities, which demonstrated just how popular he had become. For example, most of the cast of *Iron Man* showed up at a 2007 panel at the San Diego Comic-Con to publicize the film and launch the word-of-mouth buzz. When director Jon Favreau announced a special guest, Downey Jr. glanced to his left and then raised his arm in a victory salute, a monumental grin spreading across his devilish face. The surprise visitor was Lee, who immediately drew hugs from the main star, as well as costar Gwyneth Paltrow and the other cast members and crew in attendance. The audience applause thundered through the hall. Several of the hottest celebrities in the world reacted with equal amounts of passion.

While fans might never get within a million miles of Downey Jr. or Paltrow, part of Lee's popularity centers on his availability. They can see his larger-than-life image up on the screen but also meet him at a local comic book convention or appearance. Lee's accessibility sets him apart from other iconic artists (a Bob Dylan or Bruce Springsteen), who have countless fans but are essentially walled off.

Lee presses the flesh and constantly meets new generations of crazed fans who just want a moment with the master, even if they are too overcome with nerves to pose a question or squeak out a "thank you." Not many iconic figures of Lee's age, or even those decades younger, would attract similar crowds. How many people well past ninety years old have 2.42 million Twitter followers?

Lee's role as the elder statesman of the Marvel Universe and quasi-formal role as chairman emeritus, as well as his desire to keep producing new characters and stories, have given him a unique place in the early decades of the twenty-first century. He is the walking, talking, joking, clowning, self-deprecating heritage of the comic book world.

On November 17, 2008, President George W. Bush honored Lee by bestowing on him the National Medal of Arts and the National Humanities Medal in a ceremony at the White House. The honor stands as the highest and most prestigious granted by the United States government in the humanities disciplines. Ever the joker, Lee waited for his turn, directly after famed Academy Award–winning actress Olivia de Havilland. In placing the medal over her head, the president bent down and kissed the *Gone with the Wind* actress on the cheek. Next, Lee stepped forward and reached out his hand, Bush took it in both hands. As he smiled at the president, Lee blurted out, "You're not gonna kiss me, are you?" Bush burst out laughing. The next day, media sites around the globe revealed Lee and the president sharing a good belly laugh, the photographs catching the precise moment in time.[1]

While career retrospectives like these have become more frequent, at the same time, Lee is focused on new projects and only slowing down to the degree that his body forces him to. When it comes to his work with POW! Entertainment, Lee is outside the Marvel system, yet his most visible presence is on the big screen in cameo Marvel film roles and at comic book conventions where everyone wants to rehash the past.

Lee keeps a big smile on his face, but it must be challenging for him to never shake those wonder years in the early to mid-1960s when he and his artist partners created the characters the world loves so deeply. For example, at the press conference for the 2009 joint venture with Disney, a journalist asked Lee if he might attempt to get Superman for the Marvel universe when the copyright reverted back to the families of Joe Shuster and Jerry Siegel. Lee replied that he liked the idea, but explained, "I'm with Marvel, but I'm not really part of the Marvel decision-making team. . . . I think my title is Chairman Emeritus, but it doesn't really mean much. . . . To prove they haven't forgotten me, I get these cameos in the movies, which is kind of nice."[2]

During the last decade, Lee has been the subject of lifetime tribute efforts while he still works to remain productive. In late 2007 and 2008, two comic book industry trade publications focused entire issues on Lee's career. Edited by Lee's former protégé Roy Thomas, *Alter Ego* no. 74 came out in December 2007, while Danny Fingeroth's *WriteNow!* no. 18 was published in summer 2008. These publications drew from interviews with Lee and discussions of his place in comic book history with historians, aficionados, and artists and writers who worked with and for him. In each case, the magazines attempted to provide detailed context about Lee's preeminent role for a new generation of readers, as well as sort through contentious issues that more hardcore people might question.

In 2008 Lee brought out *Election Daze*. Under the "Stan Lee Presents" banner, the volume poked fun at political leaders, harkening back to the 1940s and 1950s when he self-published books of humorous photos of celebrities and others with funny captions and took a tongue-in-cheek look at golf and its odd habits. The cover, for example, satirized George W. Bush's mispronunciation of the word "nuclear" and Hillary Clinton's allusion to potential intern challenges. The tongue-in-cheek nature of the publication clearly attempted to capitalize on Lee's satire, but the effort lacked bite in an era when political commentators essentially wage rhetorical warfare on one another twenty-four hours a day.

Lee continued to search for the franchise superhero universe that would rival his Marvel work. In 2009, POW! teamed with Walt Disney Studios Home Entertainment to produce *Time Jumper*, an animated comic book series made explicitly for release on the Web and mobile phones. Adopting his role as carnival barker and famous spokesperson of the comic book age, Lee created the characters and series as well as a character for himself—"Lee Excelsior"—the leader of an anticrime operation dubbed H.U.N.T. Corporation.

On the *Time Jumper* project, Lee took on a role that someone of his stature should hold, as producer, which meant that a creative team put together the script and storyboards and then Lee made comments as necessary. He told a reporter that he did not engage with the other voice actors while they recorded, but he did show up from time to time for his own parts. The show's lead actress, Natasha Henstridge, however, joked about Lee flirting with her and talked about what fun they had on set.[3]

Naturally, as Lee's film cameos expanded, he appeared on other programs, from late-night talk shows to popular sitcoms. In March 2010, for example, Lee appeared as himself in "The Excelsior Acquisition" on *The Big Bang Theory*, a show that highlights the growing popularity of "geek" culture. Seen by about sixteen million viewers, the episode focused on the show's lead characters attempting to meet Lee at a comic book store signing. Later, as the convoluted hijinks that define the show unfolded, theoretical physicist Sheldon visited Lee's house (Stan answers the door wearing a navy Fantastic Four robe). When he barges into Lee's home, the character gets arrested, leading to a restraining order being issued. As the show ends, the off-beat scientist gleefully proclaims that he will hang the restraining order next to the one he received from *Star Trek*'s Leonard Nimoy.

In April 2012, Lee launched a YouTube channel, dubbed *Stan Lee's World of Heroes*, with the program *Fan Wars*. Dedicated to the "hero lifestyle and enthusiast culture," the channel featured scripted and unscripted shows, as well as comic book convention and news coverage. Google originally funded the channel as part of its Channel Initiative, an effort to generate premium content for its wildly popular video service. Other celebrities and entertainers who received seed money included Madonna and former basketball superstar Shaquille O'Neal. Lee's POW! Entertainment company partnered with Vuguru, a multimedia production company founded by former Disney chief executive Michael Eisner, to create the show.

One of the most popular features on *Stan Lee's World of Heroes* turned out to be "Stan's Rants," a kind of live-action version of his Soapbox columns that used to appear in Marvel comics during his heyday. In each rant, Lee explored a topic that bothered him with a mix of his distinctive wise-guy style and a healthy dose of curmudgeonly charm thrown in for good measure. One rant, for example, had Lee railing against people who claimed that they were his "biggest fan." In another he implored people to spell "comic book" in his preferred one-word style: "comicbook." Lee delivered the diatribes in vintage, tongue-in-cheek Lee fashion, exclaiming about a video game version of himself: "Anybody could be Stan Lee! What if a guy isn't worthy? And I'm pretty particular! Never again will I put myself in a position where you, who may not be deserving, can be me!"[4]

From a pretty quick start and initial popularity (as of late 2016, it had about half a million subscribers and approximately 163 million views), the Lee YouTube page kind of died on the vine. YouTube thrives on endless streams of new content delivered to an audience that constantly demands fresh material. Though Lee's page showed promise, it just could not keep pace with the relentless pressure. Similarly to other POW! Entertainment initiatives, the YouTube channel launched with a bang, then withered as Lee's attention turned to other ideas. For Lee, this work more or less epitomized his recent efforts—full throttle when he had the time, but soon falling by the wayside. He is a one-man show, and the difficulty in turning over the reins to a successor causes many fits and starts.

The early YouTube content gave fans a way to watch Lee, but another initiative enabled them to become their hero. In 2012, Activision turned the comic book creator into an animated superhero in *The Amazing Spider-Man* video game released to coincide with the movie opening. As Lee, players could swing high above the streets of New York City, shooting webs and confronting villains, just like Lee's iconic character. Voicing the part, Lee begins his electronic adventure by announcing that he is the "king of cameos" and exclaims: "take that Hitchcock!"[5]

In late 2013, Lee again appeared alongside the characters he helped create in *Lego Marvel Super Heroes.* The role-playing game grew from the tremendous popularity of the Lego versions of famous characters and film franchises, such as Batman and *Star Wars.* In the Marvel version, players can become any of 180 characters, including Lee, and operate in a Lego rendering of New York City. Lee is part of a mission called "Stan Lee in Peril," which places him in dangerous situations that require rescue.

Lee is also a playable character with a variety of superpowers in the Marvel game, including being able to shoot rays like Human Torch and Cyclops and becoming a Lee version of the Hulk. The game also features other celebrities in their Marvel film guises, such as Robert Downey Jr. as Tony Stark and Samuel L. Jackson as Nick Fury.

In January 2014, Lee returned to Springfield, the fictional home of *The Simpsons,* in the episode "Married to the Blob" from the show's twenty-fifth season. Once again, as in the 2002 appearance, Lee is teamed with Comic Book Guy. Early in the episode, he urges the shop owner to ask Kumiko, a Japanese manga writer touring America's most tragic cities, out on a date. At the end, he marries the couple in the fabled comic book shop.

Early in 2016, Lego capitalized on the success of the Avengers franchise, releasing *Lego Marvel's Avengers.* Lee again returns to the video game as a character and voices himself. In this version, Lee can be played as "Iron Stan" (in Iron Man–like armor), but in a humorous nod, the facemask has a built-in moustache.

While these kinds of appearances might have seemed like nothing more than gimmicks, young video game–playing fans might get their first interaction with Lee this way, in turn leading them to know more about him and the characters. Just like a new legion of fans turned on to classic rockers Aerosmith based on the popularity of *Guitar Hero,* young video gamers would learn about Lee through the Spider-Man action pack. They could bound through the skyscrapers of New York City as Lee, fighting villains and leaping from the rooftops. YouTube videos posted of people playing the Spider-Man video game as Lee have eclipsed three million views.

While fans can become Lee in video games, they can also own a variety of versions of him, ranging from a five-inch minibust statuette to a lifelike action figure that came out in 2015 retailing at $250. Only one thousand of these dolls were sold, with interesting, interchangeable parts, like different versions of Lee's glasses, and even a couple heads that allowed users to make Lee look like the 1970s version of himself.

In January 2016, *Stan Lee's Lucky Man* debuted on British television's Sky 1, a drama about a troubled police officer working in homicide who can control luck (for decades Lee told interviewers that this was the superpower he wished to have). Drawing about 1.9 million viewers per episode, the series became Sky 1's most successful original drama and moved toward a second season in 2017.

In July 2016, Lee unveiled Nitron, a new comic book franchise centered on a super-intelligent species called "Nitronians" that secretly live among us in modern times. To transform the comic book series into feature films, television, and digital content, Lee is partnering with Keya Morgan and Michael Benaroya, whose Benaroya Pictures is anchoring the $50 million funding and production development. The three plan to write the comics and then serve as producers for subsequent film projects. Benaroya Publishing will also release the comic books. "Stan is the greatest story teller of all time," Morgan exclaimed, "the billions of dollars his stories have generated at the box office is a testament to his genius."[6]

In mid-2016, the *Hollywood Reporter* presented *Stan Lee's Cosmic Crusaders*, its first show to debut under its brand. Fabian Nicieza, who cocreated the superhero Deadpool, wrote the animated online series, while the magazine and Genius Brands International coproduced it, along with Lee's POW! Entertainment. Lee conceived the series, then edited the script and voiced himself, since he played a starring role.

On *Cosmic Crusaders*, Lee leads a group of seven aliens who have crashed on Earth. They lose their superpowers on this planet, but under Lee's tutelage they figure out how to employ the powers available to them on Earth. The partnership with *THR* coincided with the magazine's "Stan Lee: 75 Years in the Business" special Comic-Con issue. For Lee, the series provided another opportunity to expand his brand outside of Marvel. The involvement with Comic-Con included the first episode being presented in virtual reality, with smartphone viewers handed out at the convention. *THR* also marketed the series across its platforms, including its website, YouTube channel, Facebook, and Twitter, a combined social media audience of about fifteen million people monthly.[7]

As 2016 came to a close, Lee prepared to celebrate his ninety-fourth birthday just a couple days after Christmas. Rarely at rest, he unveiled two new projects that essentially symbolize the roles he plays in contemporary pop culture. The first project drew from the awful state of race relations in the United States. Lee hoped to find an alternative path with Hands of Respect—a campaign he created with his artist daughter J.C. to alleviate divisiveness between blacks and whites. With her advice and help, Lee created a lapel pin depicting black and white hands interlocked in a handshake, with the word "respect" above them. Lee told a reporter: "As a believer in the inert goodness of man, I'm hoping that the pin will serve to remind people that America is made of different races. . . . We're all co-travelers on the spaceship Earth and must respect and help each other."[8] The sentiment Lee used in describing Hands of Respect is certainly reminiscent of the values exemplified in his heroic African American and female characters in Marvel comics, as well as his promotion of diversity issues in *X-Men* and other franchises. His words about humankind's "goodness" reflect his most foundational beliefs.

As the year ended, POW! Entertainment announced a deal with Box Blvd to produce "The Stan Lee Box," a subscription delivery every eight weeks of collectibles "personally curated" by Lee, featuring exclusive comic book variants from Marvel, DC, and other publishers, as well as other character- and art-driven items. For just under $50 per delivery, Lee promised that fans would receive products exceeding $125 in retail value in each box. The subscription offer came after another product, "The Limited Edition Stan Lee Block" from a partnership with Nerd Block. The $49.99 block contained "hand-curated exclusives," including an "officially licensed" Lee T-shirt and other collectibles (valued over $150). When Lee posted a brief announcement about the box full of goodies, more than twenty-seven thousand people viewed the clip in its first hour after being posted.

Cavorting in the near corner of the massive convention floor are five Deadpools, mimicking the outlandish swordplay and violence that the character engages in. Over in line, two young girls are wearing T-shirts emblazoned with Captain America shields and delicately clutching comic books in their tiny hands. A sea of attendees with backpacks, water bottles, and selfie-snapping cell phones wait patiently to ride up and down escalators or to buy a soda at the concession stand. Behind tables, anxious young men wear logo-inscribed shirts and peddle action figures, posters, yellowing comic books, and an endless array of other products. Everywhere, people mill about, some in long lines to meet the guy who played Lando Calrissian (Billy

Dee Williams) or the artist who drew their favorite superhero. Three days, tens of thousands of one's closest friends—welcome to the comic convention world.

Throughout 2016, at age ninety-three and arguably never more popular, Lee embarked on a long series of "final appearance" tour stops, similar to the way generations of professional athletes would play their last games at stadiums or arenas across the nation. A number of cities, including Los Angeles and Kansas City, paid tribute to Lee, proclaiming it "Stan Lee Day" and showering him with attention that drove more and more fans to the convention centers. The tremendous success of Marvel films, a broader acceptance of geek culture, and Lee's status as the industry's eminent statesman fueled not only the tour, but tens of thousands of fans willing to do just about anything—and pay any amount of money—to see Lee and get his autograph. "There is an excitement about these comic conventions that nothing can match," Lee explained. "These people are so in love with the pop culture of comic books."[9]

Late in the year, Lee stormed into relatively small comic book conventions, such as the Cincinnati Comic Expo, but then later followed with an appearance at the enormous New York Comic Con in early October, which drew more than one hundred eighty thousand from around the globe. In New York, his birthplace and longtime home base, Lee explained to a *New York Daily News* interviewer:

> It's the most incredible thing in the world, because wherever I go, people want my autograph and people say 'thank you for the enjoyment that you brought me.' . . . I must be one of the luckiest guys in the world. . . . It's just great to know that you're wanted and that people actually appreciate the work that you've done.[10]

In October 2016, Lee paused his cross-country tour to attend his own convention, the renamed "Stan Lee's Los Angeles Comic Con," which he had run as "Stan Lee's Comikaze" since 2012.[11] The three-day celebration of geek culture kicked off with Friday being designated "Stan Lee Day" in L.A. The event drew ninety-one thousand fans, a new attendance record. At the end of the year, Lee took the tour overseas, visiting the Tokyo Comic Con, where fans flashed buttons announcing "Stan Lee for President" beneath his smiling, animated likeness. He also announced a visit in May 2017 to ConQue, a Mexican Comic Con in Queretaro City.

Since leaving New York for California in the 1970s, Stan Lee has worked tirelessly to promote Marvel and the beloved superheroes and villains he created or cocreated. The outcome of that effort has culminated with the Marvel superheroes dominating film and television. More significantly, the superhero narratives dominate storytelling, thus fundamentally changing entertainment in the contemporary world. Lee stands at the center of this transformation.

The challenge for icons as they age is the questions they face about living up to their own past accomplishments. This is a tall order, whether for Bob Dylan, Robert De Niro, or the Rolling Stones. In recent years, it has been easy for Lee to become the "king of the cameo," a fan-favorite scene-stealer in Marvel films, but his other work in the entertainment business necessitates cooperation and coordination with others, unlike the more personal acts of producing music or writing books.

The film, television, Web, and video game industries are unique and present immense challenges in moving from idea to completed project. Lee explained, "It goes on forever. I'm used to doing comic books, where every month there's a new comic book! I find that the movie business is not quite the same. It doesn't move quite as fast."[12] As a matter of fact, there are thousands of projects in development at any given moment in the entertainment business, but scant few make it to a screen, theater, or other distribution channel. Lee's work with POW! seems to have nearly slowed to a trickle, but that is only within the context of how the entertainment industry operates and in comparison to the halcyon days at Marvel in the 1960s when he controlled a much smaller operation, albeit with lasting significance for contemporary culture.

As a result, detractors might point to Lee's post-Marvel work and conclude that he has coasted on past successes (or the work of Kirby and Ditko) for far too long. Closer examination, however, reveals a more accurate portrait of an artist still producing well past ninety years of age, as well as an icon still among his fans, cementing his legacy as one of the most important creative figures in American history.

In late 2016 at the Cincinnati Comic Expo, several hundred people stood in line and many hundreds more waited outside the hall for the chance to see Lee and get his autograph. They slowly shuffled ahead through a series of roped-off areas, trying to contain their excitement, and chatting at length with the fans around them in a communal lovefest. When their big moment with Lee finally took place—almost to a person—the fans were too dumbstruck to say anything to their hero. Some managed to get out a whispered "thanks."

On paper, the moment might read as anticlimactic. However, being in Lee's presence seemed enough for the fans. After getting their Spider-Man poster or Doctor Strange comic book signed, they turned away from Lee with huge grins, as if they had just scored a major victory. Finally out of the lines and with the moment starting to settle in, fans immediately searched out family members or friends who had accompanied them. They shared in the glory and wanted to acknowledge the event. Some people viewed getting their cherished comic book signed by Lee as the culmination of a lifetime of experiences with Marvel and its superheroes.

One might mistake Lee's POW! Entertainment office in Santa Monica for a kind of stand-in Stan Lee museum. The bright space is bursting with shelves of Lee trinkets, including various dolls and action figures of the comic book icon and his many creations. An old-school Captain America sits at the front of the desk, daring visitors to lean closer. A stuffed Hulk guards the computer monitor. Walls are lined with photos of Lee—from a group shot with the cast of *The Big Bang Theory* to a drawing of Lee as Clark Kent pulling his shirt open to reveal a red Superman "S" emblazoned across his chest. Another photo shows Lee and Joanie on the red carpet at a Hollywood premiere, another is of Lee shaking hands with President Reagan. A large Silver Surfer awash in deep blue and riding a teal-striped surfboard adorns the wall behind the desk, as if emerging directly out of the wall.

Max Anderson, Lee's longtime personal assistant and cofounder of Stan Lee Collectibles, tells a story about a day that Stan and Joanie invited him to their home. They asked him to haul away mountains of mementos and memorabilia that had accumulated since the Lees moved to Los Angeles decades before. Stan just wanted to toss it all. Anderson realized the significance of pieces of Lee's past and instead carted it away for safekeeping. Later the items from that surprising housecleaning would serve as the foundation for a pop-up Stan Lee Museum on display at Lee's Comikaze comic book convention. Later, Anderson stored the items for possible use in a permanent museum dedicated to Lee and his legacy.[13]

As someone steeped in comic book and pop culture history, and the creator of a new storytelling sensibility, Lee has a keen sense of his past. However, he has little use for nostalgia. Most journalists and fans ask Lee inane, simplistic questions about who his favorite superhero is or what was running through his mind decades ago when he created the characters. Always polite to journalists and media people, Lee dutifully tells the superhero origin stories over and over again. New waves of journalists, interviewers, and fans continue to want to hear them. His own outlook, though, is constantly looking ahead, off toward the next creation or idea, and he still scribbles down these thoughts on the tiny notepads that he carries in his front shirt pocket, as he has for his entire career.

Meeting Lee, one senses that his public persona grew out of a teenage desire to be an actor and later morphed into a kind of celebrity identity that enabled him to play up the brash, New York City attitude that he saw all around him in his youth. The caricature, however, falls by the wayside in one-on-one conversation. In these moments, Lee is thoughtful and reflective, answering questions as if after all these years he still can't believe his good fortune or why the fans line up to see him by the hundreds and thousands. Lee's youthful, appreciative outlook offsets the exaggerated public displays of braggadocio. In his mid-nineties, he no longer hears well, and a 2012 operation installed a pacemaker to regulate his heartbeat, yet he continues to make appearances, relishing his role as the Marvel Universe's spiritual leader.

Asked in 2016 how it felt to inspire generations of fans and artists with his flawed hero narrative, Lee paused for a moment. "It's an incredibly great feeling, when I think about it. I don't have that much time to think about it, but when I do . . ."[14] His voice trails off. The thing about creative icons is that they never really stop creating. Lee's worldview isn't based on what he did in the 1960s. He believes in the next spark, the new work, always charting a course toward the future.

CONCLUSION
AMERICAN ICON

At the conclusion of *Captain America: Civil War* (2016), a FedEx delivery driver appears at the Stark Enterprises headquarters of the Avengers. Knocking on the glass, he asks, "Are you Tony Stank?"

James "Rhodey" Rhodes, Tony Stark's best friend, points to his buddy and exclaims, "Yes, this is Tony Stank. . . . You're in the right place. Thank you for that!"

The FedEx employee is played by Stan Lee, his twenty-ninth cameo in superhero films. The scene ends the movie on a humorous note and, more importantly, demonstrates Lee's place in the Marvel Universe. The package contains a letter from Captain America to Iron Man, turning over leadership of the Avengers to him, but also letting Stark know that he will still show up if the Earth faces peril. Lee's cameo may seem a throwaway, but the moment is central to the plot, and points to how the Marvel Universe unfolds in the future. As Rhodes explains, Lee's character is definitely "in the right place"—at the center of the action.

The cheerful conversation between Stark and Rhodes counterbalances the previous scene in which Rhodey—veteran military hero and War Machine combatant—struggles to walk again after breaking his back in the earlier superhero melee. Despite the dramatic edge, the tone and voice sounds as if Lee wrote the exchange in the early 1960s. Rhodes and Stark trade smirks and jokes, with Rhodes laughing, "Please, table for one for Mr. Stank, preferably by the bathroom." The dialogue is a Lee line, set during a Lee cameo, in Lee's Marvel Universe—his personality imprinted on a grand scale. Lee certainly fulfilled Martin Goodman's early directive—create a bunch of superheroes. No one realized that the order would transform storytelling and American popular culture.

When Stanley Lieber became Stan Lee, he was hiding his real identity behind a pseudonym that he thought protected him from the disdainful scorn of those who looked down on the meaningless work he did in a trivial industry. Lee explained, "Early in my career, before *The Fantastic Four*, I struggled. I felt I was never going to get anywhere. Even afterward, I was embarrassed to say I wrote comic books for a living. I had a lot of shame about that."[1] He carried that concept—the notion that what he did each day didn't really matter—for decades.

Then, rising from his own anguish (and with goading from wife Joanie), Lee took ownership of who he was and what he might create if he changed his outlook and wrote what he wanted. Then, he turned the ideas over to some of the greatest artists to ever work in comics to create them visually. The Fantastic Four came to life, he birthed the Hulk, and soon Thor dropped down from the heavens. Countless additional characters endowed with otherworldly powers and unfathomable evil joined the early superheroes. Most significantly, Lee created the least likely hero around: a geeky teenager with a boatload of personal problems whose life changes when a supercharged spider bites him. The Amazing Spider-Man was born.

The Marvel Universe did not begin with Spider-Man, but he was the one fans gravitated to the most—as did Lee. For his creator,

Spider-Man is more than a comic-strip hero. He's a state of mind. He symbolizes the secret dreams, fears, and frustrations that haunt us all. We all have our hidden daydreams, daydreams in which we're stronger, swifter, and braver than we really are—than we can ever hope to be. But, to Spider-Man, such dreams are reality.[2]

Spider-Man sparked a revolution in comic books and storytelling by giving readers a fresh way of viewing superheroes. Finally, they seemed real, with feet of clay, just like people everywhere. Marvel's characters possessed emotional weaknesses. They had to deal with their human emotions, not simply vulnerabilities like Superman's, which came from unearthly rocks that bad guys stumbled upon. In the final frame of his debut in *Amazing Fantasy* #15, Lee wrote the famous line that Spider-Man had become "aware at last that in this world, with great power there must also come—great responsibility!" The way Spider-Man has since been popularized and immortalized across American culture, this line alone might have forever cemented Lee as an iconic writer.

In short order, Lee created an interlocked network of superheroes and supporting characters that reflected the way people with extraordinary powers might actually live in the real world. Long before people could look back and realize Lee's influence on the broader culture, they had to read the comic books. The genius he brought to the business, which launched the Marvel Age, centered on the way the characters spoke, their feelings, and the convincing issues they faced. The equation seemed almost too simple: If superheroes can be like you, then you can be like a superhero. Readers responded to Lee's ideas, and his authorial imprint developed into a central facet of popular culture.

Cocreating the characters and writing the stories with Marvel's gifted artists, inkers, letterers, and colorists, however, did not end the process or Lee's influence. He served other critical functions at Marvel that expanded his role far beyond the creative staff he worked with, including editing the comics, approving the artwork, and keeping the full-time staff and freelancers on task to meet the deadlines the publishing industry demanded. Then, realizing that his duties did not end there, he stumbled into serving as a mouthpiece for Marvel, first in the press, and then barnstorming the nation's (and later the world's) college campuses and public stages. The superhero stories went global and Lee told them again and again to whoever would listen.

On many occasions, Lee wondered when the superhero craze would wear off and he'd be onto another genre, fully expecting the boom-and-bust cycle to continue. From this perspective, the creative aspects of the job were tightly wound to the financial. "If *Spider-Man* hadn't sold, we'd have forgotten about it," Lee said. "To us they were just scripts. We were making them up, and we'd hope they'd sell, and some sold better than others, so those we kept."[3]

There is no shortage of controversy or crisis in the entertainment industry. Often it seems as if these forces—not talent or success—fuel popular culture. Lee has faced various levels of condemnation for decades. To his critics, many of Lee's actions have seemed inauthentic, centered on his own fame at the expense of others who should have been included in the spotlight's glow. Even now, some antagonists have found his recent work focused mainly on making him money, not creating anything of lasting value. And, as well, the battle lines are tightly drawn between Lee and the pro-Kirby and pro-Ditko camps regarding who actually created the Marvel Universe.

With all the challenges Marvel faced as an organization, the answer often came back to Spider-Man. The character's enduring popularity saved the day. Lee's willingness to promote the superhero ensured that Marvel also stayed securely on the nation's popular culture radar. In turn, the effort solidified Lee's own place in the cultural pantheon.

While people often credit Lee for his role in gradually turning comic books into a more respected medium and establishing Marvel's place among the world's great brands, he is rarely given enough credit simply as a writer. Just like novelists and filmmakers had always done, it is as if Lee put his hands up into the air and pulled down fistfuls of the national zeitgeist. As a writer, Lee did what all iconic creative people do—he improved on or perfected his craft, thus creating an entirely new style that would have broad impact across the rest of the industry, and then around the globe.

At the time Spider-Man appeared, Lee had already been working in the industry for more than twenty years. By this point, his writing process grew out of his fascination with dialogue. He explained, "Whenever I write a story of any sort, I usually recite all the dialogue aloud as I'm writing it. . . . I act it out, with all the emotion and corny emphasis that I can muster." What this kind of writing and narration forces is what all great writers understand: "It's got to sound natural."[4] These innovations—focusing on realistic dialogue, speaking directly to the reader, and allowing the reader into the character's thinking via thought bubbles—created the Marvel style that would soon dominate the comic book industry and then gradually extend to film, television, literature, and other forms of storytelling.

Generations of artists, writers, actors, and other creative types have been inspired, moved, or encouraged by the universe Lee voiced and birthed. While he did not invent the imperfect hero (one could argue that such heroes had been around since Homer's time and even before), Lee delivered the message to a generation of readers hungry for something new. Although the nerd-to-hero story line seems like it must have sprung from the earth fully formed, Lee gave readers a new way of looking at what it meant to be a hero and spun the notion of who might be heroic in a way that spoke to the rapidly expanding number of comic book buyers. They gobbled up his superheroes with their dimes, nickels, and quarters. Spider-Man's popularity revealed the attraction to the idea of a tainted hero, but at the same time, the character also hit the newsstands at the perfect time, when the growth of the baby boomer generation and the optimism of John F. Kennedy's Camelot resulted in a second golden age for comic books.

Regardless of the opinions of nay-sayers, there is something heroic in Lee himself. Like others at the apex of American popular culture, Lee transformed his industry, which subsequently had much broader implications. Lee became Marvel madman, mouthpiece, and all-around maestro—the face of comic books for six decades. The man who wanted to pen the Great American Novel did so much more. Without question, Lee became one of the most important creative icons in contemporary American history.

NOTES

PROLOGUE

1. *Stan Lee's Mutants, Monsters, and Marvels,* directed by Scott Zakarin (Burbank, CA: Sony Pictures, 2002), DVD.
2. Ibid.
3. Ibid.
4. David Anthony Kraft, "The *Foom* Interview: Stan Lee," in *Stan Lee Conversations,* ed. Jeff McLaughlin (Jackson: University Press of Mississippi, 2007), 63.
5. Ibid.
6. Stan Lee, *Origins of Marvel Comics,* revised edition (New York: Marvel, 1997), 12.
7. Quoted in Stan Lee and George Mair, *Excelsior! The Amazing Life of Stan Lee* (New York: Simon and Schuster, 2002), 113.
8. Lee, *Origins,* 12.
9. Lee and Mair, *Excelsior!,* 114.

CHAPTER 1

1. The sum equates to about $3,500.
2. Gur Alroey, *Bread to Eat and Clothes to Wear: Letters from Jewish Migrants in the Early Twentieth Century* (Detroit: Wayne State University Press, 2011), 10.
3. Dana Mihailescu, "Images of Romania and America in Early Twentieth-Century Romanian-Jewish Immigrant Life Stories in the United States," *East European Jewish Affairs* 42, no. 1 (2012): 28.
4. Ibid., 29.
5. Ibid., 32.
6. Alroey, *Bread to Eat and Clothes to Wear,* 12.

7. For a man who has lived most of his life on the public stage—and written two different memoirs—Lee says little about his parents, relatives, ethnicity, or religion. In his first memoir, he claims that his parents were "both Romanian immigrants." However, in the graphic novel memoir (2015), Lee says that his father was a Romanian immigrant, but that his mother "was born in New York." Actually, Lee got it right in the first memoir—his mother was born in Romania as well, though her past in her native land is a mystery to us today. For Lee's discussion of his youth, please see: Stan Lee and George Mair, *Excelsior! The Amazing Life of Stan Lee* (New York: Simon and Schuster, 2002), 5; Stan Lee, Peter David, and Colleen Doran, *Amazing Fantastic Incredible: A Marvelous Memoir* (New York: Touchstone, 2015), n.p.

8. Sifting through tens of thousands of United States Census records, a rudimentary picture emerges about Lee's parents and his extended family. Although these records shed light on a part of Lee's life he rarely discusses, recordkeeping in that era relied on census-takers rendering accurate documentation. Accuracy ebbed, however, under the difficulties the census workers faced: language barriers, privacy concerns, and other challenges. The enumerators were forbidden to ask for proof to corroborate the information they received, so they would try to get pertinent details correct, assuming that the interviewee even had a handle on the truth. The effort took on added difficulty in New York City, where numerous families might be living in the same apartment building with extended family and boarders, a common practice at the time. As a result, some records flip-flop first and last names, which then skews electronic database searches. Other times, entire families slip out of the official documentation. Given that the documents were handwritten, simple legibility is a challenge. The enumerators had little incentive for getting the information perfect; they were poorly compensated for their work, with speed more important than accuracy. Many were political appointees who knew the right people in the local power structure to be awarded the job.

9. With Lee's family, like so many others that arrived in the early years of the twentieth century, uncertainties even exist about the most basic facts. For example, in the Census records, his father's name changed from Hyman in 1910 to Jacob in 1920, while his birthdate is listed alternately as 1886 or 1888. If the latter date is correct, then he is only seventeen years old when he makes the transatlantic journey. His relative, Abraham, who is living with him in a boarding home with an older Russian-Romanian couple and their children in 1910, disappears in later documentation, leading to speculation that Jacob's younger brother may have been among the thousands of Romanian immigrants who later returned to the homeland. Alternatively, Abraham could have moved away from New York City and into the throngs of immigrants spreading westward. Later, Lee mentioned his brother's sisters (Becky and Bertha) but they do not show up in any further documentation, nor does he mention them in his memoirs. Joanna Lieber to Stan Lee, e-mail message, April 26, 1998, Correspondence, 1998, Box 196, Stan Lee Papers, American Heritage Center, University of Wyoming.

10. Unfortunately there are no surviving records to fill us in on Celia and Jack's courtship or wedding. We do not know if it was elaborate, simple, or somewhere in between.

11. Only four children remained at home, but of the four, only Celia is listed as not being employed. In one Census report, Celia's birthdate is listed as 1894, two years later than previously identified, but there is no reason given for why the twenty-six-year-old did not work. Greater mystery regarding Stanley Lieber's family history occurs in the 1930 Census.

12. Basically, the Liebers disappeared from the 1930 Census. There are many reasons that the family might have vanished, ranging from shoddy work on the part of census enumerators who often misspelled or skipped over information that wasn't easily determined, to the

transiency of families in that era as the Depression raged. Under difficult circumstances, enumerators would turn to neighbors, young children, or non-English-speaking family members to provide information. In this environment, many people disappeared from the official documentation. As a result, the family could have been in transition from one part of the city to another and simply missed the census taker's visit. Alternatively, they might have dodged the local enumerator in an attempt to go unnoticed, basically ashamed of their plight.

13. Mark Lacter, "Stan Lee Marvel Comics Always Searching for a New Story," *Inc.*, November 2009, 96.

14. Stan Lee, "Excelsior!" Outline, July 30, 1978, Box 96, Stan Lee Papers, American Heritage Center, University of Wyoming.

15. Lee and Mair, *Excelsior!*, 7.

16. Lee, David, and Doran, *Amazing Fantastic*.

17. Lee and Mair, *Excelsior!*, 8.

18. Lee, "Excelsior!" Outline.

19. Jordan Raphael and Tom Spurgeon, *Stan Lee and the Rise and Fall of the American Comic Book* (Chicago: Chicago Review Press, 2003), 4.

20. Lee and Mair, *Excelsior!*, 11.

21. Quoted in Raphael and Spurgeon, *Stan Lee and the Rise and Fall*, 4.

22. Lee and Mair, *Excelsior!*, 12.

23. Ibid., 9.

24. Lee, "Excelsior!" Outline.

25. Lee and Mair, *Excelsior!*, 10.

26. Stan Lee, "Comic Relief: Comic Books Aren't Just for Entertainment," *Edutopia*, August 11, 2005, www.edutopia.org/comic-relief.

27. Lee and Mair, *Excelsior!*, 13.

28. Lee, "Excelsior!" Outline.

29. Quoted in Mike Bourne, "Stan Lee, the Marvel Bard," in *Alter Ego*, ed. Roy Thomas, vol. 3, no. 74 (2007): 26.

30. Quoted in *With Great Power: The Stan Lee Story*, directed by Terry Douglas, Nikki Frakes, and William Lawrence Hess (Los Angeles: MPI Home Video, 2012), DVD.

31. Stan Lee, "History of Marvel (Chapters 1, 2, 3)," unpublished, 2. Marvel Comics—History (Draft of "History of Marvel Comics"), 1990, Box 5, Folder 7, Stan Lee Papers, American Heritage Center, University of Wyoming.

32. Quoted in Raphael and Spurgeon, *Stan Lee and the Rise and Fall*, 8.

33. Ibid.

34. Lee and Mair, *Excelsior!*, 15.

35. Raphael and Spurgeon, *Stan Lee and the Rise and Fall*, 7.

36. United States, Bureau of the Census, 1940 U.S. Census, New York, Bronx County, New York, enumeration district 3-1487, household 61, Jacob Lieber Family, Sheet 6-B. Barb Sigler, *HeritageQuest Online*, http://www.ancestryheritagequest.com: accessed March 30, 2016.

37. Lee and Mair, *Excelsior!*, 6.

38. David Hochman, "*Playboy* Interview: Stan Lee," *Playboy*, April 11, 2014, http://www.playboy.com/articles/stan-lee-marvel-playboy-interview.

39. Lee and Mair, *Excelsior!*, 7.

40. Mark Alexander, "Lee and Kirby: The Wonder Years," in *The Jack Kirby Collector* 18, no. 58 (Winter 2011): 5.

CHAPTER 2

1. Blake Bell and Michael J. Vassallo, *The Secret History of Marvel Comics: Jack Kirby and the Moonlighting Artists at Martin Goodman's Empire* (Seattle: Fantagraphics, 2013), 98.

2. Quoted in Kenneth Plume, "Interview with Stan Lee (Part 1 of 5)," *IGN*, June 26, 2000, accessed June 1, 2016, http://www.ign.com/articles/2000/06/26/interview-with-stan-lee-part-1-of-5.

3. Young Stanley Lieber's hiring at Timely has changed repeatedly over the years. In an unpublished draft of the history of Marvel, Lee wrote "early 1940," but in other publications and places he says or infers 1939. Stan Lee, "History of Marvel (Chapters 1, 2, 3)," unpublished, 1. Marvel Comics—History (Draft of "History of Marvel Comics") 1990, Box 5, Folder 7, Stan Lee Papers, American Heritage Center, University of Wyoming.

4. Gerard Jones, *Men of Tomorrow: Geeks, Gangsters, and the Birth of the Comic Book* (New York: Basic, 2004), 97.

5. Ibid., 108.

6. Ibid., 158.

7. Ibid., 159.

8. Sean Howe, *Marvel Comics: The Untold Story* (New York: Harper, 2012), 14.

9. Ibid.

10. Quoted in Mark Evanier, *Kirby: King of Comics* (New York: Harry N. Abrams, 2008), 45.

11. Joe Simon, *Joe Simon: My Life in Comics* (London: Titan, 2011), 92.

12. Howe, *Marvel Comics*, 20.

13. "The Marvelous Life of Stan Lee," *CBS News*, January 17, 2016, http://www.cbsnews.com/news/the-marvelous-life-of-stan-lee.

14. Stan Lee and George Mair, *Excelsior! The Amazing Life of Stan Lee* (New York: Simon and Schuster, 2002), 26.

15. "Stan Lee Speaks at the 1975 San Diego Comic-Con Convention," YouTube, uploaded January 6, 2010, https://youtu.be/MhJuBqDTM9Q.

16. *Captain America Comics* #3, May 1, 1941, 37.

17. Simon, *Joe Simon*, 114.

18. Ibid., 113.

19. Ibid.

20. Ibid., 114.

21. Quoted in Stan Lee, Peter David, and Colleen Doran, *Amazing Fantastic Incredible: A Marvelous Memoir* (New York: Touchstone, 2015), n.p.

22. Lee and Mair, *Excelsior!*, 30.

23. Lee, "History of Marvel (Chapters 1, 2, 3)," 9.

24. Quoted in Shirrel Rhoades, *A Complete History of American Comic Books* (New York: Peter Lang, 2008), 36.

25. Jim Amash, "The Goldberg Variations," *Alter Ego* 3, no. 18 (October 2002): 6.

26. Arie Kaplan, *Masters of the Comic Book Universe Revealed!* (Chicago: Chicago Review Press, 2006), 49.

27. Quoted in Rhoades, *A Complete History*, 36.

28. Lee and Mair, *Excelsior!*, 30.

CHAPTER 3

1. Rebecca Robbins Raines, *Getting the Message Through: A Branch History of the U.S. Army Signal Corps* (Washington, DC: Center of Military History, U.S. Army, 1996), 256.

2. Mike Benton, *The Comic Book in America: An Illustrated History* (Dallas: Taylor, 1989), 35.

3. Ibid., 35–41.

4. Sean Howe, *Marvel Comics: The Untold Story* (New York: Harper, 2012), 24.

5. Catherine Sanders, et al., eds., *Marvel Year by Year: A Visual Chronicle* (New York: DK, 2013), 20.

6. Quoted in Howe, *Marvel Comics*, 25.

7. During the time Lee was stationed at Fort Monmouth, Julius Rosenberg carried out a clandestine mission spying for Russia. He also recruited scientists and engineers from the base into the spy ring he led in New Jersey and funneled thousands of pages of top-secret documents to his Russian handlers. Rosenberg and his wife Ethel were arrested, convicted, and in 1953 executed.

8. Quoted in Steven Mackenzie, "Stan Lee Interview: 'The World Always Needs Heroes,'" *Big Issue*, January 18, 2016, http://www.bigissue.com/features/interviews/6153/stan-lee-interview-the-world-always-needs-heroes.

9. Stan Lee, "Excelsior!" Outline, July 30, 1978, Box 96, Stan Lee Papers, American Heritage Center, University of Wyoming.

10. Quoted in Stan Lee and George Mair, *Excelsior! The Amazing Life of Stan Lee* (New York: Simon and Schuster, 2002), 37.

11. Ibid., 40.

12. Stan Lee, "Comic Relief: Comic Books Aren't Just for Entertainment," *Edutopia*, August 11, 2005, www.edutopia.org/comic-relief.

13. Lee and Mair, *Excelsior!*, 44.

14. Ibid., 45.

15. Blake Bell and Michael J. Vassallo, *The Secret History of Marvel Comics: Jack Kirby and the Moonlighting Artists at Martin Goodman's Empire* (Seattle: Fantagraphics, 2013), 158.

16. Stan Lee, "Only the Blind Can See," *Joker* 1, no. 4 (1943–1944): 39, reprinted in ibid., 159.

17. Lee and Mair, *Excelsior!*, 43–44.

18. Lee, "Excelsior!" Outline.

CHAPTER 4

1. Stan Lee and George Mair, *Excelsior! The Amazing Life of Stan Lee* (New York: Simon and Schuster, 2002), 56.

2. Timely script editor Al Sulman claims that he created the character after Lee asked him to come up with a Wonder Woman–like heroine.

3. Joe Simon, *Joe Simon: My Life in Comics* (London: Titan, 2011), 166–67.

4. A great deal of uncertainty exists regarding how comic books were numbered, titled, retitled, and renumbered. Part of the answer had to do with the publisher's printing and distribution processes. There are also indications that postal regulations for mailing magazines had

some influence. Finally, tradition or heritage also played a role. Many pulp publishers opera-ted this way, which led to similar tactics in the comic book business. For more information, see John Jackson Miller, "Where Did Comics Numbering Come From?" *Comichron*, July 10, 2011, http://blog.comichron.com/2011/07/where-did-comics-numbering-come-from.html.

5. Lee and Mair, *Excelsior!*, 64.

6. Stan Lee, *Secrets behind the Comics* (New York: Famous Enterprises, 1947), 6.

7. Ibid., 22.

8. Blake Bell and Michael J. Vassallo, *The Secret History of Marvel Comics: Jack Kirby and the Moonlighting Artists at Martin Goodman's Empire* (Seattle: Fantagraphics, 2013), 72.

9. David Anthony Kraft, "The *Foom* Interview: Stan Lee," in *Stan Lee Conversations*, ed. Jeff McLaughlin (Jackson: University Press of Mississippi, 2007), 68.

10. Stan Lee, "Excelsior!" Outline, July 30, 1978, Box 96, Stan Lee Papers, American Heri-tage Center, University of Wyoming.

11. Ibid.

12. Stan Lee, "Where I Span a Hero's Yarn," *Sunday Times* (London), May 12, 2002, F3.

13. Jordan Raphael and Tom Spurgeon, *Stan Lee and the Rise and Fall of the American Comic Book* (Chicago: Chicago Review Press, 2003), 38.

14. Lee, "Where I Spun a Hero's Yarn."

15. Lee, "Excelsior!" Outline.

CHAPTER 5

1. "Urges Comic Book Ban," *New York Times*, September 4, 1948, 16.

2. Quoted in Thomas F. O'Connor, "The National Organization for Decent Literature: A Phase in American Catholic Censorship," *Library Quarterly: Information, Community, Policy* 65, no. 4 (1995): 390.

3. Ibid., 399.

4. Ron Goulart, *Great American Comic Books* (Lincolnwood, IL: Publications Internati-onal, 2001), 210–12.

5. See Lee's glib discussion of the debates in Stan Lee and George Mair, *Excelsior! The Amazing Life of Stan Lee* (New York: Simon and Schuster, 2002), 92–94.

6. Ibid., 91.

7. Ibid., 92, 93.

8. Quoted in David Hajdu, *The Ten-Cent Plague: The Great Comic-Book Scare and How It Changed America* (New York: Farrar, Straus and Giroux, 2008), 264.

9. Ibid., 269ff.

10. Ibid., 270–73.

11. Goulart, *Great American Comic Books*, 217.

12. Lee and Mair, *Excelsior!*, 93

13. Ibid., 94.

14. Alexandra Gill, "Captain Comics," *Globe and Mail*, September 29, 2003, R1.

15. Jim Amash, "The Goldberg Variations," *Alter Ego* 3, no. 18 (October 2002): 9.

16. Richard Harrington, "Stan Lee: Caught in Spidey's Web," *Washington Post*, February 4, 1992, D1.

17. Lee and Mair, *Excelsior!*, 99.

18. Quoted in Sean Howe, *Marvel Comics: The Untold Story* (New York: Harper, 2012), 32.

19. Lee and Mair, *Excelsior!*, 87, 88.

20. Blake Bell and Michael J. Vassallo, *The Secret History of Marvel Comics: Jack Kirby and the Moonlighting Artists at Martin Goodman's Empire* (Seattle: Fantagraphics, 2013), 158.

21. Quoted in Howe, *Marvel Comics*, 35.

CHAPTER 6

1. John Romita, "Face Front, True Believers! The Comics Industry Sounds Off on Stan Lee," *Comics Journal* 181 (October 1995): 83.

2. Roy Thomas, "All-Schwartz Comics: A Conversation with Editorial Legend Julius Schwartz, *Alter Ego* 3, no. 7 (2001), http://www.twomorrows.com/alterego/articles/07schwartz.html.

3. Shirrel Rhoades, *A Complete History of American Comic Books* (New York: Peter Lang, 2008), 70–71.

4. Ibid., 72–73.

5. Blake Bell and Michael J. Vassallo, *The Secret History of Marvel Comics: Jack Kirby and the Moonlighting Artists at Martin Goodman's Empire* (Seattle: Fantagraphics, 2013), 75.

6. Quoted in ibid., 45.

7. Stan Lee and George Mair, *Excelsior! The Amazing Life of Stan Lee* (New York: Simon and Schuster, 2002), 112.

8. Stan Lee, *Origins of Marvel Comics*, revised edition (New York: Marvel, 1997), 10.

9. Craig Tomashoff, "Move Over Batman . . ." *Los Angeles Reader*, January 26, 1990.

10. *Stan Lee's Mutants, Monsters, and Marvels*, directed by Scott Zakarin (Burbank, CA: Sony Pictures, 2002), DVD.

11. Roy Thomas, "A Fantastic First," in *The Stan Lee Universe*, ed. Danny Fingeroth and Roy Thomas (Raleigh, NC: TwoMorrows, 2011), 17.

12. Stan Lee and Jack Kirby, *Marvel Masterworks: Fantastic Four, Nos. 1–10* (New York: Marvel, 2003), n.p.

13. *Stan Lee's Mutants*.

14. Stan Lee, Peter David, and Colleen Doran, *Amazing Fantastic Incredible: A Marvelous Memoir* (New York: Touchstone, 2015), n.p.

15. Quoted in Les Daniels, *Marvel: Five Fabulous Decades of the World's Greatest Comics* (New York: Harry N. Abrams, 1995), 87.

16. The popularity of *The Fantastic Four* enabled Goodman to raise the price of all comics from the traditional ten cents to twelve cents per issue. The increase took place with the third issue dated March 1962.

17. "*Fantastic Four* #1 Synopsis," reprinted in Thomas, "A Fantastic First," 16.

18. Ted White, "Stan Lee Meets [Castle of] Frankenstein: An Early Marvel Age interview with Stan," in *The Stan Lee Universe*, ed. Danny Fingeroth and Roy Thomas (Raleigh, NC: TwoMorrows, 2011), 11.

19. Lee and Mair, *Excelsior!*, 124.

20. Stan Lee and Jack Kirby, *Marvel Masterworks: Fantastic Four, Nos. 11–20* (New York: Marvel, 2003), n.p.

21. Quoted in Daniels, *Marvel: Five Fabulous Decades*, 85, 87.

22. Stan Lee, *Bring on the Bad Guys*, revised edition (New York: Marvel, 1998), n.p.

23. Ibid.

24. Lee and Kirby, *Marvel Masterworks, Nos. 11–20*, n.p.

CHAPTER 7

1. Mark Lacter, "Stan Lee Marvel Comics Always Searching for a New Story," *Inc.*, November 2009, 96.

2. Don Thrasher, "Stan Lee's Secret to Success: A Marvel-ous Imagination," *Dayton Daily News*, January 21, 2006, sec. E.

3. Lacter, "Stan Lee, Marvel Comics Always Searching," 96.

4. Quoted in ibid.

5. Stan Lee and George Mair, *Excelsior! The Amazing Life of Stan Lee* (New York: Simon and Schuster, 2002), 126–27.

6. Ibid., 126.

7. Roy Thomas, "Stan the Man and Roy the Boy: A Conversation between Stan Lee and Roy Thomas," in *Stan Lee Conversations*, ed. Jeff McLaughlin (Jackson: University Press of Mississippi, 2007), 141.

8. Ibid.

9. Lee and Mair, *Excelsior!*, 127.

10. Thomas, "Stan the Man," 141.

11. Lee and Mair, *Excelsior!*, 127.

12. Ibid., 128.

13. Ibid., 128.

14. Leonard Pitts Jr., An Interview with Stan Lee, in *Stan Lee Conversations*, ed. Jeff McLaughlin (Jackson: University Press of Mississippi, 2007), 96.

15. Quoted in Lee and Mair, *Excelsior!*, 128.

16. Stan Lee, Peter David, and Colleen Doran, *Amazing Fantastic Incredible: A Marvelous Memoir* (New York: Touchstone, 2015), n.p.

17. Lee and Mair, *Excelsior!*, 135–36.

18. Stan Lee, "That's My Spidey," *New York Times*, May 3, 2002, http://www.nytimes.com/2002/05/03/opinion/that-s-my-spidey.html.

CHAPTER 8

1. Stan Lee and George Mair, *Excelsior! The Amazing Life of Stan Lee* (New York: Simon and Schuster, 2002), 120.

2. Stan Lee, *Son of Origins of Marvel Comics*, revised edition (New York: Marvel, 1997), 69.

3. Pierre Comtois, *Marvel Comics in the 1960s: An Issue by Issue Field Guide to a Pop Culture Phenomenon* (Raleigh, NC: TwoMorrows, 2009), 20.

4. Stan Lee, *Origins of Marvel Comics*, revised edition (New York: Marvel, 1997), 165.

5. Larry Lieber, interviewed by Danny Fingeroth, *WriteNow!* 18 (Summer 2008): 5.

6. Quoted in Will Murray, "Stan Lee Looks Back: The Comics Legend Recalls Life with Jack Kirby, Steve Ditko, and Heroes," in *Stan Lee Conversations*, ed. Jeff McLaughlin (Jackson: University Press of Mississippi, 2007), 182.

7. Lee and Mair, *Excelsior!*, 160.

8. Quoted in Les Daniels, *Marvel: Five Fabulous Decades of the World's Greatest Comics* (New York: Harry N. Abrams, 1995), 99.

9. Lee, *Origins of Marvel Comics*, 215.

10. Lee, *Son of Origins*, 110.

11. Ibid., 10.

12. Quoted in Dick Cavett, "*The Dick Cavett Show*: An Interview with Stan Lee," in *Stan Lee Conversations*, ed. Jeff McLaughlin (Jackson: University Press of Mississippi, 2007), 15.

13. Quoted in Dewey Cassell, ed., *The Art of George Tuska* (Raleigh, NC: TwoMorrows, 2005), 57.

14. Ibid., 58.

15. Gene Colan, interviewed in Tom Field, "The Colan Mystique," *Comic Book Artist* 13 (May 2001), http://twomorrows.com/comicbookartist/articles/13colan.html.

16. Dennis O'Neil, interviewed in Danny Fingeroth, *The Stan Lee Universe*, ed. Danny Fingeroth and Roy Thomas (Raleigh, NC: TwoMorrows, 2011), 53.

17. Ibid.

18. *Stan Lee's Mutants, Monsters, and Marvels*, directed by Scott Zakarin (Burbank, CA: Sony Pictures, 2002), DVD.

19. Ibid.

20. Quoted in Chris Gavaler, "Kirby vs. Steranko! Silver Age Layout Wars," *Hooded Utilitarian*, July 12, 2016, http://www.hoodedutilitarian.com/2016/07/kirby-vs-steranko -silver-age-layout-wars/.

21. Ibid.

22. Lee, *Origins of Marvel Comics*, 164.

CHAPTER 9

1. *Stan Lee's Mutants, Monsters, and Marvels*, directed by Scott Zakarin (Burbank, CA: Sony Pictures, 2002), DVD.

2. Ibid.

3. Quoted in Paul Lopes, *Demanding Respect: The Evolution of the American Comic Book* (Philadelphia: Temple University Press, 2009), 65.

4. Craig Tomashoff, "Move Over Batman . . ." *Los Angeles Reader*, January 26, 1990.

5. David Kasakove, "Finding Marvel's Voice: An Appreciation of Stan Lee's Bullpen Bulletins and Soapboxes, *Write Now* 18 (Summer 2008): 57

6. Mark Alexander, "Lee & Kirby: The Wonder Years," in *The Jack Kirby Collector* 18, no. 58 (Winter 2011): 8.

7. Ibid.

8. Quoted in Danny Fingeroth, *The Stan Lee Universe*, ed. Danny Fingeroth and Roy Thomas (Raleigh, NC: TwoMorrows, 2011), 52.

9. Ibid.

10. Stan Lee interview in Dan Hagan, "Stan Lee," *Comics Interview*, July 1983, 55.

11. Leonard Sloane, "Advertising: Comics Go Up, Up and Away," *New York Times*, July 20, 1967.

12. Ibid.

13. Quoted in ibid.

14. Lopes, *Demanding Respect*, 66.

15. Mike Benton, *The Comic Book in America: An Illustrated History* (Dallas: Taylor, 1989), 71.

16. Stan Lee, "Excelsior!" Outline, July 30, 1978, Box 96, Stan Lee Papers, American Heritage Center, University of Wyoming.

17. Stan Lee and George Mair, *Excelsior! The Amazing Life of Stan Lee* (New York: Simon and Schuster, 2002), 142.

18. Quoted in Dick Cavett, "*The Dick Cavett Show*: An Interview with Stan Lee," in *Stan Lee Conversations*, ed. Jeff McLaughlin (Jackson: University Press of Mississippi, 2007), 16.

19. Ibid.

20. M. Thomas Inge, "From the Publisher's Perspective: Comments by Stan Lee and Jenette Kahn," in *Stan Lee Conversations*, ed. Jeff McLaughlin (Jackson: University Press of Mississippi, 2007), 105.

21. Stan Lee, Peter David, and Colleen Doran, *Amazing Fantastic Incredible: A Marvelous Memoir* (New York: Touchstone, 2015).

22. Lee and Mair, *Excelsior!*, 179.

23. Quoted in Sean Howe, *Marvel Comics: The Untold Story* (New York: Harper, 2012), 92.

24. Ibid., 100ff.

25. Quoted in ibid., 104.

26. Quoted in Cavett, "*The Dick Cavett Show*: An Interview with Stan Lee," 18.

CHAPTER 10

1. Norman Mark, "The New Super-Hero (Is a Pretty Kinky Guy)," in *Alter Ego* 3, no. 74 (2007): 20.

2. Michael Goldman, "Stan Lee: Comic Guru," *Animation World Magazine*, July 1997, 8.

3. Quoted in Mark, "The New Super-Hero," 20.

4. Ibid.

5. Quoted in ibid., 21.

6. Quoted in Brian Cunningham, ed., *Stan's Soapbox: The Collection* (New York: Marvel, 2009), 16.

7. Quoted in Mike Bourne, "Stan Lee, the Marvel Bard," in *Alter Ego*, ed. Roy Thomas, vol. 3, no. 74 (2007): 30.

8. Quoted in Cunningham, *Stan's Soapbox*, 31.

9. Mark Evanier, *Kirby: King of Comics* (New York: Harry N. Abrams, 2008), 157.

10. Joe Simon, *Joe Simon: My Life in Comics* (London: Titan, 2011), n.p.

11. Ibid., n.p.

12. Lawrence Van Gelder, "A Comics Magazine Defies Code Ban on Drug Stories," *New York Times*, February 4, 1971, 37.

13. Quoted in ibid., 38.

14. Ibid.

15. Ibid.

16. "Stan Lee," Billy Ireland Cartoon Library & Museum Biographical Files, The Ohio State University Billy Ireland Cartoon Library & Museum.

17. "Comics Come to Carnegie," *New York Post*, January 6, 1972, 44.

18. Ibid.

19. Quoted in Van Gelder, "A Comics Magazine Defies Code Ban," 28.

20. Ibid., 33.

21. Roy Thomas, interviewed in Jon B. Cooke, "Son of Stan: Roy's Years of Horrors," in *Comic Book Artist* 13 (May 2001), http://twomorrows.com/comicbookartist/articles/13thomas.html.

22. Ibid.

23. *Stan Lee's Mutants, Monsters, and Marvels*, directed by Scott Zakarin (Burbank, CA: Sony Pictures, 2002), DVD.

24. Quoted in Thomas J. McLean, "Unique Collaborations Set Marvel Apart," *Variety*, July 19–25, 2004, B12.

25. Quoted in Cooke, "Son of Stan."

26. Ibid.

27. Stan Lee, *The Best of Spider-Man* (New York: Ballantine, 1986), 10.

CHAPTER 11

1. Memo, "Marvel Comics, Classification and Frequency of Titles," January 16, 1973, Memoranda 1969–1976, Box 7, Folder 1, Stan Lee Papers, American Heritage Center, University of Wyoming.

2. Ibid.

3. Stan Lee, Memo, "Approval of Covers, Etc.," n.d., Memoranda 1969–1976, Box 7, Folder 1, Stan Lee Papers, American Heritage Center, University of Wyoming.

4. Quoted in David Anthony Kraft, "The *Foom* Interview: Stan Lee," in *Stan Lee Conversations*, ed. Jeff McLaughlin (Jackson: University Press of Mississippi, 2007), 65.

5. Mike Benton, *The Comic Book in America: An Illustrated History* (Dallas: Taylor, 1989), 74.

6. "ABC Audit Report-Magazine: Marvel Comic Group," Memoranda 1969–1976, Box 7, Folder 1, Stan Lee Papers, American Heritage Center, University of Wyoming.

7. Jonathan Hoyle, "Comic Sales (Monthly Average in Millions) for Marvel and DC, 1950 to 1987," *The Fantastic Four 1961–1989 Was the Great American Novel*, http://zak-site.com/Great-American-Novel/comic_sales.html.

8. Quoted in Brian Cunningham, ed., *Stan's Soapbox: The Collection* (New York: Marvel, 2009), 59.

9. Quoted in Les Daniels, *Marvel: Five Fabulous Decades of the World's Greatest Comics* (New York: Harry N. Abrams, 1995), 156.

10. Memo, "We Must Be Doing Something Right!" Memoranda 1969–1976, Box 7, Folder 1, Stan Lee Papers, American Heritage Center, University of Wyoming.

11. Peter Gorner, "Stan Lee's Superheroes," *Chicago Tribune*, July 17, 1975, B1.

12. Stan Lee and George Mair, *Excelsior! The Amazing Life of Stan Lee* (New York: Simon and Schuster, 2002), 183.

13. Sherry Romeo, "Inter-Office Memo," December 17, 1974, Memoranda 1969–1976, Box 7, Folder 1, Stan Lee Papers, American Heritage Center, University of Wyoming.

14. Stan Lee, "Introduction," in George Lucas, *Star Wars* (New York: Del Rey, 1977), 1.

15. Daniels, *Marvel*, 177.

16. Ibid.

17. Stan Lee, "Streaking," *Crazy*, July 1973, 16. San Francisco Academy of Comic Art Collection, The Ohio State University Billy Ireland Cartoon Library & Museum.

18. Quoted in David Hench, "Maine Artist Recalls Spider-Man Work," *Portland Press Herald*, May 5, 2007, A1.

19. Stan Lee and Frank Springer, *The Virtue of Vera Valiant* (New York: Signet, 1976), 9, 10.

20. Dan Hagan, "Stan Lee," *Comics Interview*, July 1983, 57.

21. Stan Lee, *The Best of Spider-Man* (New York: Ballantine, 1986), 6.

22. Dewey Cassell, ed., *The Art of George Tuska* (Raleigh, NC: TwoMorrows, 2005), 105.

23. Lee, *Best*, 8.

24. Stan Lee interviewed in Jim Salicrup and David Anthony Kraft, "Stan Lee," *Comics Interview*, July 1983, 57.

25. Memo, "S&S Sales," Marvel Comics Group—Facts and Figures 1976–1978, Box 6, Folder 4, Stan Lee Papers, American Heritage Center, University of Wyoming.

26. Kraft, "The *Foom* Interview, 67.

27. Stan Lee, *The Superhero Women* (New York: Simon and Schuster, 1977), 8.

28. "Fireside Paperbacks Marketing Flyer," Articles—1977, Box 32, Folder 2, Stan Lee Papers, American Heritage Center, University of Wyoming.

29. Quoted in Kraft, "The *Foom* Interview, 67.

30. Stan Lee, *Stan Lee Presents the Best of the Worst* (New York: Harper & Row, 1979), 10.

31. Quoted in Mike Gold, Jenette Kahn, "Stan Lee, and Harvey Kurtzman Discuss Comics," in *Stan Lee Conversations*, ed. Jeff McLaughlin (Jackson: University Press of Mississippi, 2007), 43.

32. Mark Evanier, *Kirby: King of Comics* (New York: Harry N. Abrams, 2008), 189.

33. George Kashdan interviewed in Jim Amash, "Sales Don't Tell You Everything," *Alter Ego* 3, no. 94 (June 2010): 49.

34. Evanier, *Kirby*, 191.

35. "'Spider-Man' to be Featured in Action Film," *New Castle (PA) News*, April 16, 1975, 8.

36. Lee Stewart, "Spinner Takes All," *Sunday Times* (London), May 12, 2002, accessed February 21, 2015, http://www.stewartlee.co.uk/written-for-money/spinner-takes-all/.

37. N. R. Kleinfield, "Superheroes' Creators Wrangle," *New York Times*, October 13, 1979, 25.

38. Quoted in ibid.

39. Ibid.

40. Quoted in ibid., 26.

41. Paul Lopes, *Demanding Respect: The Evolution of the American Comic Book* (Philadelphia: Temple University Press, 2009), 71.

42. Quoted in Sean Howe, *Marvel Comics: The Untold Story* (New York: Harper, 2012), 215.

CHAPTER 12

1. Stan Lee and George Mair, *Excelsior! The Amazing Life of Stan Lee* (New York: Simon and Schuster, 2002), 202.

2. "Marvels of the Mind: The Comics Go Hollywood," *Time*, February 5, 1979.

3. Quoted in Paul Weingarten, *"The Hulk," Chronicle-Telegram* (Elyria, OH), October 30, 1978, B-9.

4. Ibid.

5. Craig Tomashoff, "Move Over Batman . . ." *Los Angeles Reader*, January 26, 1990.

6. Pat Jankiewicz, "The Marvel Age of Comics: An Interview with Stan Lee," in *Stan Lee Conversations*, ed. Jeff McLaughlin (Jackson: University Press of Mississippi, 2007), 108.

7. Tomashoff, "Move Over Batman."

8. Quoted in Jim Salicrup, and David Anthony Kraft, "Stan Lee," *Comics Interview*, July 1983, 48.

9. Tomashoff, "Move Over Batman."

10. Letter, Stan Lee to Alain Resnais, May 23, 1979, Correspondence—1977–1980 (Folder 1 of 2), Box 14, Folder 1, Stan Lee Papers, American Heritage Center, University of Wyoming.

11. Stan Lee, Peter David, and Colleen Doran, *Amazing Fantastic Incredible: A Marvelous Memoir* (New York: Touchstone, 2015), n.p.

12. Letter, Stan Lee to Alain Resnais, Stan Lee Papers.

13. Letter, Michael Herz to Sam Arkoff, July 5, 1979, Correspondence—1977–1980 (Folder 1 of 2), Box 14, Folder 1, Stan Lee Papers, American Heritage Center, University of Wyoming.

14. "Marvel Entertainment Group Forms Marvel Productions Ltd.," *Marvel Update*, Summer 1980, 6, Scrapbook Feb. 1980–Nov. 12, 1984, Box 129, Stan Lee Papers, American Heritage Center, University of Wyoming.

15. "Marvel Entertainment," 1, Stan Lee Papers, American Heritage Center, University of Wyoming.

16. Quoted in ibid., 2.

17. "Marvels of The Mind."

18. Salicrup and Kraft, "Stan Lee," 47.

19. Ibid., 48.

20. Ibid.

21. "Comic Characters Put a Zing in Product Promotion," *Sales Executive*, April 1, 1980, 4.

22. Quoted in Judy Klemesrud, "Savage She-Hulk New Comic Heroine," *New York Times News Service*, January 20, 1980.

23. Terry Young, "Spider-Man's About to Get Real, Says His Creator," *Toronto Star*, July 6, 1986.

24. Stan Lee to Francelia Butler, November 21, 1980, Correspondence, Box 14, File 4, Stan Lee Papers, American Heritage Center, University of Wyoming.

25. Stan Lee interviewed by Margaret Jones and John R. Gambling, "Good Afternoon New York," WOR/Radio, June 22, 1984, Interviews with Stan Lee 1970–1989, Box 3, Folder 10–11, Stan Lee Papers, American Heritage Center, University of Wyoming.

26. Stan Lee, *The Best of Spider-Man* (New York: Ballantine, 1986), 9.

27. Ibid., 10, 12.

28. Ibid., 12–16.

29. Quoted in Sean Howe, *Marvel Comics: The Untold Story* (New York: Harper, 2012), 294.

30. Lee and Mair, *Excelsior!*, 209–10.

31. Quoted in Howe, *Marvel Comics*, 295.

32. Ibid., 309.

33. Quoted in ibid., 311–12.

CHAPTER 13

1. Mike Wallace, "Ronald Reagan Remembered," *CBS News 60 Minutes*, June 6, 2004, http://www.cbsnews.com/news/ronald-reagan-remembered.

2. Quoted in Dan Raviv, *Comic Wars: How Two Tycoons Battled over the Marvel Comics Empire—and Both Lost* (New York: Broadway, 2002), 12.

3. Floyd Norris, "Boom in Comic Books Lifts New Marvel Stock Offering," *New York Times*, July 15, 1991, http://www.nytimes.com/1991/07/15/business/market-place-boom-in -comic-books-lifts-new-marvel-stock-offering.html.

4. Ibid.

5. Quoted in Les Daniels, *Marvel: Five Fabulous Decades of the World's Greatest Comics* (New York: Harry N. Abrams, 1995), 225.

6. Michael E. Hill, "Where Does The Hulk Buy Clothes? Anywhere He Wants, of Course," *Washington Post*, February 18, 1990, O8.

7. Stan Lee, ed., *The Ultimate Spider-Man* (New York: Berkeley, 1994), 10.

8. Lee, *Ultimate*, 11, 13.

9. John Updike, "Cut the Unfunny Comics, Not 'Spiderman,'" *Boston Globe*, October 27, 1994, July 1994 to November 1994, Coll. 8302, Box 137, Stan Lee Papers, American Heritage Center, University of Wyoming.

10. Lee, *Ultimate*, 22.

11. Ibid., 110.

12. Ibid., 342.

13. Ibid., 7.

14. Adam Bryant, "Pow! The Punches That Left Marvel Reeling," *New York Times*, May 24, 1998, http://www.nytimes.com/1998/05/24/business/pow-the-punches-that-left-marvel -reeling.html.

15. Ibid.

16. Shirrel Rhoades, *A Complete History of American Comic Books* (New York: Peter Lang, 2008), 153–54.

17. Ibid., 155.

18. Ibid., 160–61.

19. Raviv, *Comic Wars*, 230.

20. Michael Goldman, "Stan Lee: Comic Guru," *Animation World Magazine*, July 1997, 8.

21. Ibid.

CHAPTER 14

1. Stan Lee Media Press Kit, 1999, Stan Lee Media Publicity Folder 1999, Box 127, Stan Lee Papers, American Heritage Center, University of Wyoming.

2. Quoted in Gary Dretzka, "At 77, 'X-Men' Creator Stan Lee Is as Busy as Ever," *Chicago Tribune*, July 19, 2000.

3. Stan Lee and George Mair, *Excelsior! The Amazing Life of Stan Lee* (New York: Simon and Schuster, 2002), 223.

4. Figures noted in Sean Howe, *Marvel Comics: The Untold Story* (New York: Harper, 2012), 398.

5. Quoted in Dretzka, "At 77."

6. Stan Lee Media Press Kit, 1999, Stan Lee Media Publicity Folder 1999, Box 127, Stan Lee Papers, American Heritage Center, University of Wyoming.

7. Quoted in Madeleine Brand, "Growing Trend of Online Comics," *Morning Edition*, NPR, January 20, 2000.

8. Michael Dean, "If This Be My Destiny," *Comics Journal* 232 (April 2001): 8.

9. Quoted in ibid., 8.

10. Ibid., 10.

11. Jordan Raphael, "The Invincible Stan Lee?" *Los Angeles Times Magazine*, July 16, 2000, 20.

12. Quoted in Howe, *Marvel Comics*, 408.

13. Anthony D'Allessandro, "Lee Bounces Back into Business with POW!" *Variety*, July 19–25, 2004, B14.

14. "Co-founder of Comic Company Pleads Guilty," *Los Angeles Times*, March 10, 2005, http://articles.latimes.com/2005/mar/10/business/fi-rup10.4.

15. Ibid.

16. Howe, *Marvel Comics*, 408–9.

17. Shelly Garcia, "Spider-Man's Business Brain," *Los Angeles Business Journal*, August 21, 2000, 29.

18. "Ex-Exec of Stan Lee Media Sentenced," *Los Angeles Times*, August 5, 2003, http://articles.latimes.com/2003/aug/05/business/fi-stanlee5.

19. Jon Swartz, "Stan Lee Rises from Dot-Com Rubble," *USA Today*, May 12, 2004.

20. Lee v. Marvel Enterprises, Inc. and Marvel Characters, Inc., 02 Civ. 8945 United States District Court for the Southern District of New York 765 F. Supp. 2d 440 (S.D.N.Y. 2011) LEXIS 11297 February 4, 2011, Decided February 4, 2011, Filed.

21. United States of America v. Peter Paul, Stephen M. Gordon, Jeffrey Pittsburg, Charles Kusche, Jonathan Gordon, Docket Nos. 09-3191-cr (L), 09-4147-cr (con) United States Court of Appeals for the Second Circuit, 634 F.3d 668 (2011 U.S. App.) LEXIS 4473, February 17, 2011, Argued. March 7, 2011, Decided.

22. Swartz, "Stan Lee Rises."

23. Lee and Mair, *Excelsior!*, 233.

24. Larry Schultz, e-mail message to Stan Lee, January 12, 2001, Correspondence, 1995–2010, Box 106 (2016-09-22 142037), Stan Lee Papers, American Heritage Center, University of Wyoming.

CHAPTER 15

1. Adam Chitwood, "The Epic Bryan Singer Interview: 'X-Men Apocalypse,' the Super-hero Genre, Timelines, and More," *Collider*, April 21, 2016, http://collider.com/bryan-singer-x-men-apocalypse-interview/.

2. Stan Lee, Peter David, and Colleen Doran, *Amazing Fantastic Incredible: A Marvelous Memoir* (New York: Touchstone, 2015), n.p.

3. Anthony D'Alessandro, "Lee Bounces Back into Business with POW!" *Variety*, July 19–25, 2004, B14.

4. "POW! Entertainment Partners in the Production of Three Live Action Flicks," *PR Newswire*, October 6, 2004.

5. Quoted in Virginia Rohan, "Stan Lee's Project with Pam Anderson Looks Like a Bust," *Record* (Bergen County, NJ), June 26, 2003: F5.

6. Ibid.

7. "Alta Loma Entertainment & POW! Entertainment to Develop Animated Series *Hef's Superbunnies*," *PR Newswire*, July 18, 2003.

8. Ibid.

9. Quoted in Michael Dean, "Stan Lee's Hour of Glory," *Comics Journal* 267 (April/May 2005): 23.

10. Brent Staples, "Marveling at Marvel: You Say Spider-Man, but I Say the Thing," *New York Times*, March 25, 2005, A16.

11. "Who Deserves the Credit (and Cash) for Dreaming Up Those Superheroes?" *New York Times*, January 31, 2005, C8.

12. Quoted in David Kohn, "Superhero Creator Fights Back," *60 Minutes*, October 30, 2002, http://www.cbsnews.com/news/superhero-creator-fights-back/.

13. "Marvel Settles Suit with Lee," *Los Angeles Times*, April 29, 2005, http://articles.latimes.com/2005/apr/29/business/fi-marvel29 (accessed November 7, 2015).

14. Ibid.

CHAPTER 16

1. Joel Garreau, "Stan Lee and Olivia de Havilland among National Medal of Arts Winners," *Washington Post*, November 18, 2008, http://www.washingtonpost.com/wp-dyn/content/article/2008/11/17/AR2008111701659.html.

2. Stan Lee, "Stan Lee Talks about *Time Jumper* at San Diego Comic-Con 2009," You-Tube, posted July 2009, https://www.youtube.com/watch?v=hixwR_c_R_4.

3. Ibid.

4. Stan Lee, "Stan Lee Is Spider-Man," *Stan Lee's World of Heroes*, June 21, 2012, https://youtu.be/I-lL8LD8SJQ?list=PL027ADE83FF495FA3.

5. Matt Clark, "Amazing Spider-Man Game Features Playable Stan Lee," *MTV*, May 9, 2012, http://www.mtv.com/news/2600338/amazing-spider-man-game-stan-lee/.

6. "Stan Lee Launches New Comic Franchise 'Nitron' with Keya Morgan and Michael Benaroya's Benaroya Pictures, Press release, July 20, 2016, http://www.broadcastingcable.com/thewire/stan-lee-launches-new-comic-franchise-nitron-keya-morgan-and-michael-benaroya-s-benaroya-pictures/158188.

7. "Stan Lee's POW! Entertainment Teams with *Hollywood Reporter* on New Series 'Cosmic Crusaders,'" *Hollywood Reporter*, June 21, 2016, http://www.hollywoodreporter.com/heat-vision/stan-lees-pow-entertainment-teams-904586.

8. Quoted in Michael Cavna, "Stan Lee Has a New Plan to Unite Police and Black Lives Matter," *Washington Post*, October 6, 2016, http://wpo.st/-ET42.

9. Quoted in Ethan Sacks, "Stan Lee Muses on His Final New York Comic Con," *New York Daily News*, October 10, 2016, https://www.youtube.com/watch?v=52vrHUNyFc4.

10. Ibid.

11. Peter Larsen, "Comic-book Legend Stan Lee Likes the 'Con Game,'" *Orange County Register*, October 28, 2016.

12. Quoted in Blair Marnell, "Stan Lee Talks *Lego Marvel's Avengers*, Marvel Movies, and More," *Nerdist*, November 18, 2015, http://nerdist.com/interview-stan-lee-talks-lego-marvels-avengers-marvel-movies-and-more.

13. Max Anderson in discussion with the author, Cincinnati Comic Expo, September 24, 2016.

14. Stan Lee in discussion with the author, Cincinnati Comic Expo, September 24, 2016.

CONCLUSION

1. Quoted in David Hochman, "*Playboy* Interview: Stan Lee," *Playboy*, April 11, 2014, http://www.playboy.com/articles/stan-lee-marvel-playboy-interview.

2. Memo, Marvel Comics Group—Manuscript Information, 1974, Box 6, Folder 8, Stan Lee Papers, American Heritage Center, University of Wyoming.

3. Quoted in Jeff McLaughlin, "An Afternoon with Stan Lee," in *Stan Lee Conversations*, ed. Jeff McLaughlin (Jackson: University Press of Mississippi, 2007), 211.

4. Stan Lee and George Mair, *Excelsior! The Amazing Life of Stan Lee* (New York: Simon and Schuster, 2002), 135.

INDEX

ABOUT THE AUTHOR

Bob Batchelor is a cultural historian who has written or edited more than twenty-five books on popular culture, American literature, and communications history. Batchelor teaches in the Media, Journalism & Film Department at Miami University. Among his books are *John Updike: A Critical Biography* (2013), *Gatsby: The Cultural History of the Great American Novel* (Rowman & Littlefield, 2014), and *Mad Men: A Cultural History* (Rowman & Littlefield, 2016). Visit him online at www.bobbbatchelor.com.